QA 135.5 I77 1999 c.2

ISSUES IN TEACHING NUMERACY IN PRIMARY SCHOOLS

D0033963

ISSUES IN TEACHING NUMERACY IN PRIMARY SCHOOLS

Edited by
Ian Thompson

OPEN UNIVERSITY PRESS

Open University Press
McGraw-Hill Education
McGraw-Hill House
Shoppenhangers Road
Maidenhead
Berkshire
SL6 2QL.
United Kingdom
email: enquiries@openup.co.uk
World Wide Web: www.openup.co.uk

and

Two Penn Plaza
New York, NY 10121-2289, USA

First Published 1999
Reprinted 2000 (twice), 2001, 2002, 2003 (twice), 2005. 2006, 2007

Copyright © The Editor and the Contributors 1999

All rights reserved. Except for the quotation of short passages for the purpose of criticism and review, no part of this publication may be reproduced, stored in a retrieval system, or transmitted, in any form or by any means, electronic, mechanical, photocopying, recording or otherwise, without the prior written permission of the publisher or a licence from the Copyright Licensing Agency Limited. Details of such licences (for reprographic reproduction) may be obtained from the Copyright Licensing Agency Ltd of 90 Tottenham Court Road, London, W1P 0LP.

A catalogue record of this book is available from the British Library

ISBN   0 335 20324 8 (pbk)   0 335 20325 6 (hbk)

Library of Congress Cataloging-in-Publication Data
Issues in teaching numeracy in primary schools / edited by Ian
  Thompson.
      p.   cm.
  Includes bibliographical references and index.
  ISBN 0–335–20325–6 (hbk.). – ISBN 0–335–20324–8 (pbk.)
    1. Mathematics – Study and teaching (Primary) – United States.
  I. Thompson, Ian (Frederick Ian)
  QA135.5.I77   1999
  372.7′2′0973–dc21   98–47063
                                                            CIP

Typeset by Graphicraft Limited, Hong Kong
Printed in Great Britain by The Cromwell Press Limited,
Trowbridge, Wiltshire.

Contents

Notes on contributors

Julia Anghileri is Head of Mathematics at Homerton College, Cambridge and has been involved in a number of curriculum initiatives including the Primary Initiatives in Mathematics Education (PrIME) and Calculator Aware Number Curriculum (CAN) projects. She acted as a consultant to the National Numeracy Project. She has extensive experience of working with primary school teachers and trainees through undergraduate and postgraduate courses as well as through her research and involvement in in-service courses. She is actively involved in research into children's learning of arithmetic and has published a number of books and chapters in edited books, as well as articles in professional and research journals.

Mike Askew taught in primary schools before moving into teacher education and is now a lecturer in Mathematics Education at King's College, London. His time there is split between providing in-service training and research. He was principal director of the Teacher Training Agency (TTA)-funded Effective Teachers of Numeracy in Primary Schools project and co-director, with Margaret Brown, of the Nuffield-funded Raising Attainment in Numeracy project. As deputy director of the five-year Leverhulme Numeracy Research Programme his research has involved longitudinal studies of teaching and learning. He is a regular contributor to *Junior Education* and other professional journals.

Meindert Beishuizen is a senior lecturer in the Department of Education at Leiden University. After his studies in psychology he worked on instructional technology in the Netherlands Navy, where he did his PhD research. After his move to Leiden, the cognitive shift in psychology changed his interest towards the study of learning processes. Research into mental arithmetic strategies brought him into contact with the Freudenthal Institute. In co-operation with Adri Treffers a study on the empty number line was carried out in 10 Dutch second grade classrooms. With a new grant this project continues for under-achieving children. Since his stay as a visiting scholar at

Homerton College, Cambridge, he has been interested in British discussions on early maths teaching.

Margaret Brown is a Professor of Mathematics Education at King's College, London. After teaching in primary and secondary schools, and being involved in teacher training, she has directed more than 15 research projects on teaching and learning in mathematics, specializing in the area of number. She was on the Numeracy Task Force and the Advisory Group of the National Numeracy Project, and before that the National Curriculum Mathematics Working Group. She has also chaired the Joint Mathematical Council and been president of the Mathematical Association and the British Educational Research Association.

Gill Close has worked at King's College, London for 15 years, before which she was head of mathematics in a London comprehensive school. She runs the Post Graduate Certificate in Education (PGCE) secondary mathematics course, but prior to this worked on various assessment projects including, from 1989 to 1994, directing the team which wrote the first Key Stage 3 mathematics tests. Her main research interest is test development. She has directed studies into the impact on teaching and learning of Key Stage 3 tests for the National Union of Teachers and the validity of the 1996 Key Stage 2 tests for the Association of Teachers and Lecturers.

Charles Desforges was a school teacher for 10 years before entering educational research. He has taught at the Universities of Lancaster and East Anglia, and has been Professor of Education at the University of Exeter since 1987 and Director of the School of Education since 1994. His main research interest is in classroom learning in the primary school. His books include the *Quality of Pupil Learning Experiences* (1984), *Testing and Assessment* (1989), *Understanding the Mathematics Teacher* (1987) and *Early Childhood Education* (1989). He has directed a number of major research projects, including an Economic and Social Research Council (ESRC) study of Children's Application of Knowledge at Key Stages 1 and 2. He is a member of the Quality Committee of the Teacher Training Agency, and was a recent editor of the *British Journal of Educational Psychology*.

Tony Harries is a senior lecturer in Mathematics and Mathematics Education at Bath Spa University College. He has worked in the primary and secondary sectors of the education system both here and abroad. Following a period of time as Head of Mathematics at a Bristol comprehensive school, he joined the education staff at Bath in 1991. In addition to teaching and in-service work he has been involved in various research projects related to the learning of mathematics with particular reference to the development of numeracy competence and the use of Information and Communications Technology (ICT) in the learning of mathematics.

Marja van den Heuvel-Panhuizen works at the Freudenthal Institute, Utrecht University, the Netherlands. She is involved in several developmental and research projects for primary school mathematics education. Her main point of interest is assessment which was the topic of her PhD study. She is also doing research on gender differences in mathematics achievements. An important part of her work is devoted to the development of a course for mathematics co-ordinators. This work is closely related to a recently started, government-funded, large project in which she works with many others on the description of longitudinal teaching/learning trajectories concerning the primary school mathematics curriculum.

Steve Higgins is a lecturer in Primary Education at the University of Newcastle. As part of his work he teaches primary mathematics to PGCE students. He also works with teachers on Continuing Professional Development courses. He is currently project manager for a research contract for the Teacher Training Agency. The project is investigating effective teaching methods in literacy and numeracy in primary schools using ICT. Prior to working in higher education he taught in Key Stages 1 and 2 and has been both a mathematics and an Information Technology (IT) co-ordinator.

Martin Hughes is Professor of the Psychology of Education at the Graduate School of Education, University of Bristol. His main research interests are in children's learning (particularly learning mathematics and learning with computers) and the role of parents in their children's education. His books include *Young Children Learning* (with Tizard, 1984), *Children and Number* (1986), *Parents and their Children's Schools* (with Wikeley and Nash, 1994), *Perceptions of Teaching and Learning* (1994), *Progression in Learning* (1995) and *Teaching and Learning in Changing Times* (1996). He is currently directing an ESRC project on the different knowledge bases held by parents and teachers in the areas of literacy, maths and science. From 1991–7 he co-ordinated the ESRC Research Programme on 'Innovation and Change in Education', and he is currently a member of the ESRC Research Grants Board.

Ruth Merttens has, since 1985, been the director of IMPACT, a research centre and major initiative whereby parents become involved in a structural way in their children's schooling. The project operates in the UK, Canada, the USA and Australia. She is the co-editor of *Master Classes: Texts for Professional Development* – a series of books published by Falmer Press, and her own recent writing includes 'Teaching not learning' in *For the Learning of Mathematics*, and two books, *Learning in Tandem* (1996) and *Teaching Numeracy: Maths in the Primary Classroom* (1996). As a co-director of the Hamilton Maths Project, she was heavily involved with the National Numeracy Project (NNP) and the development of the National Numeracy Strategy. The experience from which she continues to learn most is being a mother to six children, from 24 to 8 years of age.

Christine Mitchell has co-ordinated mathematics in primary schools and developed a specialist interest in early years mathematics writing. One outcome of this interest is *Teaching and Learning Mathematics at KS1* (with Williams, 1998). Since 1984 she has lectured in primary mathematics education for Initial Teacher Training (ITT) and provided consultancy in assessment and management as well as in mathematics for primary teachers. She developed assessment materials in the early stages of the National Curriculum assessment process and developed formative assessment approaches with practising teachers, publishing *Effective Teacher Assessment* (with Koshy 1995). Her current research interests centre on using and applying mathematics and the use of writing frames to develop young children's reasoning and thinking skills.

Daniel Muijs is a Research Associate at the Newcastle Educational Effectiveness and Improvement Centre. He was involved in research for, and was an observer on, the National Numeracy Task Force, and is currently involved in the evaluation of the Gatsby Foundation's Mathematics Enhancement Programme (Primary). Research interests include effective (mathematics) teaching, school effectiveness, media use, self-concept and quantitative research methodologies.

David Reynolds, originally at the University of Cardiff, Wales, has been Professor of Education at the University of Newcastle upon Tyne since 1993. He has researched and written in the areas of school effectiveness, school improvement and educational policy for over 20 years. He is the author/editor of 15 books and 150 papers and chapters. He is also co-editor of the *School Effectiveness and School Improvement* journal. He was chair of the government's Numeracy Task Force and a member of the Literacy Task Force, both of which are transforming the teaching of basic skills in Key Stages 1 and 2 in English primary schools.

Kenneth Ruthven taught in schools in Scotland and England before taking up his current post at the University of Cambridge School of Education. There he trains mathematics teachers and educational researchers, and researches issues of curriculum, pedagogy and assessment, particularly in the light of technological change. He advises curriculum projects and national agencies in the UK and USA, and acts as editor-in-chief of the journal, *Educational Studies in Mathematics*.

Anita Straker is the Director of the National Numeracy Strategy, having formerly directed the National Numeracy Project which piloted many of the initiatives incorporated in the strategy. After completing an MSc in mathematics, she worked as a teacher, school inspector and teacher trainer in Surrey, Wiltshire, the Inner London Education Authority (ILEA) and Berkshire before becoming Deputy Director of Education in Camden local education authority (LEA). From 1983 to 1986 she directed the National Primary Project which introduced computers into primary schools. She contributed to the development of the first National Curriculum for mathematics, the work of the Mathematics and Science Consultative Committee of the School Curriculum and Assessment Authority (SCAA) and the Numeracy Task Force which made recommendations for the National Numeracy Strategy. In 1991, she was awarded the OBE for her services to education.

Rosamund Sutherland is Professor of Education at the University of Bristol. Her research is concerned with modelling the interrelated process of teaching and learning, with a particular focus on mathematics. She currently chairs the Centre for Learning, Knowing and Interactive Technologies (L-KIT) which carries out research on what individuals can learn when mediated by a wide range of social, technological and epistemological resources.

Ian Thompson is a senior lecturer in Mathematics Education at the University of Newcastle upon Tyne. Observations of his own young children struggling to make sense of number operations and calculations provided the stimulus for his research into children's idiosyncratic mental and written calculation strategies which he began in 1986. He has written a substantial number of articles on this topic for academic and professional journals, and recently edited the book *Teaching and Learning Early Number* (1997). He was a member of the Advisory Group for the National Numeracy Project and was also a member of the team responsible for the training of the project's Numeracy Consultants.

Adrian Treffers is Professor of Mathematics Education in the Freudenthal Institute at Utrecht University (Holland). His major research interest has been the development of learning strands for fractions, decimal numbers, algorithms, mental calculation, estimation strategies, early arithmetic, geometry, etc. He is also the main author of an informal National Programme for mathematics education in primary school, the so-called *Proeve* ... series which contains at the moment four volumes. He has been involved in the development of Realistic Mathematics Education (RME) from the very beginning, starting with the Wiskobas project under the direction of Hans Freudenthal.

Editor's preface

This book is, to a certain extent, a sequel to *Teaching and Learning Early Number* (Open University Press 1997), which looked at research findings (mainly North American in origin) concerning children's early number acquisition and the implications of this research for classroom practice. This book also considers research, this time mainly English, dealing more generally with a range of issues relating to the teaching of numeracy in primary schools.

The book is loosely structured into five sections: historical overview, national projects, research projects, assessment issues and pedagogical issues. Chapters in all five sections discuss theory in relation to practice. However, the final section concentrates more heavily on this aspect, and makes suggestions for practising teachers to develop ideas for the teaching of specific aspects of numeracy. Most chapters contain cross-references to other parts of the book where particular ideas are dealt with in more detail. Each chapter, however, is self-contained, and is written to be read as a free-standing unit.

Some of the issues that currently confront us in England have already been addressed in other countries. For example, mathematics educators in the Netherlands have, over the years, carried out much ground-breaking curriculum development work on mental and written calculation and on 'realistic' mathematics and its assessment. The three chapters in this book that are written by colleagues from the Netherlands make an informed contribution to the debate in these areas, and also, if read as a discrete unit, provide an overview of mathematics education in what was the most successful European country in the Third International Mathematics and Science Study (TIMSS) of 9-year-olds' performance in mathematics.

The information in the table below gives details of the ages of children starting school in England and in the Netherlands. Two systems are running currently in Holland, and the newer 'Groep' nomenclature is gradually replacing the older Grade system. The information is included to help readers check the ages of children referred to by the contributors to this book.

School year England	The Netherlands		Age on entry
Reception		Groep 1	4
Year 1 (Y1)		Groep 2	5
Year 2 (Y2)	Grade 1	Groep 3	6
Year 3 (Y3)	Grade 2	Groep 4	7
Year 4 (Y4)	Grade 3	Groep 5	8
Year 5 (Y5)	Grade 4	Groep 6	9
Year 6 (Y6)	Grade 5	Groep 7	10

List of abbreviations

BSA	Basic Skills Agency
CAI	Computer Assisted Instruction
CAL	Computer Aided Learning
CAN	Calculator Aware Number Curriculum Project
CITO	National Institute for Educational Measurement (Netherlands)
CPD	Continuing Professional Development
CSILE	Computer Supported Intentional Learning Environments
DES	Department of Education and Science
DfEE	Department for Education and Employment
ESRC	Economic and Social Research Council
GEST	Grants for Education Support and Training
HMI	Her Majesty's Inspector (of Schools)
ICT	Information and Communications Technology
ILS	Integrated Learning Systems
LEA	Local education authority
MEP	Microelectronics Education Programme
NAEP	National Assessment of Educational Progress
NNP	National Numeracy Project
Ofsted	Office for Standards in Education
PrIME	Primary Initiatives in Mathematics Education
QCA	Qualifications and Curriculum Authority
RME	Realistic Mathematics Education
SAT	Standard Assessment Task
SCAA	School Curriculum and Assessment Authority
TGAT	Task Group on Assessment and Testing
TIMSS	Third International Mathematics and Science Study
TTA	Teacher Training Agency
UAM	Using and Applying Mathematics

NUMERACY: ISSUES PAST AND PRESENT

The late 1980s and the whole of the 1990s proved to be a decade of substantial change in the teaching of mathematics, which culminated in the launch of the National Numeracy Strategy in 1998 and the adoption by primary schools of the 'Numeracy Lesson' in 1999. As a key participant in many of the developments that took place in the teaching of numeracy during this time Margaret Brown gives an historical overview of these and earlier developments. In the first chapter of the book she provides the necessary background to enable the reader to understand the current situation. She focuses on Key Stage 2 mathematics in England, and in particular on the changes that have taken place since the 1960s. She discusses the reasons for these changes in relation to the prevailing social and political contexts and the key people involved. In particular, the role of international comparisons in stimulating more recent developments is described, especially in relation to the content of the National Curriculum for Mathematics, the National Numeracy Project (NNP) and the Numeracy Strategy.

In the second chapter Daniel Muijs and David Reynolds, who was Chair of the Numeracy Task Force, extend this historical account to the present day and beyond. He explores in some detail several of the themes which emerged from the work of the NTF, the *Numeracy Matters* report, the *Implementation of the Numeracy Strategy* report and the associated literature review. He pays particular attention to ideas of: 'the best of both worlds' – the importance of trying to learn from other countries; and 'blend' – the merging of different methods in a pragmatic fashion. He gives a brief review of some of the literature on country differences, school effectiveness and teacher effectiveness as the foundations for this new position within mathematics education, and he outlines those areas where he feels that further research is necessary.

Chapters 3 and 4 provide information about two important national projects designed to improve numeracy: one which started its life in 1970 – the Realistic Mathematics Education programme which developed out of the Wiskobas Project in the Netherlands, and one which began in England in

1996 – the National Numeracy Project. The respective Directors, Adrian Treffers and Anita Straker outline the philosophy underpinning each of these important developments in the continuing drive to raise standards of numeracy in both countries.

In Chapter 3 Adrian ·Treffers and Meindert Beishuizen provide a short account of the substantial influence of Hans Freudenthal and the early Wiskobas Project on the Dutch Realistic Mathematics Education (RME) programme. The authors use specific examples to outline the basic principles underlying this successful project. The way in which the developers of RME perceive the differences between 'realistic maths' and· 'real maths'; between 'context problems' and 'word problems'; and between 'mathematization' and 'problem solving' is discussed and is clearly illustrated with specific practical examples.

In Chapter 4 Anita Straker describes the background to the National Numeracy Project and explains how it worked in those local education authorities (LEAs) and schools which took part. Two particular distinguishing features of the project – its approach to calculation and its emphasis on interactive whole-class teaching – are singled out for discussion, and in order to give a feel for a Numeracy Project lesson, the chapter ends with a detailed description of a Year 5 lesson in an inner-city school.

Swings of the pendulum

Margaret Brown

Introduction

Ever since numeracy has been part of the curriculum for a significant proportion of the population in England, there has been a tension between accurate use of calculating procedures and the possession of the 'number-sense' which underlies the ability to apply such procedures sensibly. These two positions can be broadly characterized as 'procedural' and 'conceptual', respectively.

Alongside this has been a different type of tension between individualistic 'progressive' philosophies emphasizing the importance of autonomy of both pupils and teachers in order to lead to personal development and empowerment, and 'public education' philosophies emphasizing a greater degree of state intervention in the curriculum and in teaching methods in order both to protect the equal entitlement of pupils and to meet the skilled person power requirements of the state.

Over the years the pendulum has swung back and forth in both of these dimensions, depending on both the social and economic contexts. In prosperous times personal autonomy and conceptual approaches have had the edge, whereas high unemployment and internationally uncompetitive industries have tended to fix the state's attention on the uniform teaching of procedural skills in numeracy. Equally the political context has been important since it determined whose were the most powerful voices.

As with the inescapable tensions between the fundamental notions of cultural norms and individual rationality, and of freedom and equality, which respectively underlie the two dimensions, it is probably both proper and necessary that the emphases should shift from time to time to adapt to prevailing philosophies or circumstances.

In the sections which follow, these swings will be described, together with the people who have supported them. There is however one constant theme, which is that of poor standards in number skills. By quoting hand-wringing sentiments spanning over 100 years, McIntosh (1981), demonstrated that there has never been a time when those who speak for the nation have been satisfied with the level of numeracy achieved by primary children. This has always provided a reason for yet another swing of the pendulum.

Pre-1950: the rise and fall of the first national curriculum

In the first half of the nineteenth century, the state had taken a relatively *laissez-faire* attitude to education, looking on while different private and charitable systems developed. However by the end of the century concern over increasing international industrial competition and the uncivilized poor drove the state into action. The Newcastle Commission, set up to enquire into primary education in 1858, found that the majority of the pupils who did attend elementary schools were taught no arithmetic at all, and even when taught, the provision was judged to be generally ineffective.

This report formed the basis for state intervention to ensure in the 1870 Act each child's entitlement to primary education, following a national curriculum introduced in the *Revised Code* of 1862, concentrating on the three Rs of reading, writing and 'rithmetic.

In the original version the curriculum for the first three standards (intended respectively for pupils aged 7/8, 8/10 and 10+) stated:

Standard I   Form on blackboard or slate, from dictation, figures up to 20; name at sight figures up to 20; add and subtract figures up to 10, orally, from examples on blackboard.
Standard II   A sum in simple addition or subtraction, and the multiplication table.
Standard III A sum in any simple rule as far as short division.

This looks not unfamiliar, in relation to Levels 2, 3 and 4 of the national curriculum introduced over 100 years later, and most primary teachers still refer to these objectives as the major targets for their own pupils.

As with the second national curriculum introduced over a hundred years later, it is interesting to note that there were two major changes made to the *Revised Code* within the first ten years, with the aim of raising standards. As with levels in the 1989 curriculum, the standards were not necessarily tied to age, recognizing that children progressed at different rates. The difference then was that each class was focused on one standard, so that classes were of mixed age and slow children were held down.

However there were some authoritative sources even in the 1850s which considered that some form of 'number sense' was at least as important as mechanical arithmetic. Thomas Tate, a mathematician and educationist advised:

Teachers of elementary schools ... would confer a great benefit on society, by teaching the simple and fundamental principles of estimation, rather than waste the time of their pupils in giving sums ... those

investigations which have the greatest practical bearing invariably form the most healthful and instructive exercise to the intellectual powers.
(Quoted in Howson 1982: 120)

He added that 'a good teacher will vary his methods of instruction', and attacked the 'blind unreasoning attachment' to any particular system of teaching, believing that a teacher's judgement 'must be exercised in selecting those methods which are most suited to the existing conditions of his school'.

The senior member of Her Majesty's Inspectors (HMI) also took a progressive line denouncing this system. He wrote in his 1869/70 report that however brilliant the committee who drew up the curriculum, 'the teacher will in the end beat us . . . by [getting] children through the . . . examination . . . without their really knowing of these matters'. He noted that although the children 'sedulously practised all the year round', the failure rate in arithmetic was 'considerable' since the system 'gives a mechanical turn to the school teaching . . . and must be trying to the intellectual life of the school' (quoted in Howson 1982: 121).

For financial and educational reasons, the *Revised Code* was abandoned in 1898, but in spite of the removal of curriculum constraints, it would appear that there was gradual evolution rather than radical change in the teaching of arithmetic in primary schools during the first half of this century (Pinner 1981). Generally, classes became smaller and teachers better trained, which led to more humane classrooms and less punishing arithmetic. Influences of continental thinkers such as Montessori and Froebel on teacher training colleges encouraged more practical activities to be introduced for younger children.

In primary education more generally, the 1931 Hadow Report (Board of Education 1931) foreshadowed the later Plowden Report (CACE 1967) in taking a firmly progressive line backing themes rather than subjects, recommending that '. . . the curriculum of the primary school is to be thought of in terms of activity and experience rather than knowledge to be acquired and facts to be stored'.

A broader curriculum in mathematics was recommended with more emphasis on geometric form and practical measurement. The fact that 'too much time is given to arithmetic' was attributed to the influence of the examinations at 11+, which were then enabling increasing numbers of pupils from elementary schools to enter fee-paying grammar schools. Nevertheless a firmly traditional line was taken in relation to arithmetical skills: 'it is however essential that adequate drill be provided in . . . arithmetic'. Moreover it was not reasonable 'to expect a child . . . to justify the process he employs, say in subtraction or division, this is too hard an exercise of his reasoning powers'. The compromise was achieved by asserting that higher arithmetic standards could be attained in less time.

1950–80: Piaget, Plowden and Nuffield

In 1955 the Mathematical Association finally produced the long-awaited report, *The Teaching of Mathematics in Primary Schools* (Mathematical Association 1955), on which work had started 17 years earlier. The Second World War caused an interruption, but the greatest delay was because the new post-war committee changed the brief, since it '. . . did not share the belief of its predecessor that a curriculum should be drawn up prescribing the mathematics to be taught at each stage of the primary years'.

After disagreements had required yet more membership changes, the eventual report set a radical tone for the second half of the century. It adopted an unequivocal child-centred position which merged the Piagetian view of learning, as the result of an individual child's interaction with the physical environment, with the activity-oriented British primary tradition endorsed by the Hadow Report (Board of Education 1931) and to be further developed in the Plowden Report (CACE 1967). A key member of the committee throughout was Elizabeth Williams, who, while at King's College, London in the 1930s, and later as lecturer and principal at other teacher training colleges, was instrumental in introducing Piagetian ideas (Howson 1982). Many teachers will know her best through the classic text, *Primary Mathematics Today*, published in collaboration with Hilary Shuard (Williams and Shuard 1970).

The key belief of the report was that:

> Children developing at their own individual rates learn through their active response to the experiences which come to them; through constructive play, experiment and discussion children become aware of relationships and develop mental structures which are mathematical in form and are the only sound basis for mathematical techniques.

The broader curriculum recommended by Hadow was opened even wider, with no one admitting that this might allow less time for number work. Teachers were required, through their own reading and listening to children, to come to understand better how children learn, in much the same way as children were expected to come to understand mathematical concepts.

It is of course a long way from writing a report to seeing it implemented throughout England, but there were many allies in this task. Support from teacher trainers was significant, but there were also meetings with teachers all over the country. An energetic and inspiring travelling HMI, Edith Biggs, ran courses on the activity and investigation approach over more than 20 years (estimated by the Plowden Report (CACE 1967) to have reached more than 15 per cent of teachers).

A more Piagetian line was however followed by the Nuffield Mathematics Teaching Project (1964–71), led by Geoffrey Matthews, who became the first Professor of Mathematics Education at Chelsea College, part of London University which later merged into King's College. Using a conceptual progression based broadly on Piagetian research, a sequence of *Teachers' Guides* were produced on a variety of mathematical topics, including for the first time logic, 'graphs leading to algebra' and probability. These explained the underlying mathematics with ideas for different approaches and activities, attractively illustrated with pupils' work. The approach reflected the more structural ideas of modern mathematics like sets, number bases and commutativity of operations to help form a conceptual basis for calculation.

There was much debate about whether the project should have produced a set of pupil textbooks, but the philosophy was to treat the teachers in the same way as it was hoped that they would treat pupils; as one of the Nuffield team said later, '*I do and I understand* was the unofficial motto of the Project; well, it applied to teachers as well as children.' Teachers were encouraged to work together in each LEA. An important and enduring innovation of the Nuffield Project was the creation of mathematics teachers' centres where teachers could meet with LEA advisers; many of these later became general purpose centres.

The end of the selection examinations at 11+ in most areas, following the change from selective to comprehensive schooling, provided additional freedom to enable teachers to work in new ways. There is no doubt that large numbers of teachers were inspired by the new approaches of Nuffield and Edith Biggs, but with considerable staff turnover it is not clear that there was a great deal of change in what most teachers did in their classrooms. This only really took place on a large scale after new pupil materials became available after 1970, the first scheme being written by Harold Fletcher, one of the Nuffield team. Published schemes, including eventually an official Nuffield scheme, permeated most schools. Translated to text, some of the practical and investigatory spirit was inevitably lost.

The major effects on classroom teaching of the various texts were a broadening of the curriculum and many activities attempting to build up understanding through different diagrams and representations. This meant a much slower approach to algorithms, with often a variety of different methods of recording calculations presented to children. Thus there was less time for practice, the belief being that better understanding avoided the need for constant mechanical drill.

Many teachers chose to stick closely to the books, and often to let children work through them on their own. There were several reasons for this. First, the lack of confidence of teachers in their own mathematics, and especially in modern mathematics, discouraged them from departing from well-written and apparently authoritative sets of texts with many attractive activities that pupils seemed to enjoy. There was also, especially following the 1967 Plowden Report (CACE 1967), increasing emphasis on pupil autonomy; children were expected to be able to work on their own or in small groups and to organize themselves, with the teacher being seen as a resource to call upon when stuck rather than a classroom expositor.

A backlash against excessive freedom given to primary teachers and children gathered momentum during the 1970s. The well-publicized curricular anarchy at William Tyndale Junior School in London drew attention to the fact that with the demise of the 11+ there was no longer any control on what primary teachers taught. The Assessment of Performance Unit was launched in 1974 to monitor national mathematical standards at ages 11 and 15, and the idea of a common core curriculum began to be discussed. Certainly the texts like Nuffield which were published at the end of the 1970s tended to be less radical than those of Fletcher and his colleagues published earlier.

Although there were odd tirades against new mathematics in the primary schools, it was the perceived lack of numeracy of young employees which figured in a speech by the prime minister, James Callaghan, at Ruskin College in 1976, to justify a significant change in government policy towards exerting tighter control over the curriculum. However, the Labour government was keen not to upset its allies in schools and LEAs, and started by asking LEAs to work with teachers to produce curriculum guidelines. Mathematics advisers were appointed by LEAs which did not already have them, creating a national network for disseminating innovation. Advisers were able to draw on the expertise of a pool of teachers who had been appointed as mathematics co-ordinators in primary schools and had acquired a Diploma of the Mathematical Association, run mainly by teacher training colleges and universities. Guidelines were informed by the publication by DES/HMI of *Mathematics 5–11: a Handbook of Suggestions* (DES 1979); although progressive in tone this detailed list of aims and objectives marked a much firmer line in steering the contents of the primary curriculum.

One of the final acts of the Labour government was to set up a Committee of Inquiry into the Teaching of Mathematics in Schools, chaired by Sir Wilfred Cockcroft, previously associated with the Nuffield Project. While the bulk of the report was aimed at secondary schools, the presence on the Committee of Hilary Shuard, a forceful teacher trainer and Elizabeth Williams's collaborator, ensured that primary interests were not forgotten.

In fact it found much less concern from employers about standards of arithmetic than had been expected, but the surveys undertaken revealed an adult population which was fearful of mathematics, suffering from both lack of confidence and an inability to apply what they had been taught at school. In regard to primary mathematics, this tended to reassure the Committee, whose membership was in any case mainly drawn from the progressive-minded leaders within the professional bodies, that the earlier more formal styles of teaching were to blame. The more practical and investigative style which had long been recommended for, but not necessarily implemented by, primary schools would encourage confidence and self-expression and the ability to understand, and hence apply, knowledge; it was this which should be supported and extended into secondary schools.

Thus the findings led the Cockcroft Report, *Mathematics Counts*, published in 1982, to endorse the wide curriculum:

> We believe that this broadening of the curriculum has had a beneficial effect both in improving children's attitudes to mathematics and also in laying the foundations of better understanding.
>
> (DES 1982)

There was however a new utilitarian emphasis, removing some of the last vestiges of the more esoteric content brought in by the original Nuffield Project.

The report contained a whole section emphasizing the importance of mental mathematics, including:

. . . young children should not be allowed to move too quickly to written work in mathematics. It follows that, in the early stages, mental and oral work should form a major part of the mathematics which is done. As a child grows older, he needs to begin to develop the methods of mental calculation which he will use throughout his life.

Two aspects of recent research informed the recommendations: first that both children and adults tended to apply idiosyncratic methods of calculation rather than standard school methods; and, second, that there was a seven-year gap between ages when the higher and lower attaining children grasped a mathematical concept, even though they might be in the same class. This result led to an emphasis on curricular differentiation, later also stressed by inspectors, which encouraged schools to continue many of the organizational practices which they were already using, either allowing pupils to work individually at their own pace through a scheme, or grouping children by attainment to do different work.

Even though an individual learning system may be in use the teacher will often assemble a small group to begin a new topic or to draw together common strands in work which is going on. On such occasions mental mathematics is easily and naturally introduced, both in the form of mental calculation and of questions which develop new ideas . . .

Some whole-class teaching is recommended, but with an eye on the range of attainment:

. . . there are some skills, puzzles and problems which are appropriate for every child no matter what stage of learning he may have reached and short class sessions can be arranged for work of this kind . . . some problems should be posed with general discussion in mind. Both children and their teachers learn from different strategies and methods which other members of the class use . . . it is valuable experience for children . . . to explain the approach which has been used . . .

In order to enable the Cockcroft recommendations to be put into effect in classrooms, advisory teachers (known as 'Cockcroft missionaries') were appointed by LEAs, who succeeded in enthusing other teachers about mathematical investigation in the same way as Edith Biggs had started to do 20 years earlier.

Hilary Shuard, emerging as the main champion of the progressive movement in primary mathematics, succeeded in 1985 in attracting funding for a major project, Primary Initiatives in Mathematics Education (PrIME). Although this had many foci, with groups of teachers working in different LEAs, the major innovation was in the Calculator Aware Number Curriculum Project (CAN). The basic principle of this was to put into effect the firm endorsement of sensible calculator use in primary schools made by the Cockcroft Report and to fulfil the recommendation that research be undertaken to find how the use of calculators might change the primary mathematics curriculum. Children were given unrestricted access to calculators from the beginning, and there was a specific emphasis on mental calculation and investigational work with number. Teachers were asked not to teach pencil and paper algorithms at all.

The CAN project excited much national and international attention. Such results as are available suggest that pupils from the project developed better mental facility and more positive attitudes, and performed better even in non-calculator written tests. However it is not clear whether the effect was due to the increased emphasis on mental calculation, the in-service support, the investigative ethos or the calculator use. But the full effect was never to be found as it came to an abrupt end in 1989, due to other changes which are reported below.

It is clear that the changes which took place in primary mathematics between 1950 and 1985 were significant, marking a shift in attention from the teacher to the learner. They were led by a set of inspired individuals with broadly similar views, all with strong mathematical backgrounds and earlier experience of teaching in secondary schools, who occupied high-status roles in the educational establishment. It was clear that by the end of the period most teachers had come to espouse the principles underlying the changes, even if they had not always fully implemented the principles in their practice.

1985–98: the second national curriculum and beyond

The primary results in the international surveys carried out in 1990 (International Assessment of Educational Progress; IAEP) and 1994 (Third International Mathematics and Science Study; TIMSS) demonstrated that many of the Cockcroft objectives were achieved; British pupils were comparatively confident, unusually including those pupils whose attainments were modest, and they generally enjoyed mathematics. There is some evidence that many children seemed to enjoy the greater control they had over their own pace of work. More importantly, British pupils did very well in tests in applying mathematics to solve practical problems, in mathematics and science. The successful implementation of a wide curriculum was demonstrated by the fact that in 1994, English children were top of the international table in geometry, and in 1990 were second in statistics.

However, comparatively low English results in the number category suggested that the successes had had a cost. Concern about such international comparisons in the mid-1980s coincided with a continuing movement under the new Conservative government towards clearer curriculum specification as well as greater central control. In the White Paper *Better Schools* (DES 1985) came the first announcement of the intention to formulate both national objectives, to be known as attainment targets, for age 11 in mathematics, and an associated system of assessment. Formative assessment for diagnostic and planning purposes was highlighted, but it was also pointed out that the results would allow schools to evaluate their own practices.

The focus on targets and assessment at primary level reflected the national criteria for the new GCSE examinations which had been recently announced to start in 1988. At primary level, also, many LEAs were developing assessment systems, although these took a variety of forms ranging from written tests to profiling.

Related to the focus on clear targets to be found in *Better Schools*, a series of DES/HMI publications was being issued which contained objectives and assessment advice for each subject. *Mathematics from 5 to 16* (DES 1985) was, at primary level, an amalgamation of the earlier 1979 DES/HMI publication *Mathematics 5–11* (1979) with the Cockcroft Report. Thus the 24 objectives were listed under the headings of facts, skills, conceptual structures, general strategies and personal qualities, and were themselves unspecific (e.g. remembering notation, sensible use of a calculator, trial and error methods, a positive attitude to mathematics). However, a detailed list of what *most* 11-year-olds should know, under the content objectives only, was contained in the appendix. The list contained few surprises and reflected the contents of the more recent textbook series, emphasizing concepts rather than procedures, for example including equivalence of fractions rather than the four rules. Pencil and paper multiplication and division was by single digits only, using calculators for more complex cases. While underlining the progressive credentials of HMI, it was nevertheless seen as a further step towards state prescription.

Deciding that mathematics would be an easier subject than English to tackle, the Secretary of State, Sir Keith Joseph, initiated a one-year feasibility study to start in September 1986, which would define a three- to four-year programme for research, development and implementation of national attainment targets of age 11 (now stated to be expected to be 'differentiated') and corresponding assessment. The contract went to Brenda Denvir and myself, colleagues of Geoffrey Matthews at Chelsea College, then merging into King's College, London. Hilary Shuard was on the Steering Committee.

But the feasibility study was soon overtaken by events. A new Secretary of State, Kenneth Baker, swept in during the autumn of 1986, determined to make his mark. Persuaded by the recent reports that low mathematical standards compared with our competitors were responsible for industrial failure, he announced in January 1987 his decision to implement swiftly a full national curriculum determining what pupils should be taught in primary and secondary schools. This was considerably beyond the aim of his predecessor who supported attainment targets but had no desire otherwise to control the detail of what was taught.

Ignoring the feasibility study, Baker announced at Easter that there would be national testing at ages 7, 9 (later abandoned), 11 and 14, as well as GCSE at 16. The consultative document *The National Curriculum 5–16* (DES 1987) was rushed out in July in order to form the core of a new and radical Education Reform Bill that autumn. At the same time National Curriculum Working Groups in mathematics and science were set up, as well as a Task Group on Assessment and Testing (TGAT).

The brief was for the subject groups to draw up attainment targets for ages 7, 11, 14 and 16, with each target differentiated for three levels of attainment, to frame a programme of study for each key stage of education covering the

2–4 years prior to the tests, and to advise on teacher assessment and national testing. In the case of the mathematics group, among those with knowledge at primary level were Hilary Shuard (co-opted only reluctantly by the DES), a primary mathematics adviser, two primary heads and myself. Significantly Anita Straker, then developing new primary guidelines for the Inner London Education Authority as an Inspector, and writing innovative computer programs to teach mathematics, was also drafted in as an adviser.

As with the Steering Committee for the feasibility project, and not surprisingly in view of the shared membership, the group demanded a revision of the brief so that attainment targets were written, not separately for four key stages, but in the form of hierarchical strands, made up of statements of attainment describing the important steps of progression in each target. The statements of attainment could then be assigned to levels, each of which could be described as being attained by average pupils of a specific age. This would both ensure continuity through the 5–16 age range and cater for the documented wide range of attainment among pupils of any age. The result would be child-centred to the extent that it would take the progression in the learning of the child as the core of the system rather than fixing the syllabus for each key stage and measuring each child's attainment of it.

The TGAT group also favoured this solution, and persuaded Kenneth Baker to adopt it, together with a focus on ongoing teacher assessment, with theme-based Standard Assessment Tasks (SATs) used only for moderation purposes.

The mathematics national curriculum was not unexpectedly strongly influenced by the Cockcroft ethos, with a broad curriculum including investigation and problem solving. Hilary Shuard also fought to maintain the principles of the Calculator Aware Number curriculum (CAN) with its strong emphasis on mental arithmetic, estimation, and calculators. The eventual outcome mainly reflected this, but a compromise was negotiated with the DES to include some written arithmetic, but avoiding any requirement for standard methods. So the conceptual spirit of primary mathematics remained intact, even if the progressive aspect was significantly dented by effective state control of both curriculum and assessment.

The proposals, both from TGAT and from the Mathematics Working Group, received a guarded welcome by teachers as being better than they had feared, and although changes in the format of the Order (the various versions of the National Curriculum for Mathematics) took place in 1991 and 1995, the content remained substantially constant between 1989 and 2000. The immediate effect was for teachers to check that their textbooks matched the attainment targets fairly closely, which was generally the case for those bought within the previous decade. These generally emphasized concepts rather than procedures, although many teachers supplemented them with practice on tables and written computation exercises. Schemes brought out supplements and new editions to fill a few gaps like probability.

It was clear that the levels encouraged a continuing emphasis on differentiation, so that the many schools which had, with the aim of pupil autonomy, individualized their classrooms for mathematics, saw no need to change. However other teachers and schools, now wanting greater control over pace and coverage, started revising the curriculum into modules, using the national curriculum attainment targets as a basis. All the pupils would then work on, say, multiplication or measurement at the same time, although children in different attainment groups would be likely to be working on different activities, usually selected from different books in their scheme. These teachers thus moved from being what Johnson and Millett (1996) call *scheme driven planners* to *scheme assisted planners*, with the national curriculum framework liberating them from the framework imposed by the published scheme itself.

Although the 'Using and Applying Mathematics' attainment target was supposed to incorporate problem-solving and investigation skills, reasoning, and communication into the teaching of content, in practice teachers felt they were fulfilling the requirements by either using practical work and/or real-world examples, often artificial ones of shopping and cutting up fractions of cakes. At Key Stage 2, the occasional investigations, introduced following the work of the Cockcroft advisory teachers, were generally continued. Few had the resources, the confidence or the insight to introduce a fully investigatory style to the teaching of content, although some teachers used 'nice activities' or games which incorporated such principles, without always being able to justify them (see Hughes, Desforges and Mitchell, Chapter 6, this volume).

There were however changes during this period which did affect the nature of teaching. The first was as a consequence of national assessment. In the late 1980s and early 1990s, teachers, led initially by LEAs, had put much effort into devising assessment and recording systems as a result of the TGAT emphasis on ongoing teacher assessment. While these assessment sheets relating to statements of attainment became denigrated as bureaucratic tick-lists, many teachers found that concentrating on assessing pupils' attainment of particular ideas and skills was helpful in monitoring progress and in curriculum planning. The combination of teacher assessment and the first practical SATs at Key Stage 1 revealed that pupils' attainment sometimes differed from teacher expectations. By the time national assessment was introduced statutorily at Key Stage 2, a national teacher boycott of assessment ensured that there was no longer any requirement for continuous assessment, and the tasks had become externally marked class tests, leading to league tables of performance.

This led in many schools to the tests beginning to drive the curriculum, at least in Years 2 and 6. However the style of written questions in the early years of the national tests had little effect on the curriculum, since they were similar to the style of work in most of the commonly used schemes. Before 1998 there were no straightforward numerical calculations. Almost all items took the form of a word problem set in a real-world context or a puzzle, and thus required some degree of conceptual knowledge, including interpretation of the problem and selection of a strategy.

While in some ways assessment against specific criteria was confirming the range of attainment of different children in each class, it also made it clear to teachers that individualization of teaching was not necessarily delivering basic skills, especially in number. Perhaps this was not surprising given that children did not have to react orally or quickly to mental calculations while working through books, and had very little opportunity to talk about the methods they had used, which were often primitive and slow.

Problems about pupil autonomy and progressive methods more generally were featured in studies in Leicester, Inner London and Leeds, and a report commissioned by the Secretary of State (known as the Three Wise Men Report) (Alexander *et al.* 1992), proposed more whole-class teaching in primary schools. However momentum was lost due to a worsening of relations between the government and the teachers, culminating in a successful teacher boycott of national tests. Appeasement followed, led by Sir Ron Dearing, who negotiated a pause in innovation.

Concern about low standards of numeracy, and about teaching methods, surfaced again in 1996. First, unfavourable international comparisons were highlighted both by leaked new results and by a report reviewing earlier results, *Worlds Apart?* (Reynolds and Farrell 1996), which was co-authored by David Reynolds, later the chairman of the Numeracy Task Force (see Reynolds and Muijs, Chapter 2, this volume).

In June 1996 there was an announcement that mental arithmetic tests and non-calculator papers would be included in all the end-of-key stage national tests, persuading many more teachers to include whole-class sessions of mental arithmetic in their lessons.

Finally Gillian Shephard, the Secretary of State, announced the launch of parallel national numeracy and literacy projects, which would involve schools in poorly performing LEAs. The aim was to raise standards in basic skills by a prescribed programme for each year, reducing differentiation and focusing on whole-class teaching. Support would be offered by numeracy consultants, a revival of the Cockcroft advisory teachers, long since lost due to continual LEA cutbacks. Anita Straker was appointed as director of the National Numeracy Project, and worked with enormous energy to get the project started in Autumn 1996 (see Straker, Chapter 4, this volume).

This finally brings us to the National Numeracy Strategy, developed during 1997–8 because the Labour Party, as it came into power, took over the Conservatives' growing focus on raising standards in literacy and numeracy.

Postscript

The National Numeracy Strategy Framework, circulated in 1999, just over a century since the previous national curriculum was abandoned, prescribes not only an extremely detailed curriculum, year by year, for primary mathematics, but also an additional requirement specifying the type of activities which should take place in each lesson, and for how long.

While only the broader outlines are technically statutory, there are strong pressures to implement the detail since schools are inspected regularly by the Office for Standards in Education (Ofsted), which has power to advertise publicly those which are substandard, which may send them into a downward spiral leading to closure.

Thus, under the first Labour government for 18 years, we have the tightest ever control by government on primary mathematics, with central prescription not only of national curriculum and national tests, but also of teaching style. The post-war progressive era of teacher and pupil autonomy is apparently over, and the education system is to be driven by national targets and norms, and regularly inspected, like steel production in the Soviet state or rice production under Chairman Mao.

It would be easy to predict either massive improvement in standards or great disaster from the latest swing in the pendulum. However if the reality behind the headlines is examined, it seems likely that we shall see neither, although, as in earlier totalitarian regimes, targets will no doubt be perceived to be met.

The reason for this is that it is clear that most schools, most of the time, have been dependent on published schemes to set their curriculum as well as their teaching activities. These schemes have generally covered a wide curriculum, but have always had a major emphasis on number work. Most schools have continued throughout to teach and test number bonds and multiplication tables, and calculators have been used sparingly, if at all, to teach number sense rather than as a substitute for traditional calculation methods. Thus the combined good sense and inertia of the teaching profession has substantially damped the pendulum swings recommended in the past, and no doubt will do so again.

Perhaps we should always welcome money and time being spent on numeracy, and encourage teachers to use the opportunity to develop their expertise and exploit their freedom within the fashions of the day.

References

Alexander, R., Rose, J. and Woodhead, C. (1992) *Curriculum Organisation and Classroom Practice in Primary Schools*. London: DES.

Board of Education (1931) *Report of the Consultative Committee on the Primary School* (Hadow Report). London: HMSO.

CACE (Central Advisory Council for Education) (1967) *Children and their Primary Schools* (Plowden Report). London: HMSO.

DES (Department of Education and Science) (1979) *Mathematics 5–11: a Handbook of Suggestions* (HMI Matters for Discussion 9). London: HMSO.

DES (Department of Education and Science) (1982) *Mathematics Counts* (Cockcroft Report). London: HMSO.

DES (Department of Education and Science) (1985) *Better Schools*. London: HMSO.

DES (Department of Education and Science) (1985) *Mathematics from 5 to 16* (HMI Curriculum Matters 3). London: HMSO.

DES (Department of Education and Science) (1987) *The National Curriculum 5–16: a Consultation Document*. London: HMSO.

DfEE (Department for Education and Employment) (1999) *The National Numeracy Strategy Framework for Teaching Mathematics from Reception to Year 6*. London: DfEE.

Howson, A.G. (1982) *A History of Mathematics Education in England*. Cambridge: Cambridge University Press.

Johnson, D. and Millett, A. (eds) (1996) *Implementing the Mathematics National Curriculum: Policy, Politics and Practice*. London: Paul Chapman.

McIntosh, A. (1981) When will they ever learn? (Article reprinted from *Forum*, 19(3)). In A. Floyd (ed.), *Developing Mathematical Thinking*. London: Addison-Wesley, for the Open University.

Mathematical Association (1955) *The Teaching of Mathematics in Primary Schools*. London: Bell.

Pinner, Sr. M.T. (1981) Mathematics: Its Challenge to Primary School Teachers from 1930–1980. In A. Floyd (ed.), *Developing Mathematical Thinking*. London: Addison-Wesley, for the Open University.

Reynolds, D. and Farrell, S. (1996) *Worlds Apart? A Review of International Surveys of Educational Achievement involving England* (Ofsted Reviews of Research). London: HMSO.

Williams, E.M. and Shuard, H.B. (1970) *Primary Mathematics Today*. London: Longman.

Numeracy matters: contemporary policy issues in the teaching of mathematics

David Reynolds and Daniel Muijs

Introduction

The teaching of mathematics, and the standards of mathematics achievement more generally, has been an area of considerable controversy over the last 20 years. More recently, however, a number of different bodies of evidence appear to be pointing in the same direction as to what effective methods of teaching and of organizing schooling might be. This chapter aims to outline the history of these controversies, and particularly to outline the research and practice evidence that has been gathered during the recent work of the Numeracy Task Force, which issued its preliminary report *Numeracy Matters* (DfEE 1998a) in early 1998 and its final report *The Implementation of the National Numeracy Strategy* (DfEE 1998b) in summer 1998.

The 'problem' of mathematics achievement

Controversies about appropriate methods have appeared at the same time as a considerable volume of evidence about relatively poor performance by English children (and more recently Scottish children) in the various well-known international surveys of mathematics achievement (see the review in Reynolds and Farrell 1996). The publication of data from the Third International Mathematics and Science Study (TIMSS) has added to the debate (Keys *et al.* 1996).

On the one hand, the TIMSS data, which show a relatively poor performance in mathematics but an excellent performance by comparison with other countries in science, clearly indicate that *educational* rather than *socio-cultural* factors are the causes: the *same* socio-cultural factors in students' homes and communities cannot be responsible for *different* levels of achievement in the two subjects. On the other hand, the good performance in science at age 9 is delivered by schools and teachers who manage to do poorly in mathematics, which suggests a more complex set of educational factors than those suggested by the blanket condemnation of British teachers that is a notable part of national political discourse about education.

Reviewing research evidence from this country, and from other societies with a substantial literature such as the United States and Australia, can help us resolve these seemingly complex issues. First, it is clear that educational factors *are* more important in mathematics than in other comparable 'core' skill areas such as reading, for example. The well-known *School Matters* school effectiveness study of Mortimore *et al.* (1988) shows that the effect of the school attended by students was a ten times greater influence on progress over time in mathematics than the impact of family background (this with the effect of prior mathematics achievement 'controlled out'). In reading, the school impact was only four times greater than that of home.

Second, the recent evidence gives us some clues as to how it might be that our mathematics performance may be so problematic. Put simply, most studies show a clear relationship between whole-class interactive teaching and mathematics achievement, yet it seems that the amount of whole-class teaching in English primary schools has both declined over time since the primary education revolution of the late 1960s and early 1970s, and has recently been at substantially lower levels than that of other societies, particularly at lower levels than the societies of the Pacific Rim who possess such high levels of mathematics achievement.

The American and British effectiveness research

The first body of evidence to utilize in the understanding of the 'problem' of maths achievement is the American literature on teacher effectiveness (see summary in Creemers 1994), which shows that children learn more in classes when they spend time being taught or supervised by their teacher rather than working on their own. This is mainly because teachers in these kinds of classes provide more thoughtful and thorough presentations, spend less time on classroom management, enhance children's time on task and make more child contacts. The effective teacher carries the context personally to the child, rather than relying on curriculum material or textbooks to do so. However, this approach should not be equated to a conventional 'lecturing and drill' approach in which students remain passive. Effective whole-class teachers ask a lot of questions and involve students in class discussions. Differentiated questions that cater for the whole range of student achievement are also used.

A similar message comes from the limited British evidence on teacher effectiveness. The notable ORACLE study (Galton *et al.* 1980) showed that teachers labelled as 'class enquirers' generated the greatest gains in the areas of mathematics and language (this finding did not extend to reading). By contrast, the group of 'individual monitoring' teachers made amongst the least progress. It is important to note that the more successful 'class enquirers' group utilized four times as much time in whole-class interactive teaching as the 'individual monitors' (Croll 1996).

Further analyses (Croll 1996) correlated the academic gain made by different classes with different patterns of class/teacher interactions, finding a moderate positive correlation between whole-class and small group interaction and children's progress, showing as Croll (1996: 23) notes '. . . a positive association of progress and non-individualised interaction'.

The ORACLE study also looked at the children's time on task (or academically engaged time) and found that whole-class interaction was positively associated with high levels of time on task, with the 'class enquirers' having average time on task 10 per cent higher than other teachers. Further analyses by one of the ORACLE authors (Croll and Moses 1988) shows a high positive correlation between time in whole-class interaction and time on task. Time in group-based interaction showed no such association. It is important to emphasize in this context, of course, the close link between 'time on task' and learning gain, which is one of the most replicated of the American teacher effectiveness findings.

The British school effectiveness study noted earlier, *School Matters* (Mortimore *et al.* 1988), also contains material on the teaching methods employed in 'effective' schools that 'added significant value' to their intakes of pupils. Significant positive effects come from use of higher order questions and statements, frequent questioning, restricting sessions to a single specific area of work, involvement of pupils in activities and the proportion of time utilized in communicating with the class as a whole. Negative effects are shown by teachers spending a high proportion of time on individual work.

The British professional knowledge base

It is not just research knowledge that shows the superiority of whole-class interactive teaching in mathematics. Additional knowledge comes from Office for Standards in Education (Ofsted) reports, of which three are important. The first, *Teaching Quality: The Primary Debate* (Ofsted 1995), outlined a number of general teacher/teaching factors appearing to be associated with positive outcomes in general:

- good subject knowledge;
- good questioning skills;
- an emphasis upon instruction;
- a balance of grouping strategies;
- clear objectives;
- good time management;
- effective planning;
- good classroom organization;
- effective use of other adults in the classroom.

The second study was specifically related to the characteristics of the success-ful teaching of numeracy (Ofsted 1996). It outlined first the characteristics of classroom processes where standards were low, including:

- too much emphasis upon repetitive number work;
- too much individualization of work;
- too little fluency in mental calculation.

The report went on to outline in detail the characteristics of successful teaching.
  This:

- provides clear structure for the lessons and makes good use of time, main-taining challenge, pace and motivation;
- recognizes that knowing by heart and figuring out support each other in the learning of number and its applications;
- includes sessions of direct teaching, with the teacher involved proactively and not just when pupils are stuck;
- involves regular interaction with pupils, with the teacher using perceptive questioning, giving careful attention to misconceptions and providing help and constructive response.

The third study was that on *The Teaching of Number in Three Inner-Urban LEAs* (Ofsted 1997). The report notes a number of concerns, based upon an extensive programme of lesson observation, interviewing and collection of documentation in Years 2 and 6:

- poor lesson planning in one-third of schools;
- mental arithmetic being given less attention than it warranted in both Years 2 and 6;
- problem solving being taught well in only one-fifth of schools;
- assessment of pupils being a concern in two-thirds of schools;
- schools being unclear about the place and purpose of calculator use;
- mathematics co-ordinators having roles which were too ill-defined, too wide-ranging and not being resourced with enough time to work along-side colleagues in their classrooms.

Crucially, the report concluded that (Reynolds and Muijs's italics added):

In all the schools there was a mix of whole-class, group and individual work in varying proportions during the lesson. Some teachers were much more successful than others in the way they used these organizational strategies to extend and direct their teaching and to increase pupils' number knowledge, understanding and skills. *In the best lessons there was usually a higher proportion of time spent teaching the class together, often at the start and sometimes at the end of the lesson, with individual and group work closely linked to the whole-class work.* The pupils worked on tasks individually or in groups which reinforced or extended what they had been taught in the whole-class time and consolidated their learning by coming together again at the end of the lesson. The effect of this was an obvious common gain in core knowledge and skill which made it easier for the pupils to help one another and progress together. For the teacher, too, this well-structured mix of whole-class, group and individual work not only made the lesson more manageable, it also established a climate and a common language for talking about mathematics which benefited more children for more of the time.

These good lessons stood in sharp contrast to the poorer work *which suffered from a distinct, common organizational weakness, notably a debilitating overuse of individual work, and to a lesser extent, group work.* Where these weaknesses occurred there was often an over-reliance on worksheets and published schemes. While these were not necessarily poor in themselves, they simply isolated pupils in ways which made it difficult for them to receive any sustained, direct teaching at all. In other words, more often than not complex arrangements for individual work were self-defeating; they dissipated rather than intensified the quality of the teaching and reduced the opportunities for children to learn.

The importance of higher order skills

Whilst methods such as whole-class interactive teaching may be particularly useful in maximizing achievement in standardized tests and in basic skills, legitimate doubt has been cast on whether this approach is sufficient for teaching higher order mathematical problem-solving or mathematical thinking skills, the importance of which has received increased attention in recent years. A number of classroom processes may enhance higher order thinking: a sharp focus on meaning and understanding in mathematics; the direct teaching of higher level cognitive strategies; and co-operative small group work, which seems to be particularly potent.

The advantages of this latter method in developing problem-solving skills lie partly in the 'scaffolding' process whereby pupils help each other learn in the 'zone of proximal development'. Giving and receiving help and explanation may develop children's thinking skills, as well as helping them to verbalize and structure their thoughts. By co-operating in small groups children can share their own ways of thinking and reflect on them and on the thinking and ideas of others. This exchange may encourage students to engage in more higher order thinking. Children thus provide assistance and support to each other. Co-operative small groups force the accommodation of the opinions of various members, and students must therefore search, engage in problem solving and take one another's perspective. In this way students can develop an enhanced understanding of self and other, and learn that others possess both strengths and weaknesses. This may help students who are less able problem solvers to overcome their insecurity about problem solving because they can see more able peers struggling over difficult problems. (However, it would also be possible for them to become more insecure by seeing peers solve problems they themselves cannot solve!) The fact that a group contains more knowledge than an individual means that problem-solving strategies can be more powerful. This may help students see the importance of co-operation. Group members may serve as models to one another, thus enhancing learning-to-learn skills. Students also receive practice in collaboration, a skill they will require in real life.

While the benefits of co-operative small group work for enhancing students' problem-solving skills seem important, it is clear that for group work to be effective it is insufficient to put students into groups and let them get on with it. A number of conditions need to be met. The most important of these are group goals and individual accountability. Group goals are essential to motivate students to work co-operatively and thus help their groups' mathematics learning. Individual accountability increases the engagement of individual students and decreases the probability of 'free-rider' effects, whereby certain students choose to remain passive while letting other group members do all the work.

To be able to work effectively in groups, children must first learn the necessary general social and communication skills. These can be taught through direct teaching (though they may also be partly determined by the students' cognitive development). This, however, is not sufficient. Children must also learn specific academic helping skills, to enable them to give substantial explanations to one another. In the early stages of group work pupils can be coached to reflect on their metacognitive strategies by being given hand-outs with questions such as 'What exactly are you doing?', 'Why are you doing it?' and 'How does it help you?'

To make small group work effective, one needs to design tasks that encourage the group to work together. The use of shared equipment (e.g. graphs, calculator) can be useful. The task should engage all members of the group, focusing on processes. Each student should think about the problem in a meaningful way, and then participate in other students' problem-solving strategies. The task should be sufficiently challenging for it to require collective problem solving, but not so challenging that it causes group members to give up prematurely.

The need for blends of methods

In our search through the research and practice evidence, it is clear that this evidence has implications for policy. Not surprisingly, some of these implications are addressed in the Numeracy Task Force reports noted above (DfEE 1998a, b). Clearly, the amount of time pupils spend working individually should be curtailed to far lower levels than seem currently to exist in English classrooms. Some studies have found that children spend over 50 per cent of their time working on their own. This is not to say that all individual work should be eliminated from lessons. Some individual practice of skills can be useful, though a lot of this could be consigned to homework, which should be given from primary school onwards (see Merttens, Chapter 7, this volume). The supposed opposition between whole-class teaching and small group work is a false one, however. It would appear that both active, interactive whole-class teaching *and* co-operative small group work have their merits, and that the amount of time to be spent on both should depend on factors such as student age, ability and, most crucially, the task to be performed or the subject to be learnt.

Thus, for the teaching of basic skills active whole-class teaching is clearly the most effective strategy, though practice of concepts taught might fruitfully incorporate some small group work. On the other hand, mathematical problem-solving and thinking skills are probably best enhanced through co-operative small group work, although an element of whole-class teaching will be needed to explain the task and to teach the students the skills necessary to participate in co-operative group work. All in all, the question is not whether to use either whole-class teaching or small group work, but how to utilize them both, in a blended fashion.

Some authors would see an opposition between an emphasis on basic skills and an emphasis on problem solving and higher level thinking. This opposition, too, would seem erroneous. In order to function as fully numerate members of society, pupils need to have a firm grasp of the basics, while simultaneously being able to apply their knowledge in original ways in a wide range of situations. Good problem solving is built upon good basic skills, as the pupil needs to be able to retrieve easily from long-term memory those techniques and strategies needed to solve the task.

Whilst attempts to conceptualize and describe a blend of whole-class interactive teaching and individual/group-related activities occupied much of the efforts of the Numeracy Task Force and can be usefully seen in the National Numeracy Strategy, those countries which have historically shown very high levels of mathematics achievement are interestingly also searching for a rather similar kind of 'blend'. These societies, such as Singapore, South Korea, Taiwan and Japan, are increasingly of the view that their own practices in teaching at the primary or elementary age phase:

- teach basic skills much more effectively than higher order skills;
- teach 'theoretical' knowledge rather than make possible knowledge application in relevant real-world settings;
- do not develop collaborative skills in order for children to work productively together;
- do not develop children's capacities to generate new knowledge and access that knowledge;
- do not develop children's social attributes that will partially determine their knowledge use;
- do not reflect present knowledge of the multiple nature of the intelligences that are necessary to function in a rapidly changing society;
- involve excessive pressure upon children, leading to a concentration upon a limited approach to learning, rather than permitting the time and space for the development of interactions between subjects.

Accordingly, South Korea has reduced academic pressure somewhat by easing homework requirements. Singapore is actively exploring both the potential of information technology to transform the nature of the 'whole-class' experience, and how 'new' definitions of outcomes can be conceptualized, operationalized and implemented. Taiwan recently convened a government-sponsored conference to consider the evidence from other countries (including the United Kingdom, the United States and Japan) about the utility of what would be labelled in England 'progressive' approaches to instruction and learning. Whilst it seems highly unlikely that these societies will completely phase out their existing 'whole-class interactive' classroom organization, it seems likely that five or six years from now they will have generated learning situations which are 'blended' in their use of:

- whole class interactive teaching for maybe 60 per cent of the time;
- very limited time for individual practice (perhaps 10 per cent of lesson time);
- collaborative group work, probably achievement-differentiated both within and between groups, for perhaps 20/30 per cent of lesson time;
- greatly enhanced use of information and communication technology (ICT) by children and better resourced Continuing Professional Development (CPD) needs of practising teachers.

From validity to reliability

It should be clear from the above discussion that we now possess some idea of the blend of methods that is needed to generate high levels of achievement in different mathematical skill areas. Interestingly, other countries appear to be moving, from a very different start point in terms of classroom organization and teaching methodology, towards a rather similar kind of blend to that suggested by research and enshrined in the current National Numeracy Strategy in English schools.

Possessing a known-to-be-valid 'technology' of practice is, of course, only a part of what is necessary to improve achievement. Implementing this practice in schools and classrooms is likely to prove more difficult than identifying it. Historically in British education there has been a set of policies oriented towards the school as the unit of policy change and implementation, as evidenced in the recent educational agenda of 'New Labour' since the 1997 election. However, it may be that policies directed at schools, more than teachers and their teaching, may have difficulties, since:

- the within-school variation by department within secondary school and by teacher within primary school is much greater than the variation between schools on their 'mean' levels of achievement or 'value-added' effectiveness;
- the effect of the classroom level in those multilevel analyses that have been undertaken, since the introduction of this technique in the mid 1980s, is probably three to four times greater than that of the school level (Creemers 1994).

It may be that a 'classroom-based' policy orientation *as well as* the 'school-based' one may give a greater chance of affecting educational achievement than a 'school based' orientation on its own, for the following reasons:

- the departmental level in a secondary school or 'year' level in a primary school is closer to the classroom level than is the school level, opening up the possibility of any intervention generating greater change in the learning level;
- whilst not every school is an effective school, every school has within itself some practice that is more effective than some other practice. Many schools will have within themselves practice that is absolutely effective, across all schools. With a learning level orientation, every school can work on its own internal conditions;
- focusing 'within' schools may be a way of permitting greater levels of competence to emerge at the school level, since it is possible that the absence of strategic thinking at school level in many parts of the educational system is related to the overload of pressures amongst head teachers, who are having referred to them problems which should be dealt with by the day-to-day operation of the middle management system of departmental heads, year heads, subject co-ordinators and the like;
- within-school units of policy intervention such as years or subjects are smaller and therefore potentially more malleable than those at 'whole-school' level;
- teachers in general, and those teachers in less effective settings in particular, may be more influenced by classroom-based policies that are close to their focal concerns of teaching and curriculum than by the policies that are 'managerial' and oriented to the school level;
- the possibility of obtaining 'school level to school level' transfer of good practice, plus any possible transfer from LEAs in connection with their role as monitors of school quality through their involvement in the approval of schools' development plans, may be more difficult than the possibility of obtaining 'within-school' transfer of practice.

However, even a more 'learning level-based' policy orientation will have problems in ensuring reliability of take-up of new kinds of teaching practices. Variation between teachers in their initial levels of competence may well be further magnified by attempts to introduce new, apparently more effective methods. There is considerable cynicism within the teaching profession about whether methods that are currently favoured by governments and their advisers are more effective than existing methods, particularly since the existing methods involving a high proportion of individual work and a low proportion of whole-class work were espoused with equal fervour over the last two decades, sometimes by the same persons who now espouse a different orientation. For all these reasons, the next few years should be interesting ones for students, teachers and researchers in the field of mathematics.

References

Creemers, B.P.M. (1994) *The Effective School*. London: Cassell.
Croll, P. (1996) Teacher–pupil interaction in the classroom. In P. Croll and N. Hastings (eds), *Effective Primary Teaching*. London: David Fulton.

Croll, P. and Moses, D. (1988) Teaching methods and time on task in junior class-rooms. *Educational Researcher*, 30(2): 90–7.

DfEE (Department for Education and Employment) (1998a) *Numeracy Matters: The Preliminary Report of the Numeracy Task Force*. London: DfEE.

DfEE (Department for Education and Employment) (1998b) *The Implementation of the National Numeracy Strategy: The Final Report of the Numeracy Task Force*. London: DfEE.

Galton, M., Simon, B. and Croll, P. (1980) *Inside the Primary Classroom*. London: RKP.

Keys, W., Harris, S. and Fernandes, C. (1996) *Third International Study, First National Report, Part One*. Slough: National Foundation for Educational Research.

Mortimore, P., Sammons, P., Stoll, L., Lewis, D. and Ecob, R. (1988) *School Matters*. Wells, Somerset: Open Books.

Ofsted (1995) *Teaching Quality: The Primary Debate*. London: Ofsted.

Ofsted (1996) *Successful Teaching of Literacy and Numeracy in Primary Schools: A Starting Point*. London: Ofsted.

Ofsted (1997) *The Teaching of Number in Three Inner-Urban LEAs*. London: Ofsted.

Reynolds, D. and Farrell, S. (1996) *Worlds Apart? A Review of International Surveys of Educational Achievement Involving England*. London: HMSO for Ofsted.

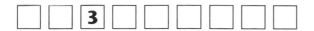

Realistic Mathematics Education in the Netherlands

Adrian Treffers and Meindert Beishuizen

Realistic Mathematics Education

The name Realistic Mathematics Education, or RME, stems from early arguments for changes in the teaching of mathematics in Holland. These arguments took the form of a demand for a greater use of problem situations from the real world. During the 1970s the movement started with the design and publication of the so-called Wiskobas projects ('Wiskunde voor de basischool' or Mathematics for Primary Schools). Hilary Shuard wrote about these projects that 'they made good use of investigative and imaginative work...' and '...exploited a style of teaching which is close to that of many British primary schools' (1986: 21). Wiskobas was based at the IOWO Institute for the Development of Mathematics Education and was greatly influenced by the views of the Institute's Director, Hans Freudenthal. The Wiskobas projects were shared with the international mathematics education community when several were published in the journal *Educational Studies in Mathematics* on the occasion of Freudenthal's retirement in 1976. He died in 1990 and in 1991 the Institute was renamed the Freudenthal Institute.

His views on mathematics education had a powerful influence on the development of Realistic Mathematics Education, particularly his strong conviction that mathematics should not be seen as subject matter that had to be transmitted but as *a human activity*. He believed that mathematics education should provide pupils with the 'guided' opportunity to 'reinvent' mathematics in the process of doing it: in short, to involve them in 'mathematization'.

As a reaction against traditional mathematics teaching, known in Holland as 'mechanistic mathematics', a greater emphasis was placed on 'applying mathematics' in many Western countries such as Britain. In Holland the reaction was also against the American 'new math' movement. The Wiskobas projects included many aspects of mathematics like measurement and geometry, ratio and fractions, column arithmetic and mental computation (see Treffers 1987, 1993). The argument for innovation, however, was not only about illustrating the applicability and relevance of mathematics in real-world situations, but also about taking realistic context situations as the starting point or as the source for learning mathematics. This important RME viewpoint goes much further than just adding a few application problems to your maths lessons. It involves a complete reversal of the teaching/learning process. No longer is the emphasis on the teacher transmitting knowledge and concepts, but on the children finding mathematical patterns and structures in realistic situations, and becoming active participants in the teaching/learning process.

'Realistic' also has a second meaning, and this relates to mathematical activities which are experientially real to a child. In the beginning, context situations taken from the real world will elicit such an experience, but later, when children become more familiar with numbers, their use of informal strategies for solving a number problem can also be experienced as a 'realistic' solution (in contrast to the execution of a standard algorithm). A similar position with respect to children's own activities as the starting point for learning can now be found in the constructivists' views.

Freudenthal (1973) was opposed to the traditional sequencing of instruction based on subject matter structure which moved from easy to complex, and to Gagné's psychological design of learning hierarchies. He believed that: 'Cognition does not start with concepts, but rather the other way around: concepts are the result of cognitive processes' (p. 18), and that 'By structuring rather than forming concepts we get a grip on reality' (p. 26).

For instance, when children use counting as an informal strategy, then structuring knowledge comes as a natural characteristic through replay and repetition, and they spontaneously discover counting in patterns and jumps. With more experience and more instruction with contextual models this develops into 'guided reinvention': schematizing and formalizing (or with a typical RME label, *mathematizing*). A well-known example is the emergence of structured counting in shorter jumps of 2s and 3s, which can be taken further towards counting in larger jumps of 10s on the model of the empty number line up to 100 (see Beishuizen, Chapter 13, this volume). The emphasis on the place-value number concept and the standard algorithms in British early mathematics teaching is the opposite approach. This more formal approach is questioned by the developers of RME and also by some authors in Britain such as Thompson (1997).

An illustrative example: long division

Long division is an example which is often used in RME publications (Figure 3.1 and see Treffers 1991b, 1993) to illustrate the development from informal context-bound solution strategies (Figure 3.1a) through what in Holland is called 'progressive mathematization' to higher level abbreviated strategies (Figure 3.1c) which come very close to formal procedures. There are, of course, some pupils who will not progress beyond intermediate levels (Figure 3.1b). However, every pupil learns to solve the long division problems at her/his own level, depending on personal abilities like knowledge of times tables facts and task-span capacity. Long division is taught in this way

Long division context problem:

1128 soldiers are transported on buses that have 36 seats.
How many buses are needed?

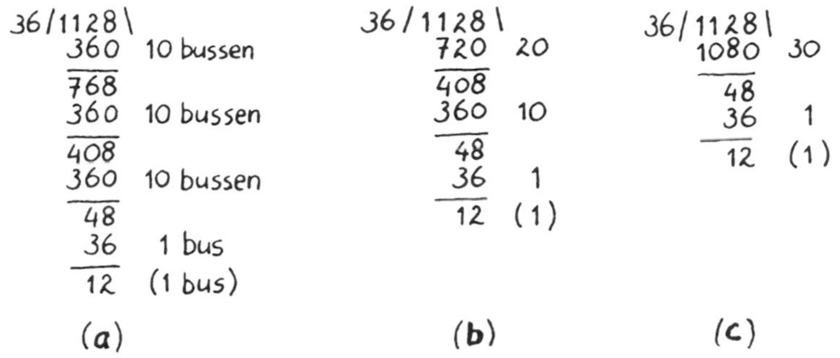

```
36/1128\                    36/1128\              36/1128\
   360  10 bussen              720  20              1080  30
   ───                         ───                  ────
   768                         408                    48
   360  10 bussen              360  10                36   1
   ───                         ───                    ──
   408                          48                    12  (1)
   360  10 bussen               36   1
   ───                          ──
    48                          12  (1)
    36   1 bus
    ──
    12  (1 bus)

   (a)                         (b)                   (c)
```

Figure 3.1 Solution levels for a long division problem.

in realistic textbooks in Holland (Anghileri and Beishuizen 1998), and under-standing is considered more important than fluency. Therefore during the initial learning, a great deal of lesson time is used for whole-class discussion of examples like the buses problem (Figure 3.1), with a range of pupils' solutions recorded on the blackboard. This also illustrates how the metacognitive aspect of pupils' verbalizing and recording of cognitive solution processes is practised in RME teaching. This aspect was mentioned as a relevant and important feature in an SCAA Discussion Paper (1997).

This 'active and interactive teaching', however, is inseparable from the role of realistic context problems as starting points, because they give pupils a better representation of the problem structure at hand and a better mental image of their solution strategies at work, compared to bare number prob-lems. For this reason context problems are preferably presented with a picture containing a modelling suggestion for the invited mathematical activity (Figure 3.2, and see also van den Heuvel-Panhuizen, Chapter 11, this volume). To depend solely on text – as happens in word problems – may well hinder the accessibility of the problem.

A further illustration of long division is given in pupils' work, collected in a collaborative research project comparing solution strategies in British and Dutch classes (see Anghileri and Beishuizen 1998). Figure 3.2 displays the first three items of a test presented in ten Cambridge and ten Leiden schools during January/February 1998 in Year 5/Groep 6 (10-year-olds), just before long division with two-digit divisors is normally taught. Later, in June 1998, the test was repeated to measure learning progress as the effect of teach-ing and practice. In this chapter some examples from the first test-round (Figures 3.3 and 3.4) will be enough to illustrate some of the aspects discussed above. The pupils were asked to show their working, which was practised with some problems at the beginning of the test.

1.

2.

98 flowers are bundled in
bunches of 7.
How many bunches can be made?

64 pencils have to be packed
in boxes of 16.
How many boxes will be needed?

3.

432 children have to be transported
by 15-seater buses.
How many buses will be needed?

Figure 3.2 First three items from a long division test.

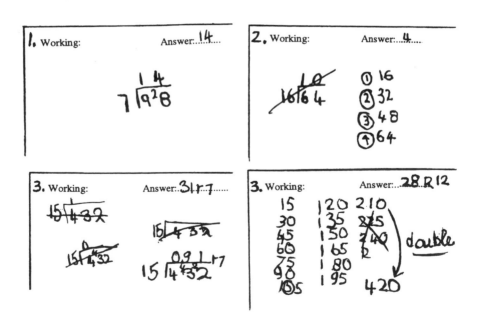

1. Working: Answer:..14....

$$7\overline{)9^2 8}$$
$$1\,4$$

2. Working: Answer:..4....

16$\overline{)64}$

① 16
② 32
③ 48
④ 64

3. Working: Answer:..31.r.7......

15$\overline{)432}$

15$\overline{)432}$

15$\overline{)432}$

15$\overline{)4\,32}$

3. Working: Answer:..28 R 12

15	20	210
30	35	215
45	50	240
60	65	R
75	80	
90	95	420
105		

double

Figure 3.3 Solutions of British pupils.

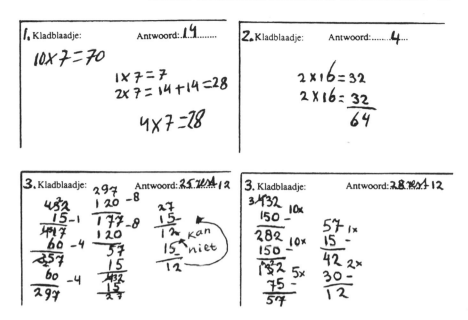

Figure 3.4 Solutions of Dutch pupils.

Most British pupils solve the first problem correctly with the standard algorithm (Figure 3.3). However, in the second and third problem solution they get stuck on the standard approach, because they have not yet practised the algorithmic division procedure with two digits. Notice that in these difficult situations many pupils revert to informal mental strategies like adding-up (problem 2) or adding-up sometimes combined with doubling as a short-cut strategy (problem 3). The context and the larger number of the dividend in the buses problem (problem 3) were deliberately chosen to invite a progression towards higher-level chunking strategies. Interestingly, this seems to work also for some British pupils – wherever they use mental strategies, but not if they hold on to the algorithmic approach (see the two problem 3 solutions in Figure 3.3). The Dutch pupils show more of these forms of mathematizing in their solutions to problem 3 (Figure 3.4), with some spontaneous use of higher level chunking ($10 \times 15 = 150$), but also many small chunks ($4 \times 15 = 60$) with transitions to larger chunks ($8 \times 15 = 120$, probably by doubling 4×15). This outcome is no surprise because Dutch pupils have had more previous experience with mental arithmetic. This can be seen in Figure 3.4 in the greater use of number facts (solutions to problem 1 and 2) as well as in the ease with which they use the subtraction procedure (solutions to problem 3).

According to the RME view, learning best takes place through offering pupils context problems in which they can discern mathematical structures and procedures through 'guided reinvention'. As explained above, pictorial context problems are designed to guide this reinvention by implicitly evoking certain (informal) strategies. Therefore all the pictures (Figure 3.2) illustrated a large quantity (the dividend) to be distributed or split into smaller ones (the divisor). The context situations also suggest that in reality the natural action or problem solution would be either taking away or adding up in consecutive steps.

This influence of context and the power of informal strategies for tackling new and unfamiliar problems – which have not yet been taught – can be observed in the solutions of the Dutch pupils and in those of some British pupils as well! Although these initial solutions are still at a low and not very efficient level, they can be used to build on teaching and reinvention of higher level strategies. However, with respect to the RME learning perspective of *progressive mathematization* (Figure 3.1) it is clear from Figures 3.3 and 3.4 that the Dutch and British pupils are not in the same position: the difference in the level of previous experience with mental arithmetic seems to make a real difference in the mental strategies they use in the long division test.

Horizontal and vertical mathematization

In the 1990s we saw a wider international recognition of mental arithmetic with whole numbers as constituting a better knowledge base for understanding number and number operations than vertical algorithmic procedures dealing with isolated digits (Pepper 1997). Emphasis on mental arithmetic has a long tradition in continental teaching (Bierhoff 1996). In the RME approach mental arithmetic regained its importance in the 1980s, when the focus of curriculum development shifted from the early Wiskobas projects to the basic computation skills of addition, subtraction, multiplication and division.

In the first decade (1970s) of the RME approach the emphasis had been on the need to make stronger connections with the real world. However, this had led to little attention being given to the systematic building up of basic knowledge in computational skills. During the second decade a more pragmatic concern developed about these neglected aspects of the early number curriculum, and this resulted in a shift in the RME approach from the first idealistic notions to an increased emphasis on the teaching of the basic skills including mental arithmetic.

Treffers (1987, 1991a, 1992) introduced the terms 'horizontal mathematization' and 'vertical mathematization' in order to characterize this difference in emphasis between the two decades. In this context the 'horizontal' dimension means what is described above: the analysing of real-world problems in a mathematical way. And, although there will always be a natural differentiation in the various levels of mathematizing in a group of pupils, the (vertical) development from lower level to higher level solution strategies is not the intention of horizontal mathematization. When, however, teaching is focusing on this development of strategies and concepts in a certain area of the mathematical system itself, this is called vertical mathematization. The difference between the two is not always clear-cut and they both are considered of equal value.

The main argument for the distinction between these two dimensions was to get a sharper grasp of the didactic design of (vertical) learning strands for the basic skills and related strategy development. 'Informal strategies as a starting point' and 'strategy development through guided reinvention' remained two leading RME principles. However, more attention was given to the didactic design of context problems (to invite specific strategies) and to the didactic improvement of models (to make mathematical structures transparent but not in a pre-structured way), so that the progressive mathematization towards higher levels of strategies and concepts would be more guaranteed. The sketch of long division and the progression in strategy levels (Figure 3.1) is given in many RME publications as an example of what is meant (Treffers 1991b, 1993). Teachers and textbook authors asked for more of such outlines for learning sequences and for teaching guidelines. Finding a balance between open and closed lesson designs is not an easy task, but since the 1980s this became a central issue in RME theory (Treffers 1987, 1993; Gravemeijer 1994). This is also covered in the proceedings of an international experts' meeting at Leiden university about 'The role of contexts and models in the development of mathematical strategies and procedures' (Beishuizen et al. 1997).

In the 1980s, the greater emphasis on mental arithmetic became central in the RME approach (Treffers 1991b, 1993). From the viewpoint of vertical mathematization it was argued that the knowledge base of memorized number facts had been neglected too much. On the other hand more attention was given to a further elaboration of the RME principle of progressive mathematization for the development of mental strategies. For instance the number operations up to 20 and up to 100 got more special attention (cf. Beishuizen, Chapter 13, this volume). It appeared that flexibility in the use of mental strategies was disappointing in existing school practice, and needed to be stimulated much more, as did the greater use of estimation strategies (Treffers 1992; van den Heuvel-Panhuizen 1998). Mental arithmetic appeared to be a ·powerful, but neglected, force, and reappeared in international research (McIntosh et al. 1992, and see Thompson, Chapter 12, this volume). RME focused on a further elaboration of mental arithmetic in mathematics teaching as well as on a better balancing of several aspects. In current British discussions similar themes like 'mental recall' versus 'mental strategies' now appear. It might, therefore, be interesting to have a closer look at our experiences in Holland (Beishuizen 1997; Beishuizen and Anghileri 1998).

During the second half of the 1980s Treffers focused more closely on the didactic implications of the RME views for teaching practice and textbook design. Existing models were reconsidered from the viewpoint of mental arithmetic and progressive mathematization (see above), which resulted in new models like the arithmetic rack up to 20 and the empty number line up to 100 as models for the development of a better basic knowledge and number sense and a more flexible use of number operations (Treffers 1991b; Treffers and De Moor 1990). Beishuizen (Chapter 13, this volume) gives the arguments and the design for a new empty number line programme in Dutch 2nd grades (Year 3). More attention was also given to the didactic design of context problems for the (guided) introduction of strategies and for the final (open) assessment of learning results (see van den Heuvel-Panhuizen, Chapter 11, this volume).

Outcomes of a first National Arithmetic Test in 1987 (half-way through and at the end of primary school) contributed greatly to a reconsideration of primary mathematics teaching in Holland. At the Freudenthal Institute proposals for revisions were formulated, which after discussions about draft versions led to the publication of the so-called *Proeve* or *Specimen of a New National Programme* (Treffers and De Moor 1990). Didactic improvements and new models for teaching were presented with examples and a further alignment of learning strands in the curriculum. This included a greater emphasis on mental arithmetic in the early grades, and by consequence a postponement of vertical algorithms until Grade 3 (Year 4). Textbook authors were, of course, influenced too by the new National Programme, which led to revisions of the existing realistic textbooks. The so-called first generation of realistic textbooks had been published in the early 1980s. Now, a second generation of revised realistic textbooks was published in the 1990s, not only including these new ideas, but also based on many comments and experiences from practising teachers.

In Dutch schools a remarkable change had taken place: in 1980 only 5 per cent of the schools used a realistic textbook whereas in 1990 this had increased to 75 per cent (Treffers 1991a). And it was not an innovatory project from the government that had caused this change, but a spontaneous process of teachers becoming attracted to, and convinced by, RME views and the realistic textbooks. Generally the experience is positive: realistic mathematics is done with more activities and pleasure, and with better results in mental arithmetic (as became evident from the second National Arithmetic Test in 1992 and also the good TIMSS results for Holland published in 1997). However, evaluation studies indicate that realistic mathematics teaching in classrooms still shows substantial shortcomings. Many teachers use their realistic textbooks in a traditional way: giving direct instruction in strategies without leaving much room for children's own activities; minimizing whole-class discussions, etc. Consequently, studies into implementation in the classroom as well as the further innovation of teacher and in-service training are high on the agenda for the near future (Treffers 1992).

Learning and teaching principles

Treffers (1987, 1991b) has formulated five learning/teaching principles as a characterization of the RME approach, and as these are still relevant they are included here as a summary of this chapter.

1 *Learning as a constructive activity and the use of context problems*
   This learning principle states that first and foremost learning mathematics is a constructive activity, and it contradicts the idea of learning as absorbing knowledge which is presented or transmitted. This principle has been

described as the main argument for the original development of RME. Later in the 1980s the distinction made between horizontal and vertical mathematization emphasized that context problems can be presented as rich contexts taken from the real world, but also as smaller and more specific introductory context problems that invite informal strategies to be built on in a new learning sequence (see Figures 3.1 and 3.2 for long division examples).

2 *Learning as the development through higher levels of abstraction and the role of models*

This principle came more into focus in the 1980s from the perspective of vertical mathematization introduced by Treffers (1987). It was illustrated in this chapter by a sketch of the possible development of long division strategies (Figure 3.1) from lower to higher levels. Different levels could also be observed in some examples from British and Dutch pupils (Figures 3.3 and 3.4). The stronger didactic role of models – and improved design of models – for 'guided' reinvention and development of strategies was then discussed in this chapter. A good example is the new model of the empty number line (Chapter 13). According to the first RME principle these models should be 'open' to children's own constructions and individual adaptations.

3 *Learning through reflection – in particular on children's own constructions*

This principle has not been discussed much in this chapter, but it is strongly connected to the first principle of learning mathematics as a constructive activity. Reflection, however, adds a dimension to children's own constructions, which is important for the progressive development towards higher level strategies and concepts. The open character of context problems is also meant to give ample opportunity for such reflections by considering one's own solution process and that of others. The teacher has the task of stimulating pupils and ensuring that they are engaged in learning through reflection. The empty number line is an example of how an improved design of instructional materials can elicit such reflection in a natural way. By drawing their jumps on the number line pupils constantly see what they are doing, which activates their mental thinking, the consideration of alternative solutions, and the discussion of different strategies.

4 *Learning as a social activity through interactive teaching*

Learning is not merely a solo activity but is also directed and stimulated by the socio-cultural context. This principle is strongly connected to the third principle of learning through reflection. The role of the teacher is seen as being crucial. Mathematics education should be interactive: as well as providing room for individual work it must also offer the opportunity for the exchange of ideas, the rebuttal of arguments, etc. One conclusion about the implementation of RME in the 1990s was that despite the widespread acceptance now in Dutch schools of RME views and realistic textbooks, classroom teaching in a genuine realistic way needs further improvement. Interactive teaching in whole-class situations with a large group of children is not an easy task. Therefore, more observational research and video examples of good interactive lessons are needed to give teachers better guidelines in their training and in-service courses.

Lieke wants to buy 4 breads costing f 1.98 each.
She has a ten-guilder coin to pay with. Is that enough?

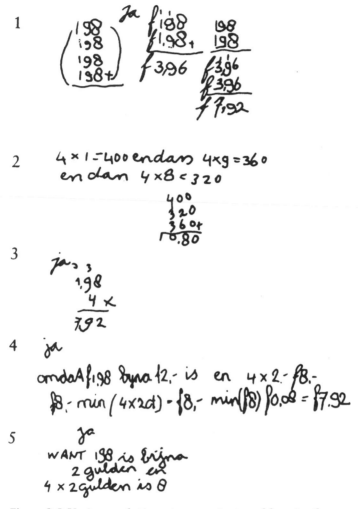

Figure 3.5 Various solutions to a context problem in the upper grade.

5 *Intertwining of the various learning strands within mathematics teaching*
This last principle takes the macro-didactic or curriculum perspective, which
became more and more important with the further progress of the RME
approach on the micro-didactic level of teaching and lesson design (Treffers
1991a, 1992). We saw how at the end of the 1980s a new proposal for
a National Programme of primary mathematics was formulated (Treffers
and De Moor 1990). Also, the authors of the so-called second generation

of realistic textbooks (published in the 1990s) paid more attention to the intertwining of the various learning strands. It is well known that the subject of mathematics has always suffered from the danger of learning strands becoming more and more separated, in particular in the upper grades of primary school. This topic is relevant but is also complicated, and needs more space than is available in this chapter.

A final example

We shall conclude this chapter by mentioning the Tussendoelen Annex Leerlÿnen (Intermediate Objectives in Learning Strands) (TAL)-project 1998 (and 1999), in which a project team at the Freudenthal Institute is working out a further renewal of the Dutch primary mathematics curriculum under the authority of the Ministry of Education (see van den Heuvel-Panhuizen 1998).

We exemplify this in Figure 3.5 where we see an increasing variety of solutions in the upper grade. About half of the pupils chose algorithmic calculation (1 and 3) and less than one-third used global estimation (4 and 5) (Treffers *et al.* 1996: 127). More emphasis on global arithmetic and on sensible estimation, based on the intertwining of learning strands as can be seen surfacing in Figure 3.5, is one of the goals for the future that are being worked out in Holland now.

References

Anghileri, J. and Beishuizen, M. (1998) Counting, chunking and the division algorithm. *Mathematics in School*, January: 2–4.

Beishuizen, M. (1997) Mental arithmetic: mental recall or mental strategies? *Mathematics Teaching*, September: 16–19.

Beishuizen, M. and Anghileri, J. (1998) Which mental strategies in the early number curriculum? A comparison of British ideas and Dutch views. *British Educational Research Journal*, 24: 519–38.

Beishuizen, M., Gravemeijer, K.P.E. and Van Lieshout, E.C.D.M. (eds) (1997) *The Role of Contexts and Models in the Development of Mathematical Strategies and Procedures*. Utrecht: Freudenthal Institute.

Bierhoff, H. (1996) *Laying the Foundations of Numeracy: A Comparison of Primary School Textbooks in Britain, Germany and Switzerland*. Discussion Paper No. 90. London: National Institute of Economic and Social Research.

Freudenthal, H. (1973) *Mathematics as an Educational Task*. Dordrecht: Kluwer Academic Publishers.

Gravemeijer, K. (1994) Educational development and developmental research in mathematics education. *Journal for Research in Mathematics Education*, 25: 443–71.

McIntosh, A., Reys, B.J. and Reys, R.E. (1992) A proposed framework for examining basic number sense. *For the Learning of Mathematics*, 12: 2–44.

Pepper, M. (1997) Mental arithmetic – back in favour. *Equals*, 3: 9–10.

SCAA (School Curriculum and Assessment Authority) (1997) *The Teaching and Assessment of Number at Key Stages 1–3*. Discussion Paper No. 10. London: SCAA.

Shuard, H. (1986) *Primary Mathematics Today and Tomorrow.* School Curriculum and Development Committee (SCDC) publication. York: Longman SCDC.

Thompson, I. (ed.) (1997) *Teaching and Learning Early Number.* Buckingham: Open University Press.

Treffers, A. (1987) *Three Dimensions. A Model of Goal and Theory Description in Mathematics Instruction – The Wiskobas Project.* Dordrecht: Reidel Publishing Company.

Treffers, A. (1991a) Realistic mathematics education in The Netherlands 1980–1990. In L. Streefland (ed.), *Realistic Mathematics Education in Primary School*, pp. 11–20. Utrecht: Freudenthal Institute.

Treffers, A. (1991b) Didactical background of a mathematics program for primary education. In L. Streefland (ed.), *Realistic Mathematics Education in Primary School*, pp. 21–56. Utrecht: Freudenthal Institute.

Treffers, A. (1992) Terug naar de toekomst [Back to the Future]. In F. Goffree, A. Treffers and J. de Lange, *Rekenen anno 2002 – Toekomstverwachtingen van het reken-wiskunde-onderwijs* [Arithmetic Anno 2002 – Expectations for the Future of Mathematics Education], pp. 11–34. Utrecht: NVORWO [Dutch Society for the Advancement of Mathematics Education].

Treffers, A. (1993) Wiskobas and Freudenthal – Realistic Mathematics Education. *Educational Studies in Mathematics*, 25: 89–108.

Treffers, A. and De Moor, E. (1990) *Proeve van een nationaal programma voor het reken-wiskunde-onderwijs op de basisschool. Deel 2: Basisvaardigheden en cijferen* [Specimen of a National Program for Primary Mathematics Teaching. Part 2: Basic Mental Skills and Written Algorithms]. Tilburg: Zwijsen.

Treffers, A., Streefland, L. and De Moor, E. (1996) *Proeve van een nationaal programma voor het reken-wiskunde-onderwijs op de basisschool. Deel 3B: Kommagetallen* [Specimen of a National Program for Primary Mathematics Teaching. Part 3B: Decimal Numbers]. Tilburg: Zwijsen.

van den Heuvel-Panhuizen, M. (1998) *Realistic Mathematics Education: work in progress* (NORMA 98 Lecture at the Nordic Conference on Mathematics Education, Kristiansand, Norway). Utrecht: Freudenthal Institute.

The National Numeracy Project: 1996–99

Anita Straker

Introduction

Many factors contributed towards the creation of the National Numeracy Project (NNP) by the Department for Education and Employment (DfEE) in September 1996 (see Brown, Chapter 1, this volume). Among these factors were three specific concerns voiced in HMI and Ofsted reports about primary mathematics teaching in the early 1990s: the level of foundation skills in arithmetic, especially mental arithmetic and other key numeracy skills; the dominance of schemes which overemphasized standard written methods at the expense of mental techniques; and a learning approach which placed undue responsibility on pupils for controlling the pace of their own learning and reduced the teacher to a classroom manager who involved the children in little direct teaching or discussion about their mathematics.

The other partners involved in the development of the NNP were the Office for Standards in Education (Ofsted), the Qualifications and Curriculum Authority (QCA), the Teacher Training Agency (TTA) and the Basic Skills Agency (BSA). Although it was originally intended that there would be five cohorts, 1996 to 2000, the last two were subsumed in the National Numeracy Strategy which was implemented in all schools in September 1999. The project was co-ordinated by a full-time Director.

Originally, there were 12 local numeracy centres and two associate centres. Each local centre had two or more full-time consultants to work with groups of schools. These consultants met regularly at the national centre to share ideas, report on progress and contribute to the development of the national programme. Schools took part in a rolling programme with about twenty schools from each LEA in each phase, and individual schools were directly involved for two years, during which time they were expected to set targets and monitor their progress against them. By the end of 1998 there were approximately 750 schools, 7000 teachers and 180,000 children taking part. The main purpose of the project was to raise standards of numeracy in the participating schools in line with national expectations for primary pupils by requiring more interactive teaching with whole classes and groups; by improving the school's management of numeracy through target setting linked to systematic action planning, monitoring and evaluation; and by encouraging family support for children's achievement.

Pupils took age-standardized numeracy tests every year which provided baseline measures, progress measures and a final result. The tests were very comprehensive and were specially commissioned for the NNP by the School Curriculum and Assessment Authority (later to become the Qualifications and Curriculum Authority (QCA)). For each of the Years 1 to 6 there was an orally administered test of mental arithmetic, and an untimed pencil and paper test (where no apparatus or calculators were allowed). As in the national tests, children could be given help with reading the written questions but not with the mathematics. The National Foundation for Educational Research administered the testing process and analysed the results in a number of ways so that each school, each LEA and the project as a whole knew what progress it was making and also what areas of numeracy needed attention.

How the project worked in the LEAs and schools taking part

The consultant started with an audit of numeracy in the school, carried out in partnership with the head teacher and mathematics co-ordinator. At about the same time, schools administered a numeracy test to pupils in three age groups to establish a baseline and to help monitor progress. They used the audit findings and test results to set clear targets for improvement and to create an action plan and training plan which the consultant supported. The mathematics co-ordinator and one other key teacher from each school attended eight days of training run by the local consultants. The head teacher attended for the first three days. Regular twilight sessions on planning and teaching aspects of numeracy were held for co-ordinators and teachers throughout the year at the local numeracy centre.

In each school, the consultant supported up to two training days for all the staff each year, and eight more days of school-based consultancy over two years. The school-based support included demonstration lessons and teaching in tandem, focusing on interactive, whole-class teaching. The mathematics co-ordinator in each school had five days of extra release each year to give extra classroom support and coaching to colleagues. Teacher assistants had the opportunity for special training in numeracy. Each class had daily lessons for mathematics, about 45 minutes in Key Stage 1, and 50 minutes to one hour in Key Stage 2. Lessons started with about 10 minutes of oral work/mental calculation, including rehearsal of 'number bonds' and tables, followed by the main teaching activity (30 to 40 minutes) and a 10-minute plenary session. Each school agreed in writing its commitment to the project, and head teachers and senior staff agreed to monitor planning and teaching regularly. LEA review days with head teachers took place each term at the local centres.

The 'Framework for teaching mathematics'

The NNP's broad definition of numeracy was:

Numeracy means knowing about numbers and number operations. More than this, it includes an ability and inclination to apply numerical understanding and skills to solve problems, including those involving money and measures. It also includes familiarity with the ways in which numerical information is gathered by counting and measuring, and is presented in graphs, charts and tables.

The project's approach to the teaching of numeracy was originally based on three key principles:

- mathematics lessons every day;
- direct teaching and interactive oral work with the whole class and groups;
- an emphasis on mental calculation.

A fourth principle, 'controlled differentiation', was added at a later stage.

The Framework for Teaching Mathematics (DfEE 1998a) set out programmes of teaching objectives for the mathematical topics to be taught in each year from Reception to Year 6 in order to help pupils become fully numerate. It gave guidance on the daily mathematics lesson in which this teaching took place and on the assessment of pupils' progress. The Framework covered all aspects of the National Curriculum for mathematics in Key Stages 1 and 2. Each year's programme was accompanied by some templates to help teachers plan a term's lessons. These showed how topics could be grouped in units of work throughout the term so that suitable emphasis could be given to numeracy. A recommended number of lessons was given for each unit, and time was built in for half-termly assessment and review. The document included supplements of examples, for Reception, Years 1–3 and Years 4–6 which illustrate, for each objective, the range of what pupils should know, understand and be able to do by the end of the year.

The Framework has four strands, three with direct links to number and one for shape and space. The first three strands incorporated the National Curriculum programmes of study for number, handling data and measures, so that computational skills could be developed through work on money and measurement and in other contexts. The fourth strand incorporated shape and space. The programme of study for using and applying mathematics was integrated throughout. The four strands, and the topics which they cover, were 'Knowledge of numbers and the number system', 'Calculations', 'Making sense of number problems' and 'Shape and space'.

The strands were described separately but had many connections between them. In the Framework mathematics was seen to be loosely hierarchical: a structure composed of a whole network of concepts and relationships. Therefore, teaching plans had to cover all four strands and teachers had to help children to appreciate the links that exist between the different parts of these strands. Teachers were advised how different kinds of activities could be structured within a lesson and a balance achieved between whole-class, group and individualized teaching.

Planning from the Framework

The Framework comprised a set of double-page *yearly teaching programmes* or 'programmes of study' summarizing teaching objectives for each of Reception and Years 1 to 6. Each programme covered the full range of the National Curriculum for mathematics that is relevant to that year group. With each year's programme were two *planning templates* to help teachers plan a term's lessons: one for the autumn and summer terms and one for the spring term (for Reception there was one for each term). Each template showed the topics to be taught in units of work, and the recommended number of days of lessons to be allocated to each unit. The first and last units in each term lasted either two or three days to allow for the start and end of term. The units could be taught in any order, and two days were set aside in each half term for assessment and the progress review.

The planning templates required 175 days of the school year, leaving about one week in each term for extra reinforcement or revision, making cross-curricular links and more extended problem solving. The templates for Reception allowed time for settling in and for new children to join the class.

Distinguishing characteristics of the project

There were many features of the National Numeracy Project which made it different from all its predecessors in this country. Two particularly interesting differences were the focus on interactive whole-class teaching and the emphasis on mental methods in the approach to calculation.

Interactive whole-class teaching

An important idea that underpinned the Project was that high-quality direct teaching is oral and interactive. It is not achieved by adopting a simplistic formula of 'drill and practice'. It is an essential craft which involves balancing different elements: demonstration, explanation, questioning, discussion and evaluation of pupils' responses and direction. For example, a teacher might: *demonstrate* how to add on by bridging through 10 on a number line or how to multiply a three-digit number by a two-digit number; *explain* a method of calculation and discuss why it works or illustrate a general statement with examples; use techniques of *questioning* to encourage children to extend and expand on their ideas or to help identify common errors and misconceptions; involve children in *discussion* to justify a particular method of calculation or to probe their understanding; give clear *directions* to ensure that pupils know what they should be doing, drawing attention to points over which particular care should be taken.

Many of these teaching strategies are particularly useful when used in an interactive whole-class teaching situation. The most important part of this phrase is 'interactive'. Good interaction is as important in group work and paired work as it is in whole-class work. Organizing children as a 'whole class' helps to maximize the direct contact they have with the teacher so that every child benefits from good interaction for sustained periods. It also keeps the class working together, as far as they reasonably can, with the aim of keeping the strugglers up with the rest.

HMI reported (Ofsted 1998) that there had been a significant improvement in the quality of teaching in Project schools, with the percentage of 'satisfactory or better' lessons increasing from 70 to 80 per cent between autumn 1997 and summer 1998. Teachers were more prepared to engage with the whole class through direct teaching, and pupils were generally eager to share their thinking and methods of calculating with the whole class. Errors were treated constructively, discussed and corrected. Pupils' attitudes to mathematics were positive in nearly all lessons, across all year groups in both key stages, and many teachers referred to the increased motivation and concentration of most pupils.

The project's approach to calculation

An important tenet underpinning the NNP is that the ability to calculate mentally lies at the heart of numeracy. Mental methods should be emphasized from an early age with regular opportunities to develop the different skills involved. These skills include:

- remembering number facts like $4 + 7$ or $21 + 3$ and recalling them instantly;
- using the facts that are known by heart to figure out new facts: for example, a fact like $8 + 6 = 14$ can be used to work out $80 + 60 = 140$, or $28 + 6 = 34$;
- having a repertoire of mental strategies for working out calculations like $81 - 26$, 23×4 or 5% of £3,000, with some thinking time;
- solving problems like: 'Will three tins of beans at 39p each cost more or less than £1?' or: 'Roughly how long will it take me to go 50 miles at 30 mph?'

This emphasis on mental calculation does not mean that written methods should not also be taught throughout the primary years but the balance between mental and written methods, and the way in which pupils progress from one to the other, is very important.

In the early years children are expected to use oral methods, generally moving from counting real or imagined objects or fingers to mental counting strategies. Later they will use a number line or square to work out their answers in different ways, depending on the numbers involved. After experience with a variety of situations, real and imagined, and problems posed in different ways, they should be taught to remember and recall number facts such as 'five add three is eight' or that 'seven taken from nine leaves two'. These early stages of mental calculation are not, however, at the exclusion of written recording. Alongside their oral and mental work they will learn first to interpret and complete statements like $5 + 8 = \square$ or $13 = \square + 5$, and then record the results of their own mental calculations using the correct symbols and a horizontal format such as $43 - 8 = 35$.

As pupils progress to working with larger numbers they will learn more sophisticated mental methods and tackle more complex problems. They will develop some of these methods intuitively and some they will be taught explicitly. Through a process of regular explanation and discussion of their own and other people's methods they will begin to acquire a repertoire of mental calculation strategies. At this stage, it can be hard for them to hold all the intermediate steps of a calculation in their heads and so informal pencil and paper notes recording some or all of their solution become part of a mental strategy. These personal jottings may not be easy for someone else to follow but they are a staging post to getting the right answer and acquiring fluency in mental calculation (see Thompson, Chapter 12, this volume).

Not everyone does a mental calculation like 81 – 26 in the same way – nor is it necessary for them to do so – but some methods are more efficient than others. By discussing and comparing different part written, part mental methods, pupils are guided towards choosing and using the methods which are most efficient and which can be applied generally. At this point, the need for more formal recording of calculation methods emerges.

Standard written methods are reliable and efficient procedures for calculating which, once mastered, can be used in many different contexts. However, they are of no use to someone who applies them inaccurately and who cannot judge whether the answer is reasonable. For each operation, at least one standard written method should be taught in the later primary years but the progression towards these methods is crucial, since they are based on steps which are done mentally and which need to be secured first.

Most countries, and in particular those which are most successful at teaching number, avoid the premature teaching of the standard methods. The bridge from recording part written/part mental methods to learning standard methods of written calculations begins only when children can calculate reliably with two-digit numbers in their heads – usually at the age of about eight and a half (see Thompson, Chapter 14, this volume).

Evaluation and assessment of mental calculation

HMI reported (Ofsted 1998) on the impact of the Project on the first cohort of schools. Three visits were made to a 20 per cent sample of the 211 schools involved, and HMI also drew on analyses of numeracy test data and National Curriculum test results carried out by the National Foundation for Educational Research (NFER) and the Department for Education and Employment (DfEE) respectively.

The NFER standardized test data showed that pupils in Years 2, 3 and 5 had made significantly better progress than predicted over the five terms in both the written and the mental tests. The improvement in mental calculation skills was especially marked. The National Curriculum test results showed that standards in Project schools as a whole had improved between 1996 and 1997, and these improvements were slightly better than the average national improvements.

Teachers had come to recognize the importance of oral and mental work and had raised their expectations of pupils' achievement. The Framework had succeeded in developing teachers' knowledge of, and confidence in, the teaching of mental calculation strategies. In the best examples, 'teachers gave a high priority to encouraging pupils to go beyond recall of number facts to explain their strategies' (Ofsted 1998: 11).

Demands on teachers

The NNP made heavy demands on project teachers who were expected to:

- structure their lessons, maintain good pace and spend minimum time on class administration or control;
- provide daily oral and mental work to develop and secure pupils' calculation strategies and instant recall skills;
- devote a high proportion of lesson time to direct teaching of whole classes and groups, involving themselves proactively, not just when pupils are 'stuck';
- demonstrate, explain and illustrate mathematical ideas, and make links between different topics in mathematics and mathematics and other subjects;
- question pupils effectively, allowing them time to think before answering;
- ask pupils to demonstrate and explain their methods, and explore reasons for wrong answers;
- pay attention to correct mathematical vocabulary and notation;
- give pupils appropriately demanding work, including some non-routine problems that require them to think for themselves; and
- ensure that differentiation is manageable and centred around work common to all the pupils in a class, with some targeted, positive support to help strugglers to keep up with their peers.

The project in action

In order to give a feel for what a Numeracy Project lesson might look like, there follows a thumbnail sketch of a lesson which took place in a large inner-city school in the London Borough of Tower Hamlets. There are 496 pupils on roll, 26 per cent of whom have special educational needs, and in this lesson the mathematics co-ordinator is working with a Year 5 mixed ability class of 30 children. Twenty-seven of the children in the class are learning English as an additional language, and over half are eligible for free school meals.

The lesson begins with the children sitting on the carpet around the teacher at a home-made flip-chart. It is clearly spelled out to the children that the overall aim of the lesson is to look at doubling, and that in the introductory part they will begin with their two times table which is also described as multiples of two. The first seven terms of the two times table are quickly generated by the teacher asking individually focused questions. She tells the children that she is aware that they all know their four times table and enlists their help to build it up. She usually calls it the four times table, but occasionally talks about multiples of four in order to extend their mathematical language.

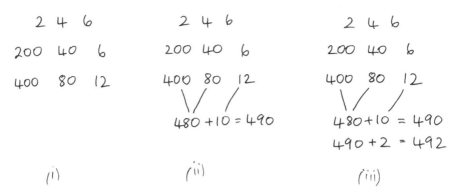

Figure 4.1 Developing stages of the teacher's board work.

The next stage is to generate the eight times table from the fours by doubling each answer. Finding the fourth entry in the eight times table produces a variety of strategies: adding eight on to the 24 ('24 add 6 is 30 and 2 more makes 32'); doubling the 16 from the four times table directly above ('10 add 10 is 20 . . . 6 and 6 is 12 . . . 20 and 12 is 32').

When the children are tackling double 56 the three different answers offered – 112, 104 and 186 – are written on the board. Answers, correct or incorrect, are passed to other children for comment. A miscalculation is shared with the class in order to emphasize that getting an answer wrong is natural, and to help others who may have made the same mistake. The situation is handled sensitively in an attempt to build up rather than destroy the child's confidence. Later in the lesson this same child is asked a question that the teacher knows she will get right.

In the main part of the lesson a discussion ensues about the reason why it is more challenging to double a number like 37 than a number like 23. Extended notation (37 is 30 and 7) is used and the children offer a variety of responses: '7 is an odd number and even ones are easier to double'; '7 is a hard number to double'; and '7 goes over the 10'. All the answers are treated with equal respect. One child doubles 37 saying, '30 and 30 makes 60 . . . 7 and 7 makes 14 . . . 60 and 14 is 64' (*sic*). This is then discussed by the group and another child suggests taking the 10 from the 14 and then adding it to the 60 to make 70 before adding on the remaining four.

Having been offered 246 as a 'favourite three-digit number' the teacher elicits from an individual child that she would double the 200 first. The child is then asked to remember the 400 that she gets as her answer. Two other children do the same with the remaining partial sums: 80 and 12. The children then say their partial answers out loud, and the teacher writes the three numbers on the board (see Figure 4.1 (i)). The class is then challenged to find the total, and one child explains her correct answer: '400 add 80 is 480 . . . and I took away 10 from 12 and added it on to 480 . . . and that became 490 . . . I added the two on to get 492.' The teacher then models this explanation on the board so that the child who miscalculated, and anyone else who got the wrong answer, can see where they went wrong (see Figure 4.1 (ii) and (iii)). The modelling also suggests how they might record their methods when asked to show how they found a particular answer.

In the main part of the lesson the class is split into two groups. Those who are still not confident with doubling work in groups at tables carrying out dice and number card activities to help them develop their doubling further so that they are ready for the next morning's carpet session. Those who are already confident and good at doubling and multiplying by two stay on the carpet with the teacher to look at the Egyptian doubling and halving method of long multiplication. This is part of the teacher's ongoing emphasis on the fact that there is not just one right way of doing calculations.

The plenary session comprises two separate parts. In the first part those working with the equipment discuss with the rest of the class the size of the numbers they have doubled, and then the whole class plays a game of 'Whizz doubles' together. The lesson ends with the teacher telling the class to give themselves a big round of applause.

This lesson can be seen on the video *Numeracy in Action* produced jointly by the NNP and the Hamilton Maths Project. It is analysed from the viewpoint of 'good practice in the teaching of mental calculation' in Chapter 12 of this volume.

Conclusion

In the final report of the Numeracy Task Force (DfEE 1998b) the recommendation was made that the *Framework for Teaching Mathematics: Reception to Year 6* (DfEE 1998a), developed and used in the National Numeracy Project, be sent, as part of the implementation of the National Numeracy Strategy, to all primary, special and secondary schools, LEAs and initial training providers in early 1999. The final version of the *Framework* became *The National Numeracy Strategy Framework for Teaching Mathematics from Reception to Year 6* (DfEE 1999), and free copies were made available in March 1999.

A great deal of work, effort and energy had gone into developing the National Numeracy Project, and its success in project schools was evident. The decision to extend its 'good practice' to all schools – inevitably with substantially less training and support – appeared to be a sensible one at the time. The proof of the pudding would be in the eating!

Resources

A number of other publications have been produced by the National Numeracy Strategy to support the *Framework for Teaching Mathematics* and the related training programme:

1 *Numeracy in Action.* A 65-minute video has been produced jointly with the Hamilton Maths Project. It features three Key Stage 1 and three Key Stage 2 numeracy lessons, and is accompanied by a booklet describing how it can be used in a whole-school in-service education and training (INSET) day or after-school training sessions. The

video costs approximately £15, plus postage and VAT, and can be obtained from Hamilton Education, tel. 01865 396613.

2 *Mathematical Vocabulary.* This 36-page booklet lists the essential vocabulary for each year group. An introductory section discusses questioning strategies. Copies of this can be obtained from the DfEE (0845 602260).

3 *Numeracy Lessons.* This book contains descriptions of six lessons for each age group from Reception to Year 7 and costs approximately £10. Each lesson is described on a double page spread. The book can be obtained at cost price from BEAM (0171 457 5535).

4 *Resource Links.* These booklets link the teaching objectives for each year to relevant parts of different published schemes. They are intended to help teachers plan day-to-day lessons and are available to Numeracy Project schools only through local numeracy centres.

5 *Assisting Numeracy.* This is a 96-page handbook intended for classroom assistants. It is the outcome of a joint venture between BEAM, the Numeracy Project and the London Borough of Tower Hamlets, which was part of the project. It can be obtained from BEAM at a cost of about £15.

References

DfEE (Department for Education and Employment) (1988a) *The Framework for Teaching Mathematics: Reception to Year 6 (Draft).* London: DfEE.

DfEE (Department for Education and Employment) (1998b) *The Implementation of the National Numeracy Strategy:* Final Report of the Numeracy Task Force. London: DfEE.

DfEE (Department for Education and Employment) (1999) *The National Numeracy Strategy Framework for Teaching Mathematics from Reception to Year 6.* London: DfEE.

Ofsted (Office for Standards in Education) (1998) *The National Numeracy Project: An HMI Evaluation.* London: Ofsted.

CURRICULUM AND RESEARCH PROJECT ISSUES

The 1990s saw an increase in the number of funded research projects related to the teaching and learning of numeracy, particularly in primary schools. In this section several experienced researchers report on specific aspects of their completed projects, and discuss the implications of their findings for the teaching and learning of numeracy in the primary school. These projects include a comparison of primary textbooks in several countries; teachers' conceptualizations of Attainment Target 1; involving parents in their children's learning of numeracy; the characteristics of effective teachers of numeracy; and an exploration of effective teaching of numeracy using Information and Communications Technology (ICT).

Mathematics textbooks are likely to reflect the school mathematics culture of a particular country. Although they can be used by teachers in a variety of different ways they will emerge from beliefs about mathematics, learning and the role of the teacher. In Chapter 5 Tony Harries and Ros Sutherland present the results of a research project which compared primary mathematics textbooks from England, France, Singapore, USA and Hungary. They discuss the framework used for analysing the books, which placed a particular emphasis on the ways in which external representations are used for scaffolding. They found that textbooks from each of the countries studied differed quite considerably from the point of view of what mathematics is presented, how it is presented and the relationship between the ideas covered. They use different approaches to multiplication in the textbooks to illustrate the extent to which some books made it relatively difficult for children to make sense of the mathematics presented, thereby raising questions about the ways in which these books support learning.

From the initial debate over Profile Component 3 in the earliest stages of the development of the National Curriculum for mathematics, Attainment Target 1 – 'Using and Applying Mathematics' – has been contentious, and has proved challenging in terms of its implementation by teachers. In Chapter 6 Martin Hughes, Charles Desforges and Christine Mitchell report on their

Nuffield-funded project, Using and Applying Mathematical Knowledge in the Primary School. Using three contrasting case studies of teachers teaching 'Using and Applying Mathematics', the authors illustrate how different teachers in the project conceptualized the problem of application, and make specific recommendations on how the main approaches to using and applying mathematics can be implemented in practice.

The Numeracy Task Force's final report, *The Implementation of the National Numeracy Strategy*, devoted a whole chapter to 'Creating a climate of support at home and in the wider community'. In Chapter 7 Ruth Merttens, Director of the Hamilton Maths Project and Inventing Maths for Parents and Children and Teachers (IMPACT) – two projects which have succeeded in involving parents in their children's learning of numeracy – describes the outcomes of these projects. She makes recommendations as to how schools might successfully promote a more positive attitude towards numeracy amongst parents and other adults, and gives practical suggestions for ensuring that schools maximize the number of parents involved in their children's learning and develop a culture of 'parents as partners'. The implications for schools' homework policies and their implementation are discussed, and consideration is given to the ways in which homework can be used to raise the achievement of *all* children rather than widen the differential between them.

The author of Chapter 8, Mike Askew, was principal investigator for the study *Effective Teachers of Numeracy* which was carried out by King's College in 1995–6 for the Teacher Training Agency. The aims of the study were to explore the key factors which made teachers into effective teachers of numeracy. To do this the researchers explored the knowledge, beliefs and practices of a sample of effective teachers of numeracy, where 'effectiveness' was defined on the basis of learning gains. The chapter discusses some of the difficulties the team encountered in deciding what might constitute effective teaching of numeracy; in setting about the task of finding effective teachers of the subject; and then in working out how to investigate their beliefs and practices. Several of the project's findings were surprising in that they challenged some popularly held beliefs about what it is that makes a teacher effective. The chapter includes illustrative examples of effective teachers in action; describes three different orientations to the teaching of numeracy; and discusses the relationship between these orientations and effectiveness.

In Chapter 9 Steve Higgins and Daniel Muijs discuss ICT and numeracy from the perspective of their work as, respectively, manager of the TTA-funded project Effective Pedagogy Using ICT in Primary Schools and research worker for the Numeracy Task Force. They consider the software used by teachers responding to a questionnaire completed as part of the ICT project. Specific programs are classified in terms of Higgins's and Muijs's own model for the development of mathematics with ICT. The use of Integrated Learning Systems (ILS) and palmtops is also explored. The role of the teacher and suitable aims for computer use are examined, and the chapter concludes with a detailed list of implications for teaching suggested by the research findings.

Primary school mathematics textbooks: an international comparison

Tony Harries and Rosamund Sutherland

Introduction and background

In England, primary mathematics textbooks have received very little critical attention. The dominant view is that they provoke a routine approach to teaching and learning and are likely to be used by teachers to abdicate their responsibility to prepare and teach lessons. In practice many primary teachers do not have the time or the resources to decide independently how to present and sequence mathematics for particular learning aims. Thus teachers inevitably become dependent on the very textbook schemes which the experts dismiss. Moreover reports by the inspectorate suggest that in many primary schools mathematics is learned predominantly by pupils working independently from pupil texts (Ofsted 1993a and b). This suggests that textbooks play an important role in influencing the ways in which English primary teachers think about teaching and learning mathematics, although this situation should change given the introduction of the National Numeracy Strategy in September 1999.

Many pupils, in both secondary and primary schools, do not have a textbook which they can take home and use for learning, revision and practice. This is partly because schools do not have the financial resources for such provision, which also relates to the fact that they are not prioritized as a learning resource. Increasingly the textbook is viewed as an old-fashioned source of information, soon to be replaced by electronic texts, possibly accessed at a distance on the World Wide Web. Interestingly this does not appear to be the case in many other countries, where mathematics textbooks are regarded as key elements of teaching and learning.

In this chapter we compare primary mathematics textbooks from England, France, Hungary, Singapore and the USA.[1] We take the view that within a par-ticular country textbooks reflect the dominant perspectives about what mathematics is, the mathematics that citizens need to know, and the ways in which mathematics can be taught and learned. In other words what appears in a mathematics textbook does not arise by chance. It is influenced by the multifaceted aspects of an educational culture. In this way mathematics textbooks can provide a window onto the mathematics education world of a particular country.

Primary school mathematical concepts such as addition, subtraction, multiplication and division are all interlinked in an intimate way. For example multiplication becomes a more powerful and efficient tool than repeated addition. But how do primary school pupils come to know about this web of interlinked concepts?

We maintain that pupils' construction of knowledge cannot be separated from the external representations of this knowledge. These external representations include pictures, icons and such mathematical symbols as tables, graphs and arithmetic symbols. They also include objects such as fingers for counting and representations which are developed for pedagogic purposes. These symbolic objects are transformative, in that they enable a person to do something which he/she could not do alone. For example tallies on paper support an individual to count a large number of objects; the long multiplication algorithm enables an individual to multiply numbers together which would be very difficult without such a paper-based algorithm. This perspective derives from the work of Vygotsky (1978) and Wertsch (1991) and emphasizes that human action is mediated by 'technical' and 'cognitive tools' (see Ruthven, Chapter 16, this volume). These tools are social in that they are the product of sociocultural history and are always used first as a means of influencing others and only later as a means of influencing oneself (Vygotsky 1978).

The ways in which textbook writers view teaching and learning mathematics will influence how they present mathematics on a textbook page, how they sequence activities and how they structure the links between mathematical topics. Teachers have to make decisions about how to present mathematical ideas, and primary mathematics textbooks present models from which they are likely to draw.

In analysing primary mathematics textbooks[2] we have focused on the ways in which mathematics is transformed and presented on the textbook page. Our analysis has been framed by a consideration of:

- the nature of the images with which pupils engage as they read the text; this includes pictures, diagrams and symbols;
- the ways in which pupils are introduced to links between mathematical concepts and the role of images in this respect;
- the relative emphasis on mathematical structure, mathematical processes and mathematical objects;
- the role of the teacher's guide and the advice which it gives about teaching and learning.

Organization of textbook schemes

The organization of textbook schemes varies from country to country. For example, in England texts tend to be organized according to National

Table 5.1 Comparison of age and school year across the
five countries studied

Age/School year	France	Hungary	Singapore	UK	USA
4–5 years				R	
5–6 years	GS	K	K	1	K
6–7 years	CP	1	1	2	1
7–8 years	CE1	2	2	3	2
8–9 years	CE2	3	3	4	3
9–10 years	CM1	4	4	5	4
10–11 years	CM2		5	6	5

R = Reception; GS = Grande Section; K = Kindergarten; CP = Cours Primaire; CE1 = Cours Elémentaire 1; CE2 = Cours Elémentaire 2; CM1 = Cours Moyen 1; CM2 = Cours Moyen 2.

Curriculum levels. This relates to an emphasis on differentiation from the beginning of primary school and inevitably leads to a situation where, by the end of primary school, English pupils are often working at different levels and from different texts. In the other countries which we studied the texts analysed are year-based and so, for most of their primary education, in each year all pupils are working on similar activities. The issue of different attainment levels is addressed by extra support, but all pupils were expected to cover the same core work.

In working across a number of countries it is difficult to compare school years as pupils often start in school at different ages in different countries. Table 5.1 presents an indication of the age at which pupils study in the different years of national schooling. As can be seen from the table, pupils in England start formal schooling a year in advance of the other countries in the study.

The French, Hungarian and Singapore textbook schemes consist of a pupil textbook, a work book and a teacher's guide (with possibly a single accompanying package of worksheet masters and overhead transparencies), for a particular year of schooling. In contrast, the two English schemes studied consist of a wealth of elements, which make them organizationally complex and relatively difficult to make sense of. For example, one of the English schemes analysed consists of activity books for pupils; textbooks for pupils; work books for pupils; activity masters for teachers; resource masters for pupils and teachers; answer books for pupils and teachers; teacher's guide; assessment material; differentiation material; and problem-solving material. The USA scheme studied was similar in its complexity but the teacher's guide is organized and presented in such a way that it is easier for the reader to make sense of the scheme from the point of view of teaching and learning mathematics.

Ways of introducing multiplication and division

In order to discuss the main differences between the textbook schemes we present a detailed analysis of the ways in which multiplication and division

C   Counting sides of table-tops   C I

1 Ask the children to suggest what is the same about the tables they are sitting at – four corners, legs, sides, etc.

2 Choose one of these properties, say, four sides, and ask each group to write a large numeral '4' on the blank card, one card only for each table.

3 Now talk to the class, gradually building up the total number of sides for five tables. As each table is included in the pattern, one child holds up that group's numeral card.
One table has four sides. How many sides altogether?   Two tables have . . . How many sides altogether? . . . Four and four more make . . . ?   Each table has four sides. How many sides will three tables have? How did you find out?

Resources

School
Five blank cards.*

Scheme
Activity Book 2b, page 10,
or Activity Master 38.
Resource Master 58.

4 Draw attention to the numeral cards as each table is included in the pattern.

5 Make up a written record incorporating the cards:

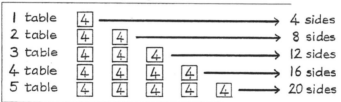

1 table	4				→ 4 sides
2 table	4	4			→ 8 sides
3 table	4	4	4		→ 12 sides
4 table	4	4	4	4	→ 16 sides
5 table	4	4	4	4	4 → 20 sides

What patterns can the children see? Can they suggest how the pattern might continue?

Activity Book 2b, page 10, or Activity Master 38; and Resource Master 58 provide individual practice.

EXTENSION

■ The child selects a set of matching objects, chooses a feature to count, and builds up a similar table.

Figure 5.1 Introduction to multiplication: function table (English text, age 6–7).

are introduced in each country for pupils aged from 6 to 8 and then provide a brief summary of the ways in which these ideas are developed at the end of primary schooling.

The main *English textbook* scheme analysed is organized into books with the second book being appropriate for most 6- to 7-year-old pupils.[3] In this book pupils are first introduced to multiplication as repeated addition of equivalent sets (using numbers up to 20). The teacher's guide suggests that pupils start by finding 'How many pairs of feet?' in a group of children. All of the activities proposed use 'everyday objects' such as legs of tables or towers of cubes. The suggested representations are: function table (Figure 5.1); written sum such as

4 + 4 + 4; intermediary notation of 2 (5) which is meant to be read as '2 sets of 5'. The standard notation of the 'x' sign is not introduced at this stage. The emphasis is more on generating numbers in a function table and then asking pupils to 'look for patterns' in the numbers produced.

Later, pupils are introduced to two aspects of division: sharing and grouping. 'In sharing a collection of objects or a quantity is divided into a given number of equal parts; in grouping we know the number of items in the collection with which we start, and the number we wish to have in each subset, but we must find the number of subsets needed to use all the items.' Again the suggestion is that pupils carry out activities with concrete objects and build on everyday experiences. Links to other curriculum areas are suggested (for example: science – when growing things such as seeds, these must be 'shared' between the pots; religious education – what is meant by fairness and a fair share).

This desire to draw on pupils' everyday experiences and other areas of the curriculum could lead pupils to develop inappropriate ideas of division. 'Sharing' as an everyday practice may or may not involve the notion of absolutely equal quantities, depending on the social situation. It also seems inappropriate that moral issues of fairness should be reduced to the notion of mathematical precision.

At the beginning of the text for Level 3 pupils (approximately 7- to 8-year-olds), multiplication is again presented as repeated addition with respect to the number of objects in an m × n array (see Figure 5.2), with the multiplication symbol 'x' being introduced for the first time. It could be argued that the emphasis in this presentation is more on 'designing stickers' than on the notion of multiplication.

This use of m × n arrays as a way of introducing multiplication is used in all the other countries studied, but we suggest that there is a subtle difference in the way in which the ideas are presented on the page. English pupils have to cope with more in the form of pictorial decoration distractors (see Santos-Bernard 1997). Presentations in textbooks from Hungary, France and Singapore structure the page so that pupils can more easily read the link between the symbolic notation for multiplication and the m × n array (see Figures 5.6 and 5.8).

Later in this Level 3 textbook multiplication is introduced as jumps on a number line. The teacher is told to revise commutativity and in the teacher's guide a number line diagram is used to show that $2 \times 5 = 10$ and $5 \times 2 = 10$ although this is not used in the pupil text. Strangely, later in this book pupils are shown an image for $2 \times 7 = 14$ and $7 \times 2 = 14$ and the accompanying text says, 'This number line shows how 2×7 and 7×2 are different', the emphasis being placed on 'difference' in ways of jumping and not on 'sameness' in terms of mathematical equivalence (Figure 5.3). This suggests that the writer of the text is not prioritizing mathematical equivalence.

Pupils are also introduced to the use of brackets and the distributive law. Whereas in the Hungarian, French and Singapore texts mathematical notation is almost always closely linked to images which support the structure of the notation, the English teacher's guide implicitly suggests that pupils

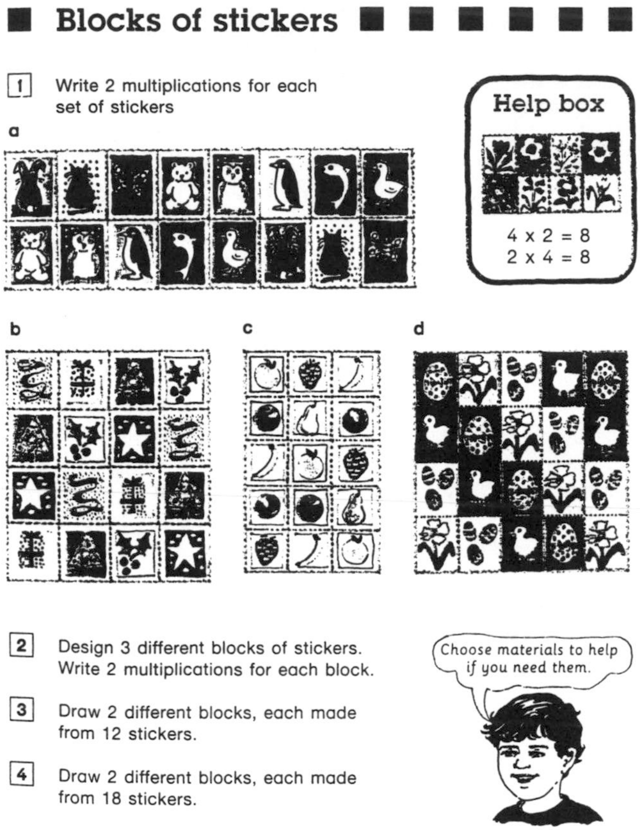

■ Blocks of stickers ■ ■ ■ ■ ■ ■

[1] Write 2 multiplications for each
     set of stickers

a

Help box

$4 \times 2 = 8$
$2 \times 4 = 8$

b   **c**   **d**

[2] Design 3 different blocks of stickers.
     Write 2 multiplications for each block.

[3] Draw 2 different blocks, each made
     from 12 stickers.

[4] Draw 2 different blocks, each made
     from 18 stickers.

Choose materials to help
if you need them.

Figure 5.2 Multiplication: arrays (English text, age 6–7).

should first understand an idea and that after this understanding the mathematical notation can be introduced. For example in the case of brackets the teacher's guide recommends: 'If the child finds using brackets difficult, the principle of separating into parts can still be practised through practical and/or pictorial examples without brackets.' Implicit in this statement is the idea of Piagetian stages in which the use of brackets is considered to be a more abstract stage.

Not only are English children introduced to a wider range of mathematical ideas at an earlier age than pupils in the other countries studied, but they are also expected to move more rapidly from the use of diagrams and pictures to the use of a more abstract representation. This, combined with the fact that much less time is spent on multiplication and division throughout primary school than in the other countries studied, suggests that we should not be surprised if many English pupils have difficulties with multiplication and division.

■ Mostly x and ÷ 3 ■ ■ ■ ■ ■ ■

> Look carefully at Polly's 4-pointed star
> to see how she used the numbers
>
> $12 \div 3 = 4$ $3 \times 4 = 12$
>
> **Rules**
>
> • She had to put a **x** or **+** sign at every corner.
> • She had to put one **3** at every corner.
>
> $4 \times 3 = 12$ $12 \div 4 = 3$

1. Make up more stars like Polly's with these numbers at the centre.

   a 24   b 15   c 27   d 21   e 30   f 18

2. Make up six **x** and **+** stars using only these numbers.

   2   3   5   6   10   15   30   90

> This number line shows how 2 x 7 and 7 x 2 are different.
>
> $2 \times 7 = 14$
>
> $7 \times 2 = 14$

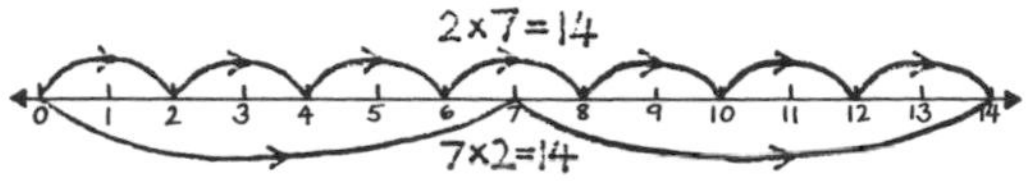

3. Design number lines to show how these are different.

   a 3 x 7 and 7 x 3   b 9 x 3 and 3 x 9

Figure 5.3 Teacher's guide (English text, age 7–8).

Multiplication and division continue to be developed in the textbooks for Level 4 and Level 5. The emphasis in the English primary school texts is on learning number facts up to 10×10, exploring the use of the calculator for multiplication and division and exploring formal and informal methods of operating. The approach tends to be one of presenting pupils with activities loosely related to multiplication and division, spread thinly between a host of other mathematical ideas which are specified in the National Curriculum. Pupils are often encouraged to find many methods for solving a multiplication problem and it is not clear whether they are expected to learn standard algorithms before they leave primary school. The teacher's guide often suggests that non-standard methods should be encouraged: 'Children may develop their own non-standard methods which, if reliable and sustainable, should be encouraged.' Pupils are shown many methods for multiplication and division, such as the Gelosia method and variations on the standard algorithm.

By the end of primary schooling pupils working on Level 5 (the top level for this textbook scheme) are being asked to solve 'word' problems such as '82 glasses of lemonade were sold at the school disco. Each glass had a capacity of 200 ml. How many 2-litre bottles of lemonade were needed?' This problem is less complex than those presented to pupils at a similar age/stage in the other countries studied.

In the *Singapore textbook scheme* the notion of multiplication is first introduced in the second semester of the first year at school (for pupils aged 6–7). As in the English texts it is introduced as 'repeated addition of equal groups'. In the teacher's guide the part–whole principle which has already been used for addition and subtraction is developed for multiplication (see Figure 5.4).

Unit 4: Multiplication

① Adding Equal Groups

Textbook 1B Pages 42 to 45
Workbook Exercises 30 to 32

Instructional Objectives

- To recognise equal groups and find the total number in the groups by repeated addition.
- To use the mathematical language such as '4 threes' and '2 groups of 5' to describe equal groups.

Notes for Teachers

When a whole is made up of two parts,   For example,

- we *add* to find the whole given the two parts;
- we *subtract* to find one part given the whole and the other part.

$$4 + 3 = 7, \ 3 + 4 = 7$$
$$7 - 3 = 4, \ 7 - 4 = 3$$

The part-whole concept of addition and subtraction can be extended to multiplication and division.   For example,

When a whole is made up of equal parts,

- we *multiply* to find the whole given the number of parts and the number in each part;
- we *divide* to find the number in each part given the whole and the number of parts; or
- we *divide* to find the number of parts given the whole and the number in each part.

$$4 \times 3 = 12, \ 3 \times 4 = 12$$
$$12 \div 3 = 4, \ 12 \div 4 = 3$$

Figure 5.4 The part–whole principle (Singapore text, age 6–7).

The pupil text presents the pupil with a pictorial image, two ways of representing repeated addition and a sentence in words (Figure 5.5), with the images being presented in a way which emphasizes the links between the different representations. The 'x' sign is introduced as, 'This is multiplication. It means putting together equal groups.' In the teacher's guide it says, 'The pupils develop and use the language of multiplication through telling number stories such as: "There are 4 vases. There are 5 flowers in each vase. There are 20 flowers altogether. 4 × 5 = 20".'

The next chapter introduces division in terms of sharing and grouping. As previously the representations used are pictures and words, and the questions in the text are related to developing the idea of equal groups. Further, word problems are used with diagrams representing a pictorial version of the word problem.

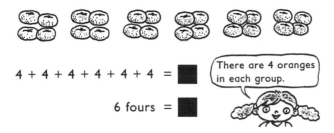

Figure 5.5 Introduction to multiplication (Singapore text, age 6–7).

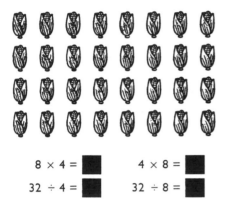

Figure 5.6 Relating multiplication and division (Singapore text, age 7–8).

Multiplication is introduced again at the end of the first semester of the second year of schooling (for pupils aged 7–8) in a 12-page chapter entitled 'Multiplication and division'. This is mainly a revision of the previous year's work with the term multiply being introduced and the commutativity of multiplication shown in the diagrams presented to pupils. This is followed by a section on division which again revises the previous work but introduces the word divide and emphasizes the idea of dividing into equal groups. It also introduces the idea that division can be thought of as finding the number of groups as well as finding how many in each group. The chapter ends by linking multiplication and division together by presenting pupils with four symbolic sentences about a given picture (Figure 5.6) and then giving pupils some practice exercises. The teacher's guide also uses diagrams to emphasize the relationship between division and multiplication.

Here we see the importance in the Singaporean text of linking the diagram/illustration to the symbolic notation, whereas in the English text illustrations bear no relation to the symbolic representation. Indeed the example of 'Polly's 4-pointed star' (Figure 5.3) could provoke some pupils to develop an incorrect link between the four points of the star and the 4 in the calculation. Also,

5.   Multiply 42 by 3.

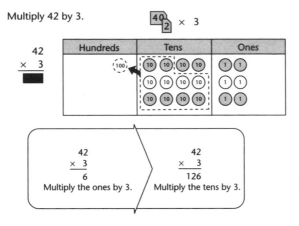

Figure 5.7 Ways of representing place value (Singapore text, age 8–9).

the 'star' representation is not related to the mathematical structure. The final chapter in the Singapore book focuses on the multiplication tables for two and three and uses the tables to explore multiplication and division further.

At the start of the second semester for 7- to 8-year-olds, pupils explore the four, five and 10 times table. Throughout this work pupils are expected to link multiplication and division together by writing and interpreting different symbolic sentences for the same picture.

In the next two years, other multiplication tables are developed. There is an emphasis on the use of word problems (1, 2 and multi-step problems) and the pupils are led towards the use of a standard algorithm. This is facilitated through the use of tabular representations, and place-value discs (Figure 5.7).

In the *Hungarian textbook* scheme, ideas related to multiplication and division are first introduced when pupils are aged 7–8 (a year later than in England and Singapore) with a large proportion of this school year being devoted to these ideas (nine out of 24 chapters in the book for the first semester and nine out of 19 chapters in the book for the second semester). Pupils are introduced to multiplication through counting in 1s, 2s, 5s and 10s which seems to be related to the coinage system. This leads to the idea of repeated addition with extensive use of diagrams representing this idea (Figure 5.8). This is followed very quickly by the introduction of the formal multiplication notation which in Hungary is a dot.

As with the Singapore and the French texts the presentation on the page supports pupils to make links between multiple representations of a mathematical idea.

Finally the idea of multiplication as jumps on a number line is introduced. Division is then introduced as the inverse of multiplication and in the context of money – using florins. It is shown as forming equal groupings from a set of coins. This is followed by an illustration of division as repeated subtraction – on a number line. For example, 'How many 5-jumps do you need to get to zero?' A summary is then given which links repeated addition to multiplication

Szorzás

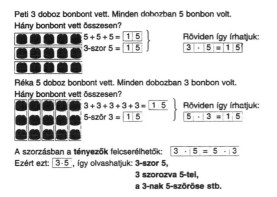

Peti 3 doboz bonbont vett. Minden dobozban 5 bonbon volt.
Hány bonbont vett összesen?

Réka 5 doboz bonbont vett. Minden dobozban 3 bonbon volt.
Hány bonbont vett összesen?

A szorzásban a **tényezők** felcserélhetők: ⸢3 · 5 = 5 · 3⸣
Ezért ezt: ⸢3·5⸣, így olvashatjuk: **3-szor 5,**
                                    3 szorozva 5-tel,
                                    a 3-nak 5-szöröse stb.

Figure 5.8 Introduction to multiplication (Hungarian text, age 7–8).

to division. Zero is introduced at the beginning of primary level which does not appear to be the case in England. Thus number tables in Hungary go from 0–99 rather than 1–100.

Pupils are then asked to work on puzzles/problem-solving activities which require them to use multiplication and division. In all these problems the pupils are encouraged to view the numbers as objects that can be split up in a variety of ways and their task is to search out the most appropriate way for the problem on which they are working. Thus the intention is that pupils will build up a flexible or even a proceptual view of numbers (Tall 1996).

As with the Singapore scheme the teacher's guide elaborates on the pupil text and attempts to give the teacher a pedagogical guide to the way in which the theme being pursued can be developed.

Hungary follows a path similar to Singapore in that the formal methods are introduced relatively quickly to 8- to 9-year-olds, with the expectation being that pupils will have already developed a good grasp of the structure of the number system. Pupils are constantly being expected to pay attention to both mathematical objects and mathematical processes.

In the *USA textbook scheme* pupils are first introduced to ideas of multiplication in the year when they are aged 7–8. As in all the other countries studied multiplication is first introduced as repeated addition using arrays which support the multiplicative structure. Pupils are asked to make up appropriate 'multiplication' stories and solve them themselves. As is the case in the English texts the notion of commutativity does not seem to be emphasized.

As the book progresses, division is introduced as equal sharing. Towards the end of this year multiplication is reviewed with pupils making up their own multiplication stories and solving them. The notion of 'multiplication facts' is introduced as the product of two one-digit numbers. Finally products tables for 1 to 10 times tables are introduced as are fact families (relationship between operations).

Throughout this textbook scheme considerable emphasis is placed on multiplication and division facts. The standard algorithm for multidigit multiplication is introduced to 8- to 9-year-old pupils, through partitioning an m × n array (similar to the approach used in the French scheme but without the extensive use of diagrams as support). Pupils are also introduced to other methods of multiplication, such as the Gelosia method, which again is similar to the English textbooks analysed. Hardly any new materials related to multiplication are introduced to 9- to 10-year-old pupils. Finally in the texts for 10- to 11-year-olds, pupils are expected to master 'whole number multiplication algorithms'.

In the USA texts there is considerable emphasis on multiplication/division facts tables. Function notation is also introduced in the context of pupils playing 'What's my rule?' As in the English texts analysed, the introduction of mathematical notation, such as brackets, is not linked to diagrams which 'scaffold' the introduction of the notation. Solving problems is a key theme and use is made of an almanac for finding real and appropriate data with which to work.

In the *French textbooks* multiplication is first introduced in the 3rd block of activities for 7- to 8-year-old pupils through the notions of 'repeated addition' and 'number of objects in a rectangular array'. From the beginning the '×' sign is introduced and the emphasis is on commutativity, both in the form of repeated addition and multiplication. The teacher's guide to this sequence of lessons suggests that the '×' sign is introduced as a valuable way of naming an m by n array (i.e. 3 × 4 is the name for a 3 by 4 array). It is suggested that pupils in groups are each given an envelope containing 36 squares formed in one of four different arrays (6 × 6, 4 × 9, 3 × 12, 2 × 18). Pupils are then asked to find their own written way of communicating to another group which array they have been given. This activity then leads to a sharing of pupils' written forms, with the teacher collecting together and presenting on the board all the pupils' 'own written representations'. This then leads to the 'institutionalization' of the '×' notation as a succinct form of notation (pupils themselves may have written down for example 4 + 4 + 4 + 4 + 4 + 4 + 4 + 4 + 4 for a 9 × 4 array). This type of activity is influenced by Brousseau's theory of didactical situations (Brousseau 1997). It illustrates the way in which mathematical representation is introduced to French pupils as a means of communication, which is not separated from the mathematical ideas being introduced. It also illustrates the emphasis in France on the 'institutionalization' of an idea with the whole class. Pupils are encouraged to start from their own ways of working and representing but they are also expected to learn more efficient ways which belong to the culture of mathematics. It should also be noticed that in the first introduction the problem chosen relates to factors of 36 and is more complex than the English pupils' first introduction to multiplication in the context of repeated addition of multiples of two. Thus the focus is on the concept of multiplication rather than learning multiplication facts.

Later in this year multiplication is introduced as the notion of repeated jumps on a number line, with the idea of commutativity still being emphasized

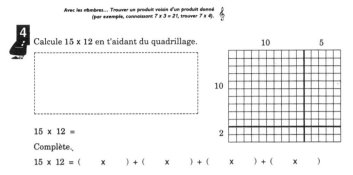

Utiliser
des parenthèses

Avec les nombres... Trouver un produit voisin d'un produit donné
(par exemple, connaissant 7 x 3 = 21, trouver 7 x 4).

4 Calcule 15 x 12 en t'aidant du quadrillage.

15 x 12 =

Complète.

15 x 12 = (x   ) + (x   ) + (x   ) + (x   )

Figure 5.9 Introduction to the use of brackets (French text, age 7–8).

through the use of diagrams. In this session the inequality sign is introduced as a way of working with the product as an object. For example $4 \times 4 < 4 \times 6$ (pupils will not always have to carry out the computation to work out the inequality). Throughout pupils are presented with 'realistic' problems which make use of mathematical ideas, and this includes problems related to multiplication and division.

Brackets are introduced as a way of representing symbolically the decomposition of numbers illustrated previously and shown in Figure 5.9.

Standard algorithms for multiplying multidigit numbers and for division begin to be introduced at the end of the year in which pupils are 8–9. Diagrams are used extensively throughout these texts to help pupils move between representations which have been introduced for pedagogic purposes (for example m by n array of squares) and standard algorithms. In this sense they are being used to 'scaffold' learning (Wood 1988). By the end of primary schooling pupils are presented with relatively complex problems to solve which use the notions of multiplication and division.

Similarities and differences between textbook schemes

A strength of the Singapore, Hungarian and French texts is the use and consistency of use of appropriate representations. These are used to draw attention to mathematical structure, mathematical objects and mathematical processes. They are also used to highlight the relationship between mathematical operations such as multiplication and division. The French texts also make extensive use of diagrams which are aimed at supporting pupils to make links between representations which are introduced for pedagogic purposes and more standard representations which are used by citizens outside school. These diagrams also provide a form of explanation which is almost entirely missing from the English texts.

The Hungarian textbooks make extensive use of networks of representations which link different mathematical operations together. This style of presentation is coupled with the view that in the first two years of schooling pupils are not exposed to formal algorithmic ways of working. It seems that external representations are used to support flexible mental approaches to solving problems.

Colour in textbooks can be used for a range of purposes which includes decoration, illustration, organization and mathematical analysis. In the textbooks from England and the USA colour is almost entirely decorative, and in the case of the English text it often dominates the texts and distracts from the mathematics. In contrast, in the French, Hungarian and Singapore schemes, colour tends to be used more as an analytical tool to support the learning of mathematics.

English pupils are introduced to a much broader curriculum than pupils in the other countries studied. More worrying than the broadness of the English curriculum is that pupils are often introduced to a wide variety of mathematical ideas and ways of solving problems without being presented with any support to make links between these ideas. The broad curriculum is often accompanied by fragmentation of mathematical ideas. For example, when ideas of multiplication and division are introduced they are surrounded by many other topics which bear little relationship to multiplication and division.

Possibly related to the broadness of the English curriculum is the fact that pupils from other countries appear to be expected to engage with more complex mathematical problems than is the case for English pupils by the end of primary schooling. These problems can be relatively authentic as is the case in the American textbook scheme, in which pupils construct problems from an almanac of real data, or they can be presented in the form of complex word problems.

In the French, Singapore and Hungarian schemes mathematical language and notation is introduced with a clear purpose in terms of communicating and understanding mathematical ideas. In the English textbooks the introduction of mathematical symbols is often delayed with pupils being expected to experience ideas first and only later being expected to learn how to represent them mathematically. We have argued that this relates to an implicit Piagetian view of learning. Our view is that mathematical language and symbols should be introduced from the beginning because they are inextricably linked to the development of ideas. We may need to understand more about the Anglo-Saxon approach as manifested in the English and USA textbooks before we can change the dominant practices in the UK.

Some concluding remarks

We suggest that in England we need to pay more attention to the use of all forms of representing mathematics on the written page. This means analysing the complexity of learning mathematics, and how mathematics has to be transformed in order to be presented to pupils. The current preoccupation with mental mathematics (see for example *Numeracy Matters*; DfEE 1998) tends to overlook the ways in which work on paper can be used both to scaffold pupil learning and to provide images for mental activity.

What appears to be more important than when ideas are introduced, is whether or not there is some background rationale for the ordering and the relationship between the introduction of different topics. It would also seem that depth of coverage is an issue which needs to be addressed since it is that which seems to be most different across the schemes studied. What depth often means is that pupils are introduced to the complexity of the interrelationship of ideas which are built up in a progressive way.

Tall (1996) suggests that the children who fail in mathematics are actually carrying out a more difficult kind of mathematics than those who succeed. He found a clear tendency with low-attaining pupils to use primitive mathematical objects and primary processes, for example counting to solve addition problems, or repeated addition to solve problems which could be more effectively solved using multiplication. We suggest that pupils should be encouraged to use forms of representation which will facilitate efficient ways of working and which allow them to engage with complexity.

We suggest that our study of textbooks has provided a window onto the different beliefs about teaching and learning mathematics which exist in different countries. Although we have also carried out some observations in mathematics classrooms in Hungary (Harries 1997) and France we believe that comparative classroom-based research would serve to illuminate further many of the issues which we have raised in this chapter.

In the future pupils may indeed be expected to work from electronic-based as opposed to paper-based texts. However unless we understand the ways in which pupils learn from engaging with texts we will not be able to produce electronic texts which facilitate and enhance the learning of mathematics.

Notes

1 This chapter derives from one of two parallel QCA-funded projects which compared primary mathematics texts from England, France, Hungary, Singapore and the USA. For a summary of the results of both projects, see Sutherland *et al.* (1998).
2 For each country one textbook scheme, recommended as being representative, was analysed in depth. We also analysed an additional scheme from England and France.
3 The National Curriculum for England is assessed on a level system and most 7-year-old pupils are expected to be working at Levels 2/3. The second book roughly corresponds to Level 2.

References

Brousseau, G. (1997) *Theory of Didactical Situations in Mathematics*. Dordrecht: Kluwer Academic Publishers.
DfEE (1998) *Numeracy Matters: Preliminary Report of the Numeracy Task Force*. London: DfEE.

Harries, A.V. (1997) *Reflections on a Hungarian Mathematics Lesson*. Mathematics Teaching No. 162. Derby: ATM.

Ofsted (1993a) *Mathematics Key Stages 1, 2 and 3*. London: HMSO.

Ofsted (1993b) *The Teaching and Learning of Number in the Primary School*. London: HMSO.

Santos-Bernard, D. (1997) The use of illustrations in school mathematics text books – presentation of information. Unpublished PhD thesis, University of Nottingham.

Sutherland, R., Harries, T. and Howson, G. (1999) *Primary School Mathematics Textbooks: An International Study (Summary)*. London: QCA.

Tall, D. (1996) Can all children climb the same curriculum ladder? In *The mathematical Ability of School Leavers*. Gresham Special Lecture. London: Gresham College.

Vygotsky, L. (1978) *Mind in Society*. Harvard University Press.

Wertsch, J. (1991) *Voices of the Mind: A Sociocultural Approach to Mediated Action*. London: Harvester Wheatsheaf.

Wood, D. (1988) *How Children Think and Learn*. Oxford: Blackwell.

Using and applying mathematics at Key Stage 1

Martin Hughes, Charles Desforges and Christine Mitchell

The problem of application

Children learn mathematics in school with a view to going beyond class-room exercises and using mathematical knowledge in all aspects of their professional and domestic lives. Unfortunately, there is now considerable evidence that learners of mathematics find great difficulty in 'using and applying' their mathematical knowledge.

Studies from a range of countries over a considerable period of time have shown that people are frequently unable to use in one context mathematics which they have acquired in another. A well-known example comes from a survey of mathematical understanding in the USA in the 1980s (NAEP 1983). As part of this survey, 13-year-old students were told that an army bus holds 36 soldiers, and asked how many buses would be needed to transport 1128 soldiers to their training site. Most of the students knew that they needed to carry out a division calculation, and many successfully divided 1128 by 36 to produce an answer of 31.33. However, nearly a third of the students proceeded to write this as the answer to the problem (i.e. 31.33 buses), thus ignoring the need for a whole number of buses. Nearly a quarter of the students made a different kind of mistake, and ignored the remainder altogether – thus leaving 12 soldiers with no transport.

In this example, the American students were having difficulty applying the mathematical knowledge they had gained in school to a novel problem situation. This is indeed a very common form of 'failure to apply'. But there is also evidence that people have difficulty in applying mathematical know-ledge which is gained *outside* school. For example, Nunes and her colleagues have carried out a number of studies of young street traders in Brazil (Nunes *et al.* 1993). These youngsters are forced by economic necessity to run stalls selling goods such as fruit and cigarettes, an activity which involves a large number of mathematical calculations. In one study, the researchers posed as buyers at the stalls and asked the young traders (aged between 9 and 15 years) a range of problems, such as working out the price of 10 coconuts. The youngsters were extremely good at such calculations, although they frequently solved them using their own idiosyncratic methods. They were then asked to do essentially the same problems but posed in the language of school arithmetic. It turned out that the young traders were much less successful at 'school maths' than they had been at 'street maths'.

Both these examples involve young people between 9 and 15 years of age. But there is also evidence that children much younger than this have problems with application. For example, Hughes (1986) showed that children start school with a range of mathematical skills, such as the ability to carry out simple additions and subtractions. However, they have difficulties in applying this knowledge to the kind of mathematics which they encounter in the early years of school. The same study also showed that young children may acquire some facility with the conventional symbolism of mathematics (numerals such as 2 and 3, and signs such as + and =). However, they are surprisingly reluctant to use this symbolism in simple practical situations where it would be helpful – such as showing how many bricks have been added to or taken from a pile. It seems that children's difficulties with using and applying mathematics are present from the very beginnings of school.

Using and applying in the mathematics curriculum

In the UK, the difficulties which pupils have in applying mathematical knowledge has been recognized for some time. For example, the influential Cockcroft Report (DES 1982) on the teaching of mathematics reported a widespread lack of ability amongst adults in applying mathematical knowledge or using it to communicate effectively. The Committee therefore recommended that the mathematics curriculum in schools should be broadened to include more practical work, problem solving, investigations and discussion, alongside the more traditional exposition and practice. The focus was on enhancing the applicability of the mathematics curriculum.

This concern with the application of mathematical knowledge has also been prominent in the development of the National Curriculum. The approach taken in the 1989, 1991 and 1995 versions of the mathematics curriculum was to identify 'Using and Applying Mathematics' as a separate attainment target or strand. In the 1995 version, for example, 'Using and Applying Mathematics' was one of three main strands at Key Stage 1, with the other two being 'Number' and 'Shape, Space and Measures'. At the same time, the official documents explicitly stated that using and applying mathematics should not be considered in isolation from these other strands, but 'should be set in the context of the other areas of mathematics' (DfE 1995: 2). Successive versions of the National Curriculum also made clear that pupils should be 'given opportunities to use and apply mathematics in practical tasks, in real-life problems, and within mathematics itself' (DfE 1995: 2) and that teachers should aim to develop the process skills of decision-making, communicating about mathematics and reasoning.

The introduction of the National Numeracy Strategy has brought with it a different approach to application. In the *Framework for Teaching Mathematics* (DfEE 1999), 'using and applying mathematics' is no longer a discrete strand. Instead, five main strands, namely 'Numbers and the Number System', 'Calculations', 'Solving Problems', 'Measures, Shape and Space' and 'Handling Data' are identified. The Framework suggests that 'Using and applying mathematics is integrated throughout' (DfEE 1999: 40) and several elements of the National Curriculum 'Using and applying' strand can indeed be found within the 'Solving Problems' strand. However, a closer inspection of the 'key objectives' of the Framework suggests that the emphasis is very much on number knowledge and calculation skills. At Year 2, for example, only one of the 13 key objectives relates to the application of numeracy, while at Year 4 the proportion is one out of 11. The impression created by these key objectives is that, despite claims to the contrary, the application of mathematics has relatively little priority within the National Numeracy Strategy.

The Nuffield Project

These concerns formed the context for a project on 'Using and Applying Mathematical Knowledge' which we carried out in the South West of England. The project was funded by the Nuffield Foundation, with the aims being to develop new ways of thinking and new teaching approaches to the problem of application in mathematics. The main work of the project revolved around 12 primary school teachers. Six of these teachers worked in Year 1/2 classes, while six worked with Year 5/6. All 12 teachers were considered to be excellent practitioners, and were committed to developing their practice in this area.

The teachers worked closely with the project team over the period of a school year. During the course of the year they developed various approaches to the problem of application, and attempted to implement these approaches in their classrooms. They met regularly with the other teachers and with the project team in order to share experiences and develop new ideas. In between meetings, each teacher was visited by a member of the project team, interviewed about his/her approach to application, and observed in his/her classroom. A full account of the work of the project is provided in Hughes *et al.* (in press).

During the course of the project, the 12 teachers explored a range of approaches to the problem of application. The project team did not insist that any particular approach had to be used. The teachers were merely asked to think carefully about how they might help their pupils apply mathematical knowledge, to implement their ideas in a systematic way, to reflect on the success or otherwise of the approach adopted, and to discuss what they had done with the other teachers and with the project team. In the rest of the chapter, we provide examples of how three project teachers at Key Stage 1 – Barbara, Alice and Diane – approached the problem of application.

Barbara: making connections with 'real life'

Barbara had recently moved to a new school where she felt that maths teaching in the past had been dominated by the use of commercial maths schemes. She felt that the children were able to carry out additions and subtractions when these were presented in the standard format in their workbooks. However, she thought they had a very limited understanding of what these standard representations meant. She wanted to encourage the children to make connections between 'maths in books' and 'real life'.

In one lesson we observed, Barbara started by asking the children why they were learning to read. The children gave a number of answers which suggested they understood that they were acquiring a skill which might prove useful in other contexts – for example, you might need to read instructions, or the words in a song book. Barbara then asked them why they were learning maths. This time it proved somewhat harder to elicit suggestions from the children, but with some persistence from the teacher ideas started to emerge. For example, it was suggested that shopkeepers might use maths to add up their money, that a teacher would need to know how to add up the dinner money in class, and that a builder would need maths to find out how many bricks to put in a house.

Barbara seemed pleased with these responses and moved on to the next part of her lesson. She wrote the following sum on a flip-chart:

$$\begin{array}{r} 12 \\ + \ 7 \\ \hline 19 \end{array}$$

and asked the children to 'tell me a story about that sum'. One child, Philip, suggested 'there were 12 caterpillars on a leaf and 7 more came along and that gave 19'. The teacher wrote another sum on the flip-chart:

$$\begin{array}{r} 20 \\ - \ 9 \\ \hline 11 \end{array}$$

and again asked for 'a story about the sum'. This time Rachel suggested, somewhat bizarrely, that 'there were 20 people reading a book and 9 went away, and that left 11'. Barbara responded to this by providing a 'story' of her own, in which there were 20 people in a cinema, and 9 left, leaving 11 inside. She attempted to situate this in a meaningful context by suggesting that the cinema doorman would need to know how many people he could now let in.

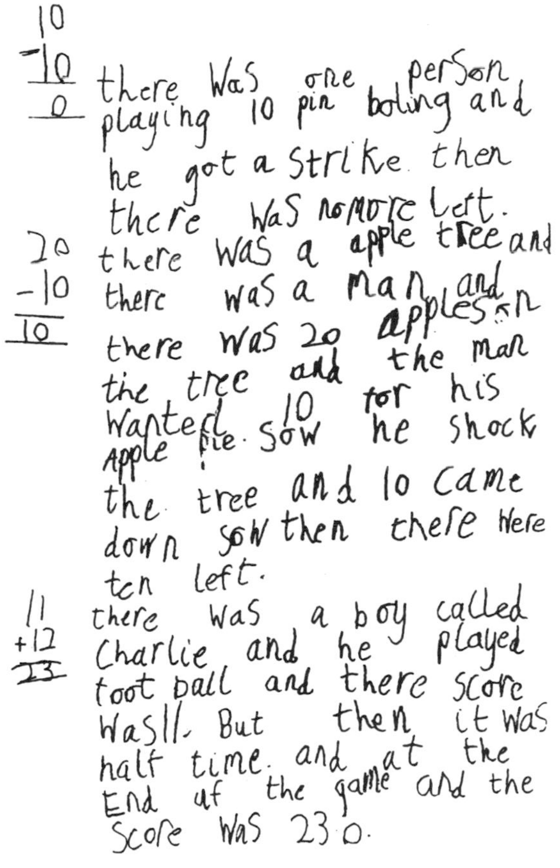

```
 10
-10
  0
```
there was one person playing 10 pin boling and he got a strike. then there was nomore left.

```
 20
-10
 10
```
there was a apple tree and there was a man and there was 20 apples on the tree and the man wanted 10 for his apple pie. sow he shock the tree and 10 came down sow then there were ten left.

```
 11
+12
 23
```
there was a boy called Charlie and he played foot ball and there score was 11. But then it was half time. and at the End of the game and the score was 23 0.

Figure 6.1 Charlie's number stories.

Barbara then gave each child a clipboard and some paper, and asked them to write some sums, as she had done, and to write underneath 'the story of that sum'. She stressed that the children should:

Think very carefully about real things that might actually happen. It's very important that you try to link it to something that might really happen. If you can't then make up a story which is close to that.

The children settled down to produce their sums and stories. For the most part they stuck to additions and subtractions up to 30. Many of their stories involved animals, food or sporting activities. Charlie, for example, produced a subtraction story involving ten-pin bowling, another subtraction involving apples being picked from a tree, and an addition story about a boy called Charlie scoring 11 goals in the first half of a football match and 12 in the second (see Figure 6.1). Rachel produced an addition involving cats

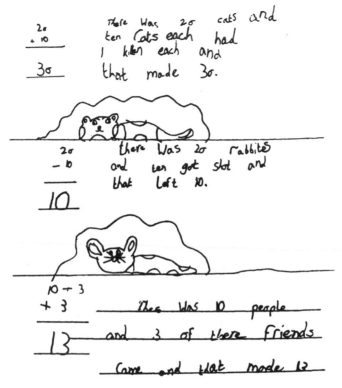

Figure 6.2 Rachel's number stories.

and kittens, a subtraction in which 10 rabbits were shot, and another addition involving people and their friends (see Figure 6.2). The teacher moved
around the class, discussing the stories with the children. At the end of
the lesson, she asked one or two of them to talk about their stories to the
whole class.

After the lesson, Barbara reflected on how it had gone. She said that she
had been trying to get the children to see some kind of relevance to school
maths, and to make some kind of connection between what they did in their
maths books and real life. She felt that some of the children had started to
make some connections, 'but it took quite a while for the penny to drop'.
She was somewhat disappointed in the stories the children had written, commenting that most of them simply reproduced the kind of 'twee' story they
encountered in their maths schemes. She commented positively on Charlie's
stories, saying that he was beginning to see how one might need maths in
the real world, and that he was 'making realistic connections.' In contrast,
she was more critical of Rachel's work, suggesting that her stories were very
typical of ones which might be found in maths schemes. She considered that
Rachel 'hadn't allowed herself to move away from that'.

Alice: introducing an authentic activity

Alice adopted a different approach to application. Instead of asking the children to imagine a real-life context, she set up a practical activity in the classroom which was intended to resemble as closely as possible an activity which might take place in 'real life'. The activity which Alice chose was a 'car boot sale'. She considered this to be an 'authentic activity', which would simulate the ways in which mathematics is used in everyday life outside school. In particular, she wanted the children to apply their classroom knowledge of addition and subtraction – and especially subtraction – in this new context.

Alice prepared for the car boot sale over several lessons. She used 'pretend' money in the home corner, and took some of the children to a 'real' shop to purchase goods and work out the change. During the car boot sale itself, she wanted the children to work in groups and be responsible to the group rather than to her. She said that she was 'not sure if application takes place if under the direct control of the teacher'.

Before the car boot sale started, Alice gave the children some practice in using subtraction as a means of calculating change. She drew a cake on a sheet of paper and told the children that it cost 5p. She suggested that they imagine they were selling the cake, and asked how much change they would give if someone gave them 50p. Several children replied '45p'. One child, Hayley, explained that she had done this by 'counting back – 49, 48, 47, 46, 45'. The teacher then drew a bigger cake with lots of candles on it, and told the children this cake cost 15p. Again, she asked them how much change they would give for 50p. This time Ruth explained that 'I had 50p and I took 10 and 5 away and I was left with 35'.

Alice then introduced the car boot sale. The children had brought in a range of articles from home which they were going to 'sell' to their classmates. The teacher organized them into four groups, and gave each group £2 (in real currency) to spend at the sale. The children priced the goods themselves, although Alice suggested that no item should be more than 5p. She told them they would need to develop their own ways of keeping track of the money. At the end of the day they would have to account for all their exchanges.

The sale started, and a long period of buying and selling ensued. As intended, many of the transactions involved the children in carrying out additions and subtractions. At the same time, some children engaged in practices which might be considered to be characteristic of a real car boot sale, such as haggling over prices. They also devised some idiosyncratic methods for keeping track of their money. One child, for example, represented on paper each item he had sold as a number with a circle around it (see Figure 6.3). Later, he was able to use this system to check that his actual takings were correct. Another group of children devised a system which resembled an old-fashioned ledger, with outgoings on one side and incomings on the other (see Figure 6.4). At the end of the day, all the books were balanced across the four groups, apart from 7p which had mysteriously disappeared!

Figure 6.3 Recording items sold in the car boot sale.

Keeping Track of our money

what we sell		what we buy	
one SHell	5p	one book	5p
one doll	5p	one MAGic GAMe	5p
one game	5p	one PArot	Ep
one watch	3p	SCAkes	6p
one car	1p	one CHell	5p
		E bisulks	Ep
		one Plano	1p
		dolls beacer	5op

Figure 6.4 Recording transactions in the car boot sale.

Alice considered that the lesson had gone very well, and that the children had found the session exciting. She also felt it had met her aim of providing a 'real life' or 'authentic' context in which the children could apply their knowledge of addition or subtraction. She commented:

They applied subtraction probably more than I expected them to. And I was really quite pleased with that, for it was a much more efficient way of dealing with some of those transactions.

Diane: understanding number sentences

The third teacher, Diane, adopted an approach which was different again from those of Barbara and Alice. Diane was less concerned with connecting children's existing knowledge to new settings, and more concerned that they should deepen their current mathematical understanding. The children in her class had already learnt to add and subtract using standard notation (such as $2 + 3 =$) to represent what they were doing. However, Diane wanted the children to develop their understanding of the meaning of this notation. She said that she wanted the children to 'explore the hidden relationships between the numbers and symbols of a simple algorithm'. By this, she meant that she wanted them to focus in depth on the meaning of one or two number sentences, rather than carrying out pages of sums.

During one activity, Diane worked closely with just two children (Karen and Simon). She started by introducing three cards on which she had written +, –, and =. She talked to the children about what these symbols meant, reminding them that 'sometimes they have a special job to do when they are in a sum'. She then illustrated these 'jobs' by writing $2 + 3 = 5$ on a flipchart, and discussed with them the role which the + and = signs played within this particular number sentence.

Diane then gave each child a set of cards. Each card had either a sign on it or a numeral. Karen's cards were: $\boxed{2}$, $\boxed{5}$, $\boxed{7}$, $\boxed{+}$, $\boxed{-}$, and $\boxed{=}$, while Simon's cards were $\boxed{3}$, $\boxed{6}$, $\boxed{9}$, $\boxed{+}$, $\boxed{-}$, and $\boxed{=}$. Diane said, 'I want you to just have a look at them and see if you can find different ways to put them all out and make them work together.' This was evidently a new activity both for the children and the teacher.

The activity proceeded with the children generating various sequences of numerals and signs. Karen, for example, produced $\boxed{7}$ $\boxed{-}$ $\boxed{5}$ $\boxed{=}$ $\boxed{2}$ followed by $\boxed{5}$ $\boxed{+}$ $\boxed{2}$ $\boxed{=}$ 7 while Simon produced $\boxed{3}$ $\boxed{+}$ $\boxed{6}$ $\boxed{=}$ $\boxed{9}$ followed by $\boxed{3}$ $\boxed{-}$ $\boxed{9}$ $\boxed{=}$ $\boxed{6}$. Each time Diane asked them whether their sequence 'worked' and how they might check whether it worked (fingers were allowed for this). The teacher also discussed with the children what 'job' the various signs were performing in each sequence. Altogether, the children spent about 20 minutes working with their particular set of cards.

Afterwards, Diane felt the session had been a qualified success. She was critical of her own role, saying that she hadn't used the kind of language which she had planned to use. However, she justified her use of terms such as 'work' and 'job', feeling they were appropriate in this context. She felt pleased with the way the children had explored various combinations, and with the ways in which they had discussed what they were doing with her. She was particularly pleased by her decision to focus intensively on one or two number sentences, and commented that she was 'amazed at how much there is going on in one simple algorithm'.

Discussion and implications

In this chapter we have presented three different approaches to the application of mathematics at Key Stage 1. These different approaches reflected the teachers' different theories about how children can be helped to apply, as well as their more immediate perceptions of what was appropriate for their children at that particular stage in their learning. Thus Barbara felt that her children's previous maths work had been dominated by commercial maths schemes, and wanted to encourage them to make more connections between their schemes and real-life situations. Her chosen method for doing this was to ask the children to write stories linking standard 'sums' to imaginary real-life settings. Alice, like Barbara, also wanted her children to apply their mathematical knowledge in a real-life setting. However, her approach differed from Barbara's in that she set up an elaborate practical activity in the classroom which was intended to serve as an 'authentic' example of a situation outside the classroom in which mathematics might be used. Diane took a different approach from either Barbara or Alice, in that she aimed to deepen her children's understanding of the various elements which form a number sentence. She did this by asking the children to explore at some length the various possible sentences which could be generated from a small range of written symbols.

In terms of the curriculum, the examples provided by these three teachers can be seen as addressing different requirements within the 'Solving Problems' strand of the *Framework for Teaching Mathematics*. For example, Barbara's activity of making up number stories is a suggested activity in the Y123 examples, within the Framework for helping children 'choose and use appropriate number operations and ways of calculating to solve problems' (DfEE 1999: 60–1). Similarly, Alice's car boot sale might be seen as meeting the objective that 'pupils should be taught to . . . solve simple word problems involving money and explain how the problem was solved' (DfEE 1999: 68). Diane's activity, on the other hand, is similar to one suggested in the Framework for encouraging children to 'reason about numbers' (DfEE 1999: 63), although in the Framework the activity is suggested for Year 2 rather than Year 1. In short, the activities described here illustrate various ways in which teachers can develop the process skills which underlie 'Using and Applying Mathematics'.

The implications for teachers would seem to be as follows. Children need to be taught from an early age how to apply their mathematical knowledge in a range of contexts and settings. Many teachers at Key Stage 1 may feel somewhat daunted by this requirement, and uncertain as to how it might be accomplished in practice. The examples shown here suggest they do not need to feel daunted. There is a range of different approaches which can be used to help young children apply their mathematical knowledge, and which can be seen to address different aspects of the *Framework for Teaching Mathematics*. Teachers need to clarify their own thinking about what might be suitable approaches to application, to plan a range of classroom activities which exemplify these approaches, and to monitor the effects of these activities on children's learning. In other words, teaching children to apply their mathematical knowledge need be no more – or no less – problematic than any other area of the primary curriculum.

Acknowledgements

We are very grateful to the Nuffield Foundation for their support of the project on which this chapter is based, and to our colleague Clive Carre for his valuable work on the project.

References

Askew, M., Brown, M., Johnson, D., Millett, A., Prestage, S. and Walsh, A. (1993) *Evaluation of the Implementation of National Curriculum Mathematics at Key Stages 1, 2 and 3*. London: SCAA.

DES (Department of Education and Science) (1982) *Mathematics Counts* (Cockcroft Report). London: HMSO.

DfE (Department for Education) (1995) *Mathematics in the National Curriculum*. London: HMSO.

DfEE (Department for Education and Employment) (1999) *The National Numeracy Strategy: Framework for Teaching Mathematics from Reception to Year 6*. London: DfEE.

Hughes, M. (1986) *Children and Number*. Oxford: Blackwell.

Hughes, M., Desforges, C. and Mitchell, C. (in press) *Numeracy and Beyond: Applying Mathematics in the Primary School*. Buckingham: Open University Press.

NAEP (National Assessment of Educational Progress) (1983) *The Third National Mathematics Assessment*. Denver: Education Commission of the States.

Nunes, T., Schliemann, A. and Carraher, D. (1993) *Street Mathematics and School Mathematics*. Cambridge: Cambridge University Press.

Family numeracy

Ruth Merttens

This chapter is really about two things – the involvement of parents in their children's education and the question of homework. This is interesting because in one sense these two topics are at opposite ends of a spectrum.

There are few things in education about which it is possible to get almost universal agreement, but the importance of involving parents is one of them. Mention parents and everyone, from the corridors of power to the chalk face, from the playground gates to the inner sanctum of Ofsted, will concur that their role is crucial, and that it is essential to incorporate ways of maximizing their involvement.

By contrast, almost no two teachers, never mind those from different sectors in education, will agree about the subject of homework. There are those who believe that any homework is a waste of time, morally indefensible and socially divisive, and those who think that requiring children to do an hour's homework from the age of 6 or 7 can do much to counter under-achievement.

Homework has also become, or perhaps has always been, something of an educational icon. It signifies something which goes way beyond what it actually means in practice. It is useful to reflect upon the reasons for this iconic status, specifically as it relates to the question of the collaboration of parents. Adults surveyed in the street tend to come across as definitively pro-homework. The giving of regular and disciplined homework is perceived as the sign of a good school, alongside a school uniform and daily assemblies. However, if parents in a class meeting at their local primary school are asked about homework, the response can be very different. They are more often inclined to complain about too much homework, or it being too hard, or of the wrong type. This apparent discrepancy is mirrored by similar findings which indicate that parents can be quite critical of education in general terms (standards are falling, teachers aren't doing a good enough job etc.), but when asked about their own child's school are generally very positive (she's got a wonderful teacher, she loves her class, the school is nice . . .).[1]

Homework here is a useful example of a more general trend. It stands for something, and is in this sense iconic. However, in practice, *how* it is done is more important than *that* it is done, because the 'how' will make the difference between it supporting children's learning and facilitating the collaboration of their parents, or it becoming yet another element in an education system in which the benefits are differentially available, according to socio-economic class, gender or ethnicity.

Should we involve parents?

We know from the evidence of both research and practice that the single biggest factor in children's educational success is their parents.[2] This fact has been recognized explicitly and implicitly by every report from Plowden (HMSO 1967), through Cockcroft (DES 1982), to the *Numeracy Matters* (DfEE 1998) report of the Task Force. Schools and teachers ignore this at their peril – whatever we do inside the school gates will never be as effective as it should be unless we turn our attention to what happens on the outside! Children's first educators are their parents; their attitudes to learning, to maths and to study in general are formed, and formulated, in the context of the home. Every teacher is aware that what happens in school is less than half the story. Furthermore, we have an increasing body of evidence to suggest that what happens *before* the child gets to school has an effectivity which reverberates throughout the rest of that child's educational career.

For all these reasons, involving the family in their child's learning is not an optional extra – it is an essential part of raising achievement. This means that it should be taken for granted within a school that getting the parents actively involved is not a peripheral matter. It is not that we can think of this as 'the icing on the cake' – if everything else is going smoothly then we can give the matter of working with parents some attention. The facts may be put very brutally:

- many children simply will not learn to read in a satisfactory manner or to a reasonable time-scale unless their parents read with them on a regular basis;
- many children will not discover how to apply the maths – and particularly the number – that they learn in class unless their parents involve them in daily numerical interactions;
- we will not reverse the so-called 'cycle of disadvantage' whereby the child of a parent who found school work difficult or unappealing is destined to do the same unless we actively intervene to prevent this happening; and
- in summary, those children whose parents take an active interest in their education are more likely to succeed and less likely to become disaffected with school and study.

The involvement of parents is therefore an essential part of the raising of achievement, since an important factor in helping those children who are not succeeding is the relationship between what they do in school and what happens outside it.

Can we involve parents?

It is a dangerous myth that some parents do not care and will not help. The overwhelming majority of parents do want their child to succeed at school, are worried about how this is to be achieved (especially if they do not feel that they themselves succeeded, educationally speaking) and will do what they can to help bring it about. If reasonable tasks are provided with clear guidance for parents as to what we want them to do and how, most parents will be keen to help.

Furthermore, what the teachers and the school do is crucial. From the Hamilton Projects, as well as others,[3] we know that it is possible to create a climate in which being an active partner in the child's education simply becomes 'what happens at this school': it is taken for granted. Although teachers are sometimes resistant to hearing the evidence, it *is* unequivocal. Although it may be harder to involve the parents in one area than it is in another, it is certainly possible to do so, given enough energy and the right sequence of actions.[4] Two schools in similar catchment areas may have a very different proportion of parents actively involved in their child's learning, and this difference will be due to the attitude of the teachers and the actions that they take.

How can schools and teachers maximize the number of parents who are actively involved in their children's learning and of what exactly does this sequence of actions consist? The answer to the second part of this question is much easier than the first. It is relatively simple to provide a set of suggestions, or even imperatives, and hope that this will produce the desired outcome. However, the sequence of actions will only prove effective if the climate for its success has been produced. And this is very much a matter of creating a culture of 'parents as partners' within the school community. The difficulty here is plain – creating a culture has to be a long-term aim; it cannot be achieved overnight. In some schools, several years of sustained effort has produced a community of educators – parents, carers, classroom assistants, special needs support workers and others – all of whom have a valued and expected role in the education of the children. As parents start their children at school they are inducted into the community and become very much an active partner in the schooling process. This is simply 'what happens' or 'what we do at this school'. Only, in fact it is not simple at all – years of hard work, careful planning and energy have gone into bringing about the culture of 'this is what happens'.

Each specific action or initiative that we plan and implement as a school has to be conceived as part of a definite and deliberate policy in which this 'parents as partners' culture is engendered and sustained. This often involves a change of attitude on the part of staff as well as parents. Schools where notices such as 'No pushchairs' or 'Please make an appointment to see your child's teacher' are displayed are declaring, probably without realizing it, that parents are on the outside of the process and peripheral to the main endeavour of the school. It is the small, and often unspoken, messages that count, frequently more than the grand invectives of official whole-school policies.

The fact that I can poke my head around the teacher's door any Tuesday or Wednesday and know that she will talk through some matter to do with my child is of infinitely more importance than the policy, and speaks volumes to the nervous or 'school-shy' parent. And the way in which the teacher writes and speaks to me about my child's reading record, which passes back and forth between home and school, is a crucial factor in my regular sharing of books with that child.

What makes the difference here is the official recognition on the part of governors, as well as senior management, that parents matter, and that creating a climate of partnership and collaboration needs specific efforts and actions which need to be timetabled and allowed for and, above all, valued! Time to talk to parents, to do home visits, to write twice weekly in the children's 'home diaries' or 'reading records', to encourage talk about and draw upon home experiences, to plan parent meetings and special events, and countless other examples, is what is needed to generate the changed culture. And the official recognition that this is the case, that it will require a large *initial* input of time and energy, and then less to sustain it, is the first step towards achieving a status quo which will benefit not only the children and their parents, but also the teachers.

In pursuit of this goal, there are some very practical actions and events which make a difference. The easiest way to get parents involved with their children's learning is to start as you mean to go on. On entry to school, parents should be involved in the formative assessment of their child as well as the settling-in process. This sometimes involves a programme of home visiting, although for obvious resource reasons most schools are concerned to keep this to a minimum. However, it is worth making the point that funding the time for the reception teacher to visit new families can pay huge dividends in terms of their subsequent involvement with their child's schooling.

Most schools will have a programme of home- or shared-reading, where children take home books, and parents are encouraged to share these. In addition, it is important to have a parallel programme of home-maths, whereby children take home weekly or fortnightly maths activities which are shared and discussed by parents and their children. The IMPACT project (Merttens 1994) has provided a huge bank of suitable resources[5] which enable teachers to match the shared maths to the topic being taught in class. Many teachers also invent their own 'home' maths tasks which draw upon the out-of-school context. We shall return to this later when discussing homework.

It is popularly held by teachers that the responses to both the home-reading and the home-maths will primarily depend upon the nature of the catchment area of the school. However, as we mentioned earlier, in fact it is possible to achieve an excellent response in any school. Doing so will involve teachers in a great deal of effort to start with, although once the 'we-do-this-here' climate is established, the system has a momentum of its own. It is a hard and unpalatable fact that the teachers in some schools in very deprived areas achieve a higher number of parents reading and sharing number activities with their children than some teachers do in more socio-economically advantaged areas. They reply to parents' comments and make efforts to see parents who are 'dropping out'. They use a great deal of praise and encouragement and, above all, are concerned to demonstrate to parents how much they value their input, and how essential it is.

Traditionally, schools have also held parent meetings, at which parental attendance again tends to be a function of the socio-economic make-up of the catchment area of the school. Different types of research and intervention[6] have shown that attendance at such meetings can be maximized using the following strategies:

- Involve children in the preparation of an invitation to their parents. Parents are far more likely to read and pay attention to an invitation which has been written or drawn by their child than they are to an official invite.
- If possible, involve children in the meeting itself – either in demonstrating work or in talking about something they have done.
- Make sure that the objective of the meeting is clear – parents go away having learned something or with necessary information which they did not have before.
- Offer two or three times – e.g. 'We should like to meet with *all* parents to discuss how you can best support your child's learning in number. Because this is of importance to every child, we shall hold three meetings, one at 9.00 a.m., one at 4.00 and one at 7.00 in the evening. You need only come to one of these meetings!' Offering a choice of time in this way serves the double function of increasing the chances of parents being able to attend and also stressing how important a matter the school believes this to be.
- Always make provision for small children. These parents are worth the effort you put in to ensure their presence, since once they are 'on-board' in terms of collaborative activities, the school reaps the benefits, and so do their younger children.

Schools can also stage other events to involve parents further. These can include numeracy days, number walk-abouts (looking for numbers in the environment), activity sessions, maths-mornings, number assemblies, and parent-help classes. However, it remains the case that the most effective way of ensuring that parents are involved in their own children's learning is through the use of shared 'take-home' maths activities, and an efficient system of feedback and dialogue. The easy access to the teacher, and the informal contact and encouragement that this can provide, is worth its weight in gold.

What can parents do?

This is certainly one of the most contentious areas in mathematics education. On the one extreme, there are those educators who believe that doing certain things 'too early' or 'too fast', or introducing a topic or strategy before they are 'ready' for it, can damage children. At the other end of the spectrum, there are those who argue that any extra input in maths must be good, and that schools tend to underestimate what children can do anyway.

The notion of 'readiness' has been contested so heavily, both at the level of theory and practice that it is now difficult to draw upon it as a justification. Furthermore, the research evidence points in one direction as regards children's early maths experiences:[7]

- what children can do aged 5 and 6 is not a bad predictor of what they will be able to do later on, so those who start 'ahead' in their number work tend to preserve their advantage;
- very young children can perform quite complex operations with numbers and are capable of handling larger numbers in more complex ways than teachers have conventionally believed or assumed;
- numbers do not have to be presented in a concrete setting (i.e. in a situation involving the physical manipulation of objects) in order to make sense to young children. They can and should be presented orally, as linguistic entities as well as representations of some physical state of affairs;
- children's conversations with adults and with their peers involve a wide variety of number usages. Any collaboration with parents should recognize and exploit this fact.

What can be drawn from the research here? And, importantly, how do current changes in the theoretical framing of early years education affect what mathematics we can encourage parents to do with their children? It is helpful to systematize our thinking by means of two diagrams. First, what are the differences between 'home' maths and 'school' maths? Drawing upon the work of Hannon (1995) in literacy, as well as research carried out as part of the IMPACT project (Merttens 1994), we can note the following:

Maths at home	Maths at school
occurs contingently, as a result of what is happening at the time	is usually planned, and follows the teacher's agenda
is often initiated by the child who is the prime mover in the questioning process	is often initiated by the teacher who is the prime mover in the questioning process
numbers are always in a real-life context, but are only occasionally matched to a physical representation	the physical or concrete representation of numbers will often be emphasized
is taught by parents using their own idiosyncratic methods	is taught by teachers using fairly standardized and uniform methods
follows no formal curriculum and is bounded only by the child's interest and the parent's time/expertise	follows a formal curriculum and is bounded by professionally defined notions of what is appropriately taught at each stage

We can also try to systematize our uses of the different educational terms in relation to the maths which happens in the context of the home:

	Concrete	Abstract

Informal	*oral*
	• counting sweets
	  or biscuits
	• sorting coins
	• adding 1 more
	  to a pile . . .
		oral
		• counting on the stairs
		• sorting number cards
		• adding 1 more
		  to someone's
		  age . . .

	null category *written*	writing 'notes' to mum . . . *written*

Formal	*oral*
	• using counters
	• using a form-board
	• using mathematical
	  toys or jigsaws
		oral
		• chanting the number
		  names in order
		• doing 'sums' in
		  our heads
		• using 'big'
		  numbers

	null category *written*	doing 'sums' using 'workbooks' *written*

Certainly it is always true that parents can help by counting and talking about numbers with their children. Almost any discussion of how numbers work, or about how a certain calculation can be carried out can be a helpful learning experience, particularly if the parent is aware of what maths is being taught at school and how it is being taught. The *Leaflets for Parents* devised by, and available from, the Hamilton Maths Project[8] provide a very good means of explaining to parents exactly what sorts of things their child should be doing at each stage in their primary career.

Teachers can personalize these leaflets by highlighting specific and appropriate targets for each child. It is remarkable what effect making each leaflet an individual document for each child has upon the take-up by the parents. If the leaflets are just given out wholesale, not nearly as many parents will read and use them as when each child brings home a leaflet which the teacher has specifically highlighted and addressed to them personally.

The most useful thing that parents can do is to share maths activities, both formal and informal, in the context of the home. Some of these activities will be school-focused, and some will be home-focused. These activities should include:

• helping with homework, playing number games;
• playing cards or other games;
• talking about the child's number work;

Targets - Year 2

About the targets:

These targets are intended to give you some idea of the things your child should be able to do by the end of this year. We welcome your comments about how your child is progressing in relation to any target. Remember that some targets are more complicated than they seem – a child who can count from 1 to 50 may still have trouble if you ask her which number comes after 37. She may have to start at 1 and count from there!

	Comments
Count, read and write the numbers up to 100	
Know which numbers come in-between any two numbers. E.g. say which numbers are in-between 56 and 59	
Know the pairs of numbers which make ten. E.g. 4 + 6, 7 + 3, 5 + 5...	
Add two numbers by counting on. E.g. 23 + 8 is twenty-three and eight more	
Add 10, 20 or 30 or 40 to a number. E.g. 34 + 20	
Subtract one number from another when the numbers are close. E.g. 23 - 18	
Subtract one number from another when the numbers are not close. E.g. 23 - 5	
Count in 2's, 5's and 10's using their fingers	
Recognise odd and even numbers	
Double and halve small numbers	

Year 2   Some fun activities to help your child's maths

Number Frieze: Make a number frieze for your children. Make each set relevant to your child's interests.

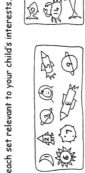

Use the frieze to help your child understand and compare numbers up to 100. E.g. pointing to the date, someone's age (!), an amount of money, a page in a book, a distance in miles. Draw children's attention to how the numbers are written. E.g. 34 is thirty-four not forty-three!

91	92	93	94	95	96	97	98	99	100
81	82	83	84	85	86	87	88	89	90
71	72	73	74	75	76	77	78	79	80
61	62	63	64	65	66	67	68	69	70
51	52	53	54	55	56	57	58	59	60
41	42	43	44	45	46	47	48	49	50
31	32	33	34	35	36	37	38	39	40
21	22	23	24	25	26	27	28	29	30
11	12	13	14	15	16	17	18	19	20
1	2	3	4	5	6	7	8	9	10

Board Game: Make a board game from a grid like this. Again make it relevant to your child's interests - space adventures, dinosaurs, superheroes...

Play these games on your board

• Throw a dice. Move along that number of spaces, BUT before you move, you must work out what number you will land on. If you are wrong, you don't move! Go around the board till the end. First one there, wins.

• Start at the top of the board. Throw the dice and move backwards. BUT you must say what number you will land on before you move your counter. Anyone landing on a multiple of ten gets an extra turn! First one to the bottom of the board, wins.

Figure 7.1 Part of a leaflet for parents of Year 2 children.

- discussing 'real-life' numeracy tasks with the child such as shopping activities;
- talking to their child's teacher;
- counting with their child;
- reading and writing numbers (including large numbers) . . .

Simply having someone at home to talk to about the maths that was done at school, or to count with as you walk up the stairs, is an important part of helping children to feel that what they do in maths is both interesting and important in the adult world.

Homework

We started with homework as an icon of 'the good school', and we have ended with shared home tasks as the most effective means of involving parents in their children's mathematical education. However, what moves us from the former to the latter is an agreement as to the *purposes* of homework. The National Numeracy Strategy training pack[9] defined the purposes as follows:

- to involve the parents in their children's learning;
- to help parents keep abreast of what their child can and cannot do;
- to utilize the context of the home and apply some numerical strategies in a non-school situation;
- to encourage children to talk about their number work and explain to their parents what they are doing and how;
- to provide some extra numerical practice;
- to help parents improve, extend or practise their own numerical strategies.

If homework is simply sent home, with little or no regard to its purpose or function, it is likely to increase the divide between those children who have parents who, for whatever reason, can offer a great deal of support when children need help with their maths, and those who cannot. Some parents, whilst not feeling mathematically competent themselves, will be able to afford to pay for some tutor assistance. Other parents will possess the necessary mathematical knowledge and confidence to help their child themselves, although this is never without attendant problems. But those parents who believe themselves to have failed at maths may well find that they are in a position of 'failing' again when they are unable to help the child who is 'stuck'.

Homework is most effective if a variety of types is sent home:

1 IMPACT-type maths tasks, games or other activities which are shared between parents and children, and where the child discusses the maths and the task itself draws upon the home context;
2 memorization games or activities to help children with the instant recall of certain number facts;
3 tasks or activities which enable the practice of numerical strategies introduced in school; and
4 investigative or problem-solving type tasks where the child, and hopefully the parent, explore a piece of maths together.

Name of Activity	PARENT		CHILD		Comments
	Was IMPACT enjoyable?	Was it too hard?	Did you like your IMPACT?	How much did you learn?	
	Great fun ☐ / All Right ☐ / Not much fun ☐	Too hard ☐ / Too easy ☐ / Just right ☐	a lot / a little / not much	a lot / a little / not much	
	Great fun ☐ / All Right ☐ / Not much fun ☐	Too hard ☐ / Too easy ☐ / Just right ☐	a lot / a little / not much	a lot / a little / not much	
	Great fun ☐ / All Right ☐ / Not much fun ☐	Too hard ☐ / Too easy ☐ / Just right ☐	a lot / a little / not much	a lot / a little / not much	
	Great fun ☐ / All Right ☐ / Not much fun ☐	Too hard ☐ / Too easy ☐ / Just right ☐	a lot / a little / not much	a lot / a little / not much	

Figure 7.2 A page from an IMPACT diary.

It is good to have specific and regular homework 'nights' so that parents and children can expect it. On the Hamilton Maths Project,[10] we have found that an ideal schedule is an IMPACT-type task at the weekend, and more traditional individual homework once or twice a week, depending on the age of the children. Thus, during the week, homework of types 2 and 3 is given, and at the weekend homework of types 1 and 4. This is a mixture that proves both practical and popular – it works out at about 10–15 minutes per session in the week and about 30 minutes of shared maths at the weekend.

All children can be encouraged to share maths activities with their parents. The proportion of individually focused homework can generally increase as children get older. However, no child should be excluded from doing a piece of homework because he or she has difficulty finding someone to share the activities at home, and so some provision for repeating or extending the shared task in the context of school or an after-school club can be made.

As has been emphasized previously, to be effective as a means of involving parents, what is done at home must be both valued by teachers and seen to be valued. A homework diary in which parents and children comment is easily the most effective way of giving a due status to this aspect of the child's work. It also provides a means of getting feedback from the parents about the child's progress.

Conclusion

Although most schools now recognize the importance of involving parents in the process of teaching children to read, there is still a long way to go when it comes to maths. On this occasion, it is not that we need more research; the evidence, and its implications are, unusually, quite clear. How much, and what, their parents do before they come to school, and to what extent they continue with this involvement, are both major factors in children's educational achievement. Furthermore, what teachers and schools do makes a great difference to the proportion of parents who are involved on a weekly basis.

With the advent of the changes in maths education which have been implemented over the last few years, we have a more formalized approach to the teaching and learning of maths. Teachers are becoming used to focusing on a limited number of objectives and to placing a strong emphasis upon the development of mental maths skills. In turn, this makes it easier to formulate activities and tasks which rehearse the prerequisite skills. These make ideal mid-week homework activities, since it is very likely that most of the children will need to practise these and will also be able to do them! The political focus on the desirability of homework, and its relatively high profile in recent times, may also assist schools in their attempts to persuade parents to participate in the weekend's shared tasks. Certainly, involving parents in the setting and attaining of individual targets will go some way towards closing the 'information gap' and helping all parents to realize that they are no longer regarded as peripheral, nor indeed as consumers. They are an integral part of the schooling process, and their collaboration is both sought and welcomed.

Useful addresses

The Hamilton Maths Project, Directors: Prof. Ruth Merttens and Mr Mike O'Regan, 6 Northmoor Rd, Oxford, OX2 6UP.
The Hamilton Reading Project, Directors: Prof. Ruth Merttens and Mr Mike O'Regan, 6 Northmoor Rd, Oxford, OX2 6UP.
Hamilton Education, Temple Court, 107 Oxford Rd, Cowley, Oxford, OX4 2ER.
The IMPACT Project, University of North London, Holloway Rd, London, N7 8BD.

Notes

1 See Hughes *et al.* 1994 for a fuller account of some of this research.
2 See Merttens, R. (1996a).
3 See Docking (1990) for a fuller account of different types of successful parental partnership initiatives.
4 For a useful account of the differences in numbers of parents involved in schools of broadly similar catchment areas see the Report to the DfEE of the IMPACT Project in Haringey (Merttens 1994).
5 See *IMPACT Maths Homework* activity books (1994), published by Scholastic Press, Leamington Spa.
6 See Merttens *et al.* (1996) for a fuller account of different models of parent meeting.
7 There is an increasing body of research which suggests (a) that we have underestimated what children can do in terms of number operations; and (b) that what young children can do is a reasonable predictor of their later achievement in education. See: Munn (1994), Merttens (1996b) and Thompson (1997).
8 These leaflets for parents can be obtained from Hamilton Education at Temple Court, 107 Oxford Rd, Cowley, Oxford, OX 4 2ER, or Tel: 01865 396613, fax: 396614.
9 The National Numeracy Strategy 'Three Day Course' Training Pack, 1999. Session 9: 'Involving parents and homework.'
10 The Hamilton Maths Project is based in Oxford and has produced materials and leaflets through Hamilton Education.

References

DES (Department of Education and Science) (1982) *Mathematics Counts* (Cockcroft Report). London: HMSO.
DfEE (Department for Education and Employment) (1998) *Numeracy Matters: Preliminary Report of the Numeracy Task Force.* London: HMSO.
Docking, J. (1990) *Primary Schools and Parents.* London: Hodder and Stoughton.
Hannon, P. (1995) *Literacy: Home and School.* London: Falmer.
HMSO (1967) *Children and their Primary Schools* (Plowden Report). London: HMSO.
Hughes, M., Wikeley, F. and Nash, T. (1994) *Parents and their Children's Schools.* Oxford: Blackwell.
Merttens, R. (1994) *The IMPACT Project in Haringey: Raising Standards in Inner City Schools.* Report to the DfEE. London: University of North London.
Merttens, R. (1996a) School effectiveness and school improvement. *International Journal of Research, Policy and Practice.* Special Issue: Improving Schools through Better Home-School Partnerships, 7(4): 411.

Merttens, R. (ed.) (1996b) *Teaching Numeracy*. Leamington Spa: Scholastic Press.
Merttens, R., Newland, A. and Webb, S. (1996) *Learning in Tandem: Parental Involvement in their Children's Education*. Leamington Spa: Scholastic Press.
Munn, P. (1994) The early development of literacy and numeracy skills. *European Early Childhood Education Research Journal*, 2(1).
Thompson, I. (ed.) (1997) *Teaching and Learning Early Number*. Buckingham: Open University Press.

It ain't (just) what you do: effective teachers of numeracy

Mike Askew

Introduction

I met John a few years ago when he was a Year 4 pupil. Sitting alone, he was working on a scheme page which asked what had to be added to several three-digit numbers to make each up to 500. He had done the first and written in his book was:

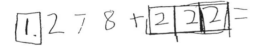

Figure 8.1 John's calculation.

As I sat down, John slipped a piece of paper under the desk. I asked him to read what he had written in his book.

'278 plus 222 makes 500.'

When I asked him how he had found the answer, John replied, 'I just worked it out.'

'Did you do it in your head?'

'No, I used a bit of paper.'

'Is that the paper that you used?' (indicating the hidden piece)

'No, it's in the bin, that's my working for the next one.'

When John reluctantly showed me the paper it became clear why, 20 minutes into the lesson, he had only done one question. Counting on from 278 to 500 in single tally marks and then recounting them is a slow process (especially if you want to get it right. I of course had interrupted the counting for the second question, so was not too popular).

Before reading on you might like to consider for a moment what your response would be to John's strategy. What would you do to help him?

I have been posing this question to many teachers at workshops and lectures. Usually there is a range of responses, including:

Figure 8.2 John's tally marks.

- work on building up his confidence. John got the right answer, so to try and show him a different method might demotivate him;
- ask him if he can think of a quicker method;
- work with much smaller numbers – he needs to be able to deal with those efficiently before working with greater numbers;
- work with much larger numbers – by asking how many more, say, 5000 is than 2780, John might realize the inefficiency of his method;
- refine his method – say, getting him to organize his tallies in tens and ones;
- show a practical method – get out tens' and ones' blocks and demonstrate how to model the situation;
- persuade him that the calculation is actually a subtraction and can be answered using a standard algorithm;
- show a more efficient method, say, shop-keeper addition (rounding up to the nearest 10 then 100) or counting on using empty number line.

I want to suggest the following simple model of the challenge that John's work poses. At one end of a continuum you have the child's methods and understanding, and at the other end the teacher's methods and understanding. The challenge is to bridge this gap.

Child's method(s) _____ Teacher's methods

So where do you focus your attention on this continuum? Do you start 'near' to where the child is (or further back than that) or do you leap in at the other end? The strength of the first option is that you build on what children can do, but a weakness is that it may take some time to move them on. On the other hand, showing a different method may increase efficiency in the short term but at the cost of longer term understanding and the ability to apply the skill in different situations.

Any decision will rest on some theory or beliefs, however informal or unarticulated, about the relationship between teaching and learning. Exploring teachers' beliefs about this relationship was one aspect of the Effective Teachers of Numeracy project carried out at King's College by myself and colleagues Margaret Brown, David Johnson, Valerie Rhodes and Dylan Wiliam and funded by the Teacher Training Agency.[1]

The beliefs of the teachers in the project appeared to be significant not only in terms of what they did in the classroom, but also in terms of children's learning outcomes. This chapter explores some of these issues. Anyone wishing to read more about the project should see Askew *et al*. 1997.

Effective teachers of numeracy

The principal aim of the Effective Teachers of Numeracy project was:

- to identify key factors which enable teachers to put effective teaching of numeracy into practice in the primary phase.

Realizing this aim posed three initial problems for us:

- what is meant by numeracy?
- how do we identify effective teaching of numeracy?
- how do we find effective teachers of numeracy?

Only when we had resolved these could we begin to identify the factors that enabled teachers to put effective teaching into practice.

Defining numeracy

Starting the project we could find no agreed definition of numeracy. We therefore decided to adopt a definition that was broad enough to encompass the ability to calculate accurately but also go beyond that to include a 'feel for number', and the ability to apply arithmetic:

Numeracy is the ability to process, communicate and interpret numerical information in a variety of contexts.

Identifying effective teaching of numeracy

Careful identification of teachers believed to be effective in teaching numeracy was crucial to the project. But before we could identify such teachers we had to decide on what we meant by effective teaching of numeracy. Our starting point was to build on our definition of numeracy, and this enabled us to be more specific about our expected outcomes of effective teaching. We defined effective teaching of numeracy as teaching that helps children:

- acquire knowledge of and facility with numbers, number relations and number operations based on an integrated network of understanding, techniques, strategies and application skills;
- learn how to apply this knowledge of and facility with numbers, number relations and number operations in a variety of contexts.

Although this definition gave some sense of the outcomes of the teaching it moved us no nearer to identifying what the actual teaching might look like.

Many people in mathematics education – researchers, inspectors, teachers – would claim to know what 'good' practice in primary mathematics should look like. However, evidence about teaching practices that are effective in terms of bringing about learning of numeracy is limited. The research in mathematics education in the UK largely separates findings on children's learning from those on teaching.

It seemed sensible therefore to base our identification of effective teaching on some measure of children's actual learning gains, rather than presumptions of 'good practice'. Once we had identified classes whose average gains were higher than others, we could go about exploring what practices appeared to be most effective in promoting this learning.

We measured children's learning by looking at the gains for individual classes over part of a school year. Specially designed tests of numeracy were administered to whole classes from Year 1 to Year 6, first towards the beginning of the autumn term 1995, and again at the end of the spring term 1996 (Year 1 being assessed only on this second occasion). The tests related as far as possible to the definition of numeracy and outcomes of effective teaching given above. Aspects of numeracy covered in the tests included:

- Understanding of the number system, including place value, decimals and fractions.

  For example, given the numbers 30, 76 and 174, Year 2 children were asked to write down the number one less than each.
- Methods of computation, including both known number facts and efficient and accurate methods of calculating.

  For example, 'share 76 equally among 4' was on the Year 5 test.
- Solving numerical problems, including complex contextualized word problems and abstract mathematical problems concerning the relationships between operations.

  For example, given that $86 + 57 = 143$ could Year 3 children quickly figure out answers to $86 + 56$, $57 + 6$, $860 + 570$, $85 + 57$, $143 - 86$?

  Or, asked how many different sandwiches can be made from six different fillings and three types of bread, could Year 4 children identify an appropriate calculation?

Average gains were calculated for each class providing an indicator of 'teacher effectiveness' for the teachers in our project.

Finding effective teachers of numeracy

In ideal circumstances, we might have chosen some teachers, judged their effectiveness through class scores on our tests, and then gone back to look at what the teachers did in their lessons.

However, the project was only funded for just over a year. By the time we had the data on children's gains there was not going to be time to go back and work with the teachers. We had to study classroom processes in the time between the two test administrations. This meant we somehow had to maximize our chances of working with teachers who were already effective.

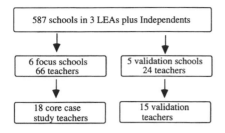

Figure 8.3 The sample of teachers.

Selecting potentially effective teachers was done through a progressive 'filtering' from LEA to school to class.

We approached three local education authorities (Berkshire, Croydon and Wandsworth) as we knew each held considerable school-level data on standards in numeracy in relation to other school variables. On the basis of this data, each LEA agreed to assist in identifying one or two *focus schools*: a total group of four schools identified as performing well above expectations in relation to numeracy. We also made sure that the sample contained schools with different socio-economic intakes in different environments (inner city, suburban, rural).

We also considered it important to include teachers in independent schools. The Incorporated Association of Preparatory Schools assisted us in identifying two further focus schools in the independent sector which were acknowledged to be effective in teaching numeracy.

Our main data on teachers was gathered from these focus schools. In order to check out these findings, a further set of five validation schools was also identified. These schools represented a range of levels of performance in mathematics.

So, from an initial sample of all the primary schools in three LEAs (some 587 schools), together with Independent schools, we had selected 11 schools – six focus schools and five validation schools – to study in detail, giving an overall sample of 90 teachers.

From the six focus schools, we worked closely with 18 teachers, three in each school. This group of 18 teachers formed our sample of *case study teachers*, providing data on classroom practices, together with teacher beliefs about, and knowledge of, mathematics, pupils and teaching. The three teachers in each school were identified as those most likely to prove effective, selected through discussion with head teachers and, where appropriate, with advice from the LEA inspectors and advisers. While the emphasis was on identifying effective teachers, the 18 were chosen so that teachers were reasonably evenly distributed across year groups 1–6.

Exploring teachers' beliefs and practices

An understanding of the teachers' beliefs and practices was built up from data from four sources:

- questionnaire data from the full sample of 90 teachers (66 in focus schools, 24 in validation);
- observations of 54 mathematics lessons with the 18 case study teachers (three for each teacher) and 30 lessons with the 15 validation teachers (two for each teacher);
- three interviews with each of the 18 case study teachers: a general interview on classroom practices, teaching intentions and experiences; a structured task to explore their mathematical understandings; an interview focused on children and the similarities and difference between them;
- two interviews with each of the 15 validation teachers.

Children test data on our tests of numeracy was gathered for all 90 classes in both core and validation schools. All the classes demonstrated gains on our test over the year.

Some findings

Some of our findings were surprising in that they challenge some popularly held beliefs about what makes a teacher effective.

For example, style of organization for mathematics teaching was not a predictor of how effective teachers were. Whole-class 'question-and-answer' teaching styles were used by both highly effective and comparatively less effective teachers. Similarly, individualized and small group work were used by teachers across the range of effectiveness.

At the school level, setting across an age group was used in schools with both high and low proportions of highly effective teachers. The same published mathematics schemes were used by highly effective and comparatively much less effective teachers.

Our findings also raised questions about the sort of mathematical knowledge that teachers need in order to be effective. Despite what might be expected, being highly effective was not positively associated with higher levels of qualifications in mathematics. The amount of continuing professional development in mathematics education that teachers had undertaken was a better predictor of their effectiveness than the level to which they had formally studied mathematics.

Levels of effectiveness

So, if styles of classroom organization and levels of mathematical qualification did not determine effectiveness, what did? On the basis of the average gains made by each class the teachers were put into three groups: highly effective, effective and moderately effective. In order to try and answer this question we looked at how our focus case study teachers were distributed across these categories.

Table 8.1 The case study teachers and levels of effectiveness

Highly effective	Effective	Moderately effective
Anne	Danielle	Beth
Alan	Dorothy	Brian
Alice	Eva	Cath
Barbara	Fay	David
Carole		Elizabeth
Faith		Erica

The initials of the pseudonyms chosen for the teachers are the same for teachers from the same school, so, for example, Anne, Alan and Alice all taught in School A. Year 1 teachers (Claire and Frances) are not included in the table since they could not be readily identified according to effectiveness on the basis of the testing of their classes on one occasion only.

By looking at the data for each group of teachers, and in particular those identified as highly effective, we noticed that some patterns began to emerge. Before discussing these, a couple of examples might provide some flavour of what the highly effective teachers did in practice. The first example is adapted from the field notes of Claire's lesson. As indicated it was not possible to determine which of the three categories Claire would be in, but her beliefs and practices were very similar to those of the group of highly effective teachers and the children's responses in class suggested that it was likely that she was a highly effective teacher.

Example 1: Place value

A Year 1 whole-class lesson. There is a large 0–99 hundred square on the board with some numbers filled in. Claire shows the children how looking at the left-hand numbers gives the name of the numbers in that row and how the top row gives the second number (i.e. row headed 20 intersects with column headed 4 at 24). She identifies an empty space (say 37) on the hundred square. The children have to work out what the missing number is and someone is invited to the board to fill it in.

On a table are a blue hoop and a yellow hoop and some interlocking cubes. Two children put three cubes into the yellow hoop and seven into the blue hoop. Claire asks each child in turn how many their cubes represent to which they respond 'ten, twenty, thirty and seven'. Under the 100 square are drawn a yellow circle and a blue circle (labelled 'tens' and 'ones' respectively). A pair of children draw squares in the circle for the appropriate number of tens and ones and, in a similar fashion to the pair with the cubes, read out the numbers.

After several numbers have been filled in, the teacher asks what the biggest number on the square is and which number would come next. The children identify 100 and a lively discussion follows on where the box for 100 should be drawn: next to 99 or under 90. They agree to under 90. A child comes and writes it in. Claire adds another hoop to the table and a third circle on the board. While the children can represent 100 using these, 102 causes difficulty and there is much discussion about recording and the order of the digits.

Example 2: Fractions, decimal fractions, percentages and ratios

A Year 6 class. Alan, the teacher, has put a chart on the white board which has columns for fractions, decimal fractions, percentages and ratios. One value has been entered in each row and the children are working in pairs to convert from one form of representation to another. They are using a variety of methods but working mainly in their heads and most are checking their results using a different method.

As they begin to complete the task Alan brings the class together. Individuals are invited to provide answers and explain methods of calculation. The class is attentive to these explanations. More efficient methods are offered and errors dealt with in a supportive manner either by the teacher or other pupils. Finally they discuss the sort of contexts where the different representations would be used.

A connectionist orientation towards teaching numeracy

From our analysis what seemed to distinguish some highly effective teachers from the others was a consistent and coherent set of beliefs about how best to teach mathematics whilst taking into account children's learning.

In particular, the theme of 'connections' was one that particularly struck us. Several of our highly effective teachers seemed to pay attention to:

- connections between different aspects of mathematics, for example, addition and subtraction or fractions, decimals and percentages;
- connections between different representations of mathematics: moving between symbols, words, diagrams and objects;
- connections with children's methods – valuing these and being interested in children's thinking but also sharing their methods.

We came to refer to such teachers as having a connectionist orientation to teaching and learning numeracy.

This *connectionist* orientation includes the belief that being numerate involves being both efficient and effective. For example while 2016 – 1999 can be effectively calculated using a paper and pencil algorithm, it is more efficient to work it out mentally. Being numerate, for the *connectionist* orientated teacher, requires an awareness of different methods of calculation and the ability to choose an *appropriate* method. As Anne put it:

> I have tried to provide them with a whole range of different ways of going about adding numbers, or taking them away, so that they will be able to become comfortable with the strategies that they like best.
>
> (Anne Y2/3/4)

Further to this is the belief that children come to lessons already in possession of mental strategies for calculating but that the teacher has responsibility for intervening, working with the children on becoming more efficient. Misunderstandings that children may display are seen as important parts of lessons, needing to be explicitly identified and worked with in order to improve understanding.

As indicated, a connectionist orientation emphasizes the links between different aspects of the mathematics curriculum.

> I think you've got to know that they are inverse operations those two (addition and subtraction), and that those two (multiplication and division) are linked, because when you are solving problems mentally you are all the time making links between multiplication, division, addition and subtraction . . . I think mental agility depends on you seeing relationships between numbers and being aware of links.
>
> (Barbara Y6)

The application of number to new situations is important to the *connectionist* orientation with children drawing on their mathematical understandings to solve realistic problems. The connectionist orientation also places a strong emphasis on developing reasoning and justification leading to the proof aspects of Using and Applying Mathematics (UAM). Reasoning about number is as important as its application, and as such UAM is integral to the teaching of number.

Associated with the *connectionist* orientation is a belief that most children are able to learn mathematics given appropriate teaching which explicitly introduces the links between different aspects of mathematics.

> But I have the same expectations for the children, I always think about it as not so much what the children are doing as what they have the potential to do. So even if I have children like Mary in the classroom who are tremendously able, I am really just as excited with the children who are having that nice slow start, because, who knows, tomorrow they may fly – you just don't know.
>
> (Anne Y2/3/4)

Within a constructivist orientation a primary belief is that teaching mathematics is based on dialogue between teacher and children, so that teachers better understand the children's thinking and children gain access to the teacher's mathematical knowledge.

> If I am honest with myself I probably spend more time talking with them than doing exercises and things like that . . . because I want them to be able not to just give an answer, I want them to explain the process and what they are doing, to be looking for these links again, and to be able to be adventurous as well.
>
> (Alan Y5/6)

Other orientations towards teaching numeracy

Two other orientations were also identified: one where the teacher's beliefs were more focused upon the role of the teacher (a transmission orientation) and one of beliefs focused upon the children learning mathematics independently (discovery orientation).

The *transmission* orientation means placing more emphasis on teaching than learning. The transmission orientation entails a belief in the importance of a collection of procedures or routines, particularly with regard to paper and pencil methods, one for doing each particular type of calculation regardless of whether or not a different method would be more efficient in a particular case. This emphasis on a set of routines and methods to be learned leads to the presentation of mathematics in discrete packages, for example, fractions taught separately from division.

Teaching is believed to be most effective when it consists of clear verbal explanations of routines. Interactions between teachers and children tend to be question and answer exchanges in order to check whether or not children can reproduce the routine or method being introduced to them. What children already know is of less importance, unless it forms part of a new procedure.

Linked to this is a view of using and applying as the application of mathematics to word problems (basic calculations set in a real-world context). These word problems can be tackled after learning to do calculations or procedures in an abstract form. The numeracy emphasis is on the ability to perform set routines, so the reasoning, logic and proof aspects of UAM are not seen as particularly relevant.

Children are believed to vary in their ability to become numerate. If the teacher has explained a method clearly and logically, then any failure to learn must be the result of the children's inability rather than a consequence of the teaching. Any misunderstandings that children may display are seen as the result of the children's failure to 'grasp' what was being taught; misunderstandings are remedied by further reinforcement of the 'correct' method and more practice to help children remember.

In the *discovery* orientation learning takes precedence over teaching and the pace of learning is largely determined by the children. Children's own strategies are the most important: understanding is based on working things out for themselves. Children are seen as needing to be 'ready' before they can learn certain mathematical ideas. This results in a view that children vary in their ability to become numerate. Children's misunderstandings are the result of pupils not being 'ready' to learn the ideas.

Teaching children requires extensive use of practical experiences that are seen as embodying mathematical ideas so that they discover methods for themselves. Learning about mathematical concepts precedes the ability to apply these concepts and application is introduced through practical problems.

The discovery-orientated teacher tends to treat all methods of calculation as equally acceptable. As long as an answer is obtained, whether or not the method is particularly effective or efficient is not perceived as important. Children's creation of their own methods is a valued process, and is based upon building up their confidence and ability in practical methods. Calculation methods are selected primarily on the basis of practically representing the operation. The mathematics curriculum is seen as being made up of mostly separate elements.

Orientation and effectiveness

The orientations of connectionist, transmission and discovery are ideal types: no single teacher is likely to hold a set of beliefs that precisely matches those set out within each orientation.

However, analysis of the data revealed that some teachers were more predisposed to talk and behave in ways that fitted with one orientation over the others. In particular, Anne, Alan, Barbara, Carole, Claire, Faith, all displayed characteristics indicating a high level of orientation towards the connectionist view. On the other hand, Brian and David both displayed strong discovery orientations, while Beth, Elizabeth and Cath were characterized as transmission-orientated teachers.

Other case study teachers displayed less distinct allegiance to one or other of the three orientations. They held sets of beliefs that drew in part from one or more of the orientations. For example, one teacher had strong connectionist beliefs about the nature of being a numerate pupil but in practice displayed a transmission orientation towards beliefs about how best to teach pupils to become numerate.

The connection between these three orientations and the classification of the teachers into having relatively high, medium or low mean class gain scores suggests that there may be a relationship between pupil learning outcomes and teacher orientations.

Table 8.2 The relation between orientation and effectiveness

	Highly effective	*Effective*	*Moderately effective*
Strongly connectionist	Anne Alan Barbara Carole Faith		
Strongly transmission			Beth Cath Elizabeth
Strongly discovery			Brian David
No strong orientation	Alice	Danielle Dorothy Eva Fay	Erica

Implications of orientations

I suggest that examining orientations towards teaching mathematics can help us understand why practices that have surface similarities may result in different learner outcomes. For example, while all the teachers in the study employed some whole-class question and answer sessions, the nature of the interaction with children within such sessions varied according to orientation. Our highly effective teachers demonstrated a range of classroom organization styles including whole-class teaching, individual and group work. On such measures their practices were indistinguishable from those of the teachers who were only moderately effective. While the interplay between beliefs and practices is complex, these orientations provide some insight into the mathematical and pedagogical purposes behind particular classroom practices and may be more important than the practices themselves in determining effectiveness.

Exhortations for teachers to adopt new practices may result either in the practices being adapted to fit with existing beliefs or in limited take-up of the practices themselves. As other research on developing teaching has demonstrated, exhorting teachers to adopt particular practices without helping them develop a deep understanding of the principles behind these practices does not in itself lead to raised standards (Alexander 1992).

Teachers may find it helpful to examine their belief systems and think about where they stand in relation to these three orientations. In a sense the connectionist approach is not a complete contrast to the other two but embodies the best of both of them in its acknowledgement of the role of both the teacher and the pupils in lessons. Teachers may therefore need to address different issues according to their beliefs: the transmission-orientated teacher may want to consider the attention given to pupil understandings, while the discovery-orientated teacher may need to examine beliefs about the role of the teacher.

Just in case anyone is left wondering what I did with John, I showed him how to find the difference using shop-keeper addition. I hoped we were on to a winner when he said, 'Oh, that's a lot quicker isn't it!' But of course, whether I had any long-term impact is another question.

Note

1 The views expressed here are those of the author and should not be interpreted as representing the views of the Teacher Training Agency.

References

Alexander, R. (1992) *Policy and Practice in Primary Education*. London: Routledge.
Askew, M., Brown, M., Rhodes, V., Wiliam, D. and Johnson, D. (1997) *Effective Teachers of Numeracy: Report of a Study Carried Out for the Teacher Training Agency*. London: King's College, University of London.

ICT and numeracy in primary schools

Steve Higgins and Daniel Muijs

Introduction

This chapter has three main aims: first, to present an analysis of some of the writing and research on Information and Communications Technology (ICT) and primary mathematics; second, to identify what we see as some trends in the way computer programs for primary maths have developed; and third, to outline what we consider are some implications for classroom teachers. The chapter arises from the authors' separate involvement in two projects: the literature analysis for the Numeracy Task Force report and the literature surveyed for a Teacher Training Agency (TTA)-funded project on 'Effective Pedagogy for the Use of ICT' in literacy and numeracy in primary schools. In addition some relevant information from the preliminary surveys and formative classroom observations from this project are discussed in the light of other research. In our recommendations we also try to take into account the changing picture of mathematics in primary classrooms and the impact of the National Numeracy Strategy.

The particular focus of this chapter is numeracy in primary schools: the focus is not therefore the development of mathematical logic or reasoning, nor the teaching of shape and space, nor even learning to use data handling and data presentation programs. There are clearly computer applications that are both helpful and desirable for the learning of mathematics in all of these areas but it is not clear that these approaches are primarily beneficial in developing numeracy or pupils' understanding of number.

The Numeracy Task Force's (DfEE 1998) definition in the final report is a useful one:

> Numeracy at key stages 1 and 2 is a proficiency that involves confidence and competence with numbers and measures. It requires an understanding of the numbers system, a repertoire of computational skills and an inclination and ability to solve number problems in a variety of contexts.

Numeracy also demands practical understanding of the ways in which information is gathered by counting and measuring and is presented in graphs, diagrams, charts and tables.

(Chapter 1, para. 15)

The breadth of this definition is important. The emphasis on 'confidence and competence' and on 'understanding' and 'inclination' as well as 'computational skills' bridges the central issue of this chapter.

We are omitting from this chapter any debate on the issue of calculators. This is partly because Ruthven (Chapter 16, this volume) deals with this issue specifically but also because the Numeracy Task Force took a particular decision about calculators, which meant that the Effective Pedagogy using ICT project did not pursue their use in Key Stage 1 and early Key Stage 2.

ICT and the teaching and learning of mathematics

There is little hard evidence for any beneficial effects of ICT on numeracy in the primary age range. Indeed there is a suggestion of possible negative effects of computers from the most recent analysis of the TIMSS data though this correlation is weak and needs to be treated with caution. Singapore, for instance, consistently does well in international surveys and is certainly forging ahead with ICT in primary schools.

The emphasis in the research literature about ICT and maths is on CAI (Computer Assisted Instruction) or CAL (Computer Aided Learning) and mainly reports studies of secondary or post-secondary mathematics teaching and learning. Overall the benefit reported by these studies is relatively low and computer use is not generally found to be as effective as other approaches such as peer tutoring or homework. There is very little research specifically on primary mathematics, and still fewer empirical studies containing information on pupils' attainment in numeracy. Where such studies are reported they are often on intervention studies with a specific and precise learning goal rather than improving numeracy more generally. Such studies are usually testing learning theory, particularly from a psychological perspective. Whilst the results of these are often informative, it can be difficult to apply the findings directly to the primary classroom. In addition there is now considerable evidence about the limited effectiveness of Integrated Learning Systems (ILS) which we consider in a separate section below.

Many studies and wider writings are enthusiastic about broader positive effects on motivation and attitude. Some doubt clearly remains over whether this motivational effect will be sustained over time, when the novelty of computer use in the classroom has waned. In mathematics this should not be ignored, especially as attitudes to mathematics tend to colour pupils' attitudes to school. Besides, as we shall argue in this chapter, the main benefit of capitalizing on such effects on attitude and motivation would be to support more effective teaching of maths by the teacher and not as an alternative to human contact.

Currently new software tends to concentrate on developing specific number skills, particularly addition and multiplication facts, following an approach we would crudely characterize as inspired by a behaviourist approach to learning. Problems or questions are presented to pupils by the computer. The computer then provides a reward of some kind (often an irritating little tune) if they provide a correct solution. Further questions follow. There are few new programs which have the potential for developing mathematical understanding in the way that some of the early BBC or Microelectronics Education Programme (MEP) software was designed to do: for example, Blocks[1] for developing calculation strategies; Grid Games[2] and Monty[3] for recognizing and predicting number patterns. More recent skills practice programs also tend to present calculations in standard and (more often than not) vertical format and do not support the development of pupils' own strategies (e.g. 10 out of 10).[4] Integrated Learning Systems (ILS), such as Successmaker[5] or Tomorrow's Promise,[6] offer plenty of appropriate examples for pupils to practise and provide feedback to teachers of the errors that pupils make but they focus again on number skills.

On the other hand constructivist or understanding-led approaches to software design have not been able to claim much success in raising attainment in numeracy either. Logo is perhaps the premier example in this area. Much was claimed for this innovative programming language which enables very young children to develop mathematical ideas through the use of precise language. However the evidence of impact on pupils' mathematical attainment has been disappointing in this area too (Yelland 1995).

Software development in maths for primary pupils seems therefore to have evolved along distinct lines. Initially very basic programs focused on skills practice. Soon however a wider range of programs was developed, many by teachers with the support of the MEP. Some of these lent themselves more to developing strategies, identifying patterns and promoting understanding. Software development today is more complex and the products are certainly more sophisticated in appearance. A similar pattern may well emerge as the more complex programs address aspects of mathematics broader than practising skills.

Integrated Learning Systems

More complex and structured skills practice programs which offer assessment summaries to teachers have been developed over recent years. These Integrated Learning Systems have been very expensive to develop and are expensive to buy. The preliminary evaluations of ILS suggested that they were not particularly beneficial for pupils in Key Stage 1, though early indications suggested that they might be more effective for older pupils. The final evaluation (Wood 1998) painted a more gloomy picture, particularly for pupils in Key Stage 3. It clearly suggests that the systems evaluated were not effective in raising attainment in mathematics, although they might possibly be effective for remediation or as a 'catch up' solution, particularly for lower attaining

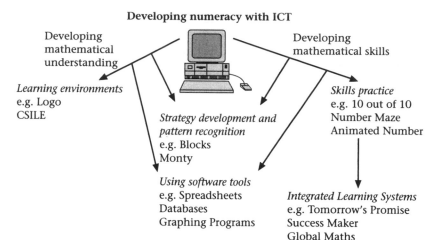

Figure 9.1 Diverging strands of development in ICT and maths.

pupils. If this approach reduces the 'tail' of under-achievement and enables more effective whole-class and group teaching with a narrower band of attainment in a class then it will have clear advantages. So far, however, the benefits are not to be found in the systems alone. They are not (yet?) capable of supporting and developing pupils' own calculation strategies, nor do they appear to be good at teaching or introducing new ideas. Overall the impact on pupils' attainment has been disappointing, particularly considering the cost of the systems. Two particularly important implications for schools can be drawn from the evaluation. First, using ILS is not good test preparation: teachers are better at preparing pupils for national tests! Second, teachers should not infer more general progress from the gains reported by ILS systems.

Our understanding of ICT and mathematics suggests to us that the development of computer applications to support mathematics for primary pupils has diverged according to the diagram in Figure 9.1.

Many mathematics educators and researchers have pursued a constructivist approach in the teaching and learning of mathematics which has emphasized understanding. This approach takes as its starting point how pupils think and learn and actively seeks to accommodate and transform their knowledge and understanding. The development of learning environments like Logo can be seen to typify this approach. Most commercial development (and therefore most software sold to schools) has concentrated on particular mathematical skills (particularly the four rules). There are clearly some exceptions to this pattern, notably where software tries to develop mental calculation strategies (e.g. Blocks), or programs like Numerator[7] or Number Connections[8] (see Figure 9.2) which seek to develop understanding by showing on screen the relationships between mathematical representations and expressions.

This separation is also reflected in the types of programs which teachers claim to use (Green 1998). In Reception and Year 1 computer use is dominated

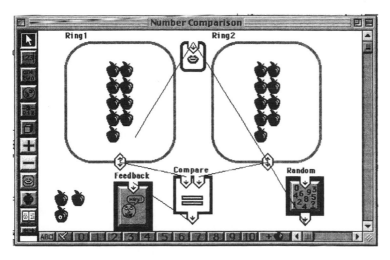

Figure 9.2 A screen from Number Connections.

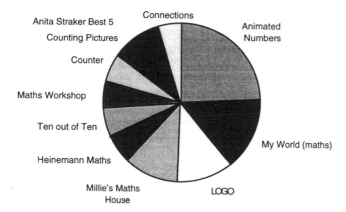

Figure 9.3 Programs primary teachers indicated they used to support numeracy.

by practice exercises and puzzles. The reported use of such programs declines steadily up to Year 6. In terms of specific software, a questionnaire to 250 teachers for the initial stages of the TTA Effective Pedagogy for the Use of ICT project found a similar picture. 87 of these teachers in Reception, Year 2 and Year 4 indicated that they used computer software to support numeracy or number activities. The programs they specified are shown in Figure 9.3. The chart clearly shows the preponderance of practice software (e.g. Animated Numbers[9] for lower primary) but also indicates the use of a range of other types of programs.

Overall this section can be summarized by saying that two strands of software development can be identified: a constructivist approach which emphasizes understanding of number and a behaviourist approach which focuses on the practice of specific numerical skills. Neither approach seems unequivocally to have had direct impact on pupils' attainment in numeracy. The implications from work on assessment (Black and Wiliam 1998) would seem to be that pupils need to identify the causes of or reasons for the errors they make so that they become aware that they can rectify mistakes themselves. Currently most maths software is unable to do this and only gives limited feedback when an answer is correct or incorrect. Typically when pupils make errors they are given an indication that they are wrong (with a sound or symbol), but they are not usually offered information either about why the answers were incorrect or how to rectify the mistakes.

Neither of these two basic directions in mathematics software, the tutoring and practice approach as exemplified by ILS and the more constructivist approach as exemplified by Logo, appear to have been particularly effective, at least so far. Possibly this might be the result of the typical weaknesses of both approaches. The more exploratory approach for pupils in a constructivist program offers a wealth of diverse experiences and opportunities to make connections within mathematics, but does not guarantee that pupils will actually be focusing on the mathematical knowledge the teacher wants them to (they might instead be 'off task' focusing on less mathematically relevant content or upon logical rather than numerical skills). In contrast, in the tightly focused tutoring system there is no guarantee that pupils are actually obtaining any meaning or understanding from their work. For example they might be learning merely how to get the best help from the system (Balacheff and Kaput 1996). This suggests to us that effective use of ICT would, like effective teaching, require use of both strategies on different occasions, depending on the specific goals of a lesson or the specific focus for part of a lesson.

Recent developments in maths and ICT

The constructivist approach to using computers is continuing. One example of this would be Computer Supported Intentional Learning Environments (CSILE),[10] based in Canada. In this approach the computer is used to support and record pupils' communication and thinking about maths. Early published results have been encouraging and suggest that pupils make demonstrable progress, particularly in mathematical problem solving. Other recent work shows that computers can support pupils' understanding in other ways. For example, the research reported by Ainsworth et al. (1998) shows software can support pupils in increasing the range of possible solutions to maths questions.

The use of portable computers and palmtops has also been investigated. Again some results have been encouraging. The use of such machines can clearly have a beneficial impact on children's mathematical thinking (e.g. Ainley and Pratt 1995). We suggest, however, that the issue here is how the machines are used. Projects like this involve considerable development work with teachers and have usually taken a constructivist approach to learning for both the teachers and the pupils. Ainley and Pratt describe the development of teachers' mathematical understanding as well as the development of their technical expertise. In addition such development work saw the particular hardware and software as mathematical tools for pupils to use, rather than seeing the technology itself as a teaching tool.

Clearly related to the way teachers approach the use of hardware and software is the difficulty teachers find in using some open-ended programs effectively. A person's understanding of mathematics limits what they see as the potential for use of a program as Bradshaw (1993) reports about Numerator. It can also be harder to organize the use of such programs in the classroom and in some instances they may take longer or be more challenging to learn how to use. These reasons perhaps explain the limited use of approaches and programs of this type. The implication for schools is that effective teaching following such approaches requires investment in both ICT training for teachers and investment in professional development in mathematics.

The World Wide Web and maths

The increase in sites on the World Wide Web about mathematics has been dramatic. Web sites exploiting the communications aspect of the technology have also appeared. (See, for example, NRICH,[11] or Math World Interactive.)[12] A clear benefit here is for teachers with small numbers of pupils in a year group, as is often the case in rural schools, or with exceptional pupils in a class who could benefit from the exchange of information with others of similar ability.

A further use of the WWW lies in the possibilities for connectivity between classrooms. In this way it would be possible for pupils in classrooms in different parts of the country or the world to challenge one another in mathematical games or activities, for example providing each other with immediate feedback on the results of their problem-solving activities.

Wider issues

Teachers in primary schools in England are currently being encouraged to change the way they teach maths. The emphasis on ICT on the one hand and imposition of an 'optional' numeracy lesson on the other are just two of the changes. The recommended structure of these lessons perhaps makes it more difficult to integrate ICT into numeracy-focused sessions, particularly where only one or two computers are available.

What evidence there is on present practice in ICT and maths in primary schools suggests that there is great variety both in the availability of equipment and its use. The range of equipment is from just about one working computer per class to some schools with networks using ILS (Green 1998). In the Effective Pedagogy using ICT project the average (modal) number of computers available to the 250 classes surveyed was one.

This is an important issue. If computers are to be used for more than demonstration by the teacher there need to be enough computers in the classroom or in accessible clusters for groups of pupils or whole classes of pupils to use them together. The alternative is that just a few pupils can work on the computer while other pupils do another activity. This, in turn, may lead to frustration for some pupils who would rather be using the computer, or may lead to teachers making sure every pupil gets a turn regardless of how appropriate the program is for them. In addition, having an ICT activity, with some technical problems on occasion, creates precisely the kind of classroom management problems that the whole-class teaching model aims to prevent, unless other helpers are also available to supervise the ICT activity. The financial constraints on providing either extra adults or a computer suite with technician on hand hardly need to be mentioned!

Why use ICT?

The implications of the evidence we have discussed is that teachers need to be clear about the aims or purposes of using ICT. There are also pragmatic considerations which are dependent upon access to appropriate equipment and software. However, the specific purpose determines the use and particular teaching emphasis. Above all, the key question is: what particular benefit does using ICT offer to making teaching or learning in mathematics more effective or more efficient?

Possible reasons

1 More effective teaching of the whole class or of large groups. This might be through demonstration or representing ideas either using a specific maths program like Counter[13] or through a presentation package like Microsoft's Powerpoint or Claris' Impact).
2 More effective discussion and use of specific mathematical language with the teacher using the computer with a group of pupils (e.g. Pond[14] with Reception children; creating a spreadsheet or discussing number patterns using Monty with older pupils).
3 Pupils learning strategies with the computer enforcing the 'rules' of the game (e.g. Blocks).
4 Exposure to multiple examples to identify patterns (e.g. Numbers[15] or Logogrid[16]).
5 Pupils learning how to use mathematical tools (working with spreadsheets or databases or presenting mathematical ideas using tables, graphs and charts).
6 Pupils practising specific skills to enable teacher to work with others more effectively.

7 Pupils getting immediate feedback from the computer to reduce the need for any marking in class time.

8 Computers providing feedback for the teacher. This could be just the basic 'Statistics' function in a program like Number Maze[17] or the more complex reporting of ILS information to increase diagnosis of errors for specific teaching at another time.

9 Pupils working individually and getting practice at an appropriate level (either by careful use of teacher's options in a program like Animated Number or in an ILS program in which the software automatically adjusts the level of challenge).

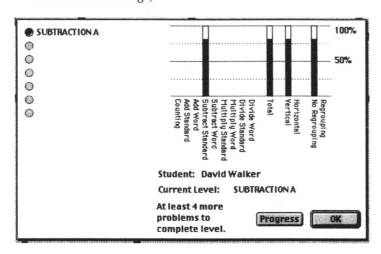

Figure 9.4 An example of the statistics function in Number Maze.

The role of the teacher

Once the teacher identifies the particular mathematical aim then further issues can be addressed. One of these is clearly identifying the appropriate role of the teacher. This role changes depending on the particular aim from the list above. For instance there will be considerable difference when the computer is used as a demonstration tool compared with when it is used to support the practice of particular skills. In the former case the teacher is central, in the second case the teacher becomes more a facilitator or manager in identifying which skills the pupils need to practise (though the pupils themselves and some programs can also play a part in this) and in obtaining information about what they have done. Alternatively having some pupils practising skills may release the teacher to work directly with other pupils.

So in an active teaching lesson the computer could be used during part of the whole-class introduction by the teacher, and then for practice or exploration by pupils as a group task either independently or with the teacher. The teacher also has to play an active role when using ICT in structured tasks. When pupils might not necessarily develop their mathematical knowledge teachers will actively have fo assist pupils in grasping the meaning of the processes they are involved in so that effective learning can occur. Pupils could easily complete examples of two-digit subtraction on a computer, but the intervention of the teacher to identify patterns or suggest strategies such as counting up when the difference is small or rounding to the nearest 10 to make the mental calculation easier would both support skills and enhance understanding. Doing this without losing the element of the pupils' contribution or 'construction' is a complex and difficult task. In part this can be achieved by adapting the computer-based environments to teachers' specific purposes, but they may have to intervene during the activity as well (Balacheff and Kaput 1996). This level of complexity may well be impractical in the normal hurly-burly of a hectic classroom's daily routine or if the teacher is to maintain a clear teaching focus with another group.

Another role of the teacher with respect to ICT in the classroom is in addressing pupils' misconceptions; this applies as much to use of ILS systems as to programs like Logo. The program itself will not be able to determine why a pupil has made a mistake, or even whether the mistake is related to mathematical content or just results from misunderstanding the computer program and its requirements. One of the benefits of Logo is that pupils see the need to 'de-bug' their routines themselves; in ILS the need to identify and address errors or mistakes is less apparent. All in all it would seem that active learning with ICT is only possible with substantial pupil and teacher input.

Some implications for teaching

The intention of this section is to offer some suggestions to support the effective use of ICT in numeracy lessons.

Develop explicit connections between mathematical activities

This might be to link computer activities and other planned activities to develop pupils' awareness of mathematical connections, for example identifying successful strategies or recognizing patterns from a maths program which could then be used in further activities away from the computer. An alternative use would be starting activities with the class or in a group which some pupils could then pursue on the computer (looking at rounding decimals from spreadsheet calculations where the data are messy and do not produce whole number solutions, for example) so as to compare and draw out the links as a specific teaching aim. This would be consistent both with the 'connectionist' view of teaching from the King's Report (see Askew, Chapter 8, this volume) and some of the preliminary survey data from the TTA Effective Pedagogy for using ICT project where the highly effective teachers planned and used activities which linked or supported computer-based work. Portable computers and palmtops clearly offer a valuable opportunity in this area to bring technology into contexts where desktop computers are impractical so as to use 'hot' data (Ainley and Pratt 1995). Discussion about representation of numerical data, whether in tables or charts, is clearly also helpful (Ainsworth *et al.* 1998).

Use the computer for direct instruction

The use of the computer by the teacher for demonstration of ideas and concepts would be consistent with both the *National Numeracy Strategy Framework for Teaching Mathematics from Reception to Year 6* (DfEE 1999) and a whole-class interactive teaching approach. At present this may mean using some older software. Alternatively using a presentation package and materials prepared by the teacher (or pupils) with a large monitor or projector may be an approach some schools are able to pursue.

Develop mathematical language and vocabulary

The teacher could also use the computer in the group teaching phase of an NNS-style lesson. This would provide a focus for discussion to promote the development of mathematical language. Pupils could also use the computer collaboratively to collect and present results. This again would be consistent with the aims of interactive whole-class teaching. Computers can also be useful during activities with smaller groups. The use of practical apparatus has been found to be an effective motivator or focus of attention in small group work; the computer can perform a similar function. Having a group of pupils working together on a computer entering data into a spreadsheet and discussing the effect of formulae or agreeing the best charting options to answer a specific question could foster co-operation and give a clear mathematical focus (which is the recommended aim of small group work).

Emphasize understanding of number when using software tools

The effective use of tables, spreadsheets, data handling and charting software offers opportunities to develop pupils' practical understanding of number and of the way numerical information can be represented. The teaching emphasis needs to be on answering questions using the data and on identifying what the strengths of different representations are, rather than seeing the completed table or graph as the finished product.

Support pupils in developing essential mathematical skills

Specific software could be used to remediate or improve basic skills (e.g. ILS or simpler drill and practice programs as 'catch-up'). This might be with regular use for particular pupils for perhaps half a term (three to four times per week for 15–20 minutes at a time). Again for such skills practice it is probably better for one pupil to use the computer alone rather than in pairs or threes. Such use of the computer would then need to be complemented by activities (whether ICT-based or not) which promoted the application and understanding of the mathematical ideas involved. In addition a clear teaching point to bear in mind when using technology in this way would need to be to help the pupils to identify where they were making errors and to support them in correcting any mistakes, perhaps through involving them in setting targets.

Use ICT to motivate and focus attention on how to improve

Computers motivate pupils to practise and they may well increase speed of their responses. Teachers would however need to be careful that pupils did not focus only on extrinsic rewards. In maths programs this would be feedback only of the number of correct responses or scores of performance. This type of feedback does not help pupils to correct errors, other than by trying again.

Identify mathematical feedback

Some skills programs, particularly early counting programs with speech, give direct feedback, which can help children mathematically. Another example of specifically mathematical feedback would be from trial and improvement methods which use a floor robot to improve estimation and measurement skills; pupils would know from where the robot stops how accurate their estimate was. Using a spreadsheet or a calculator to refine an answer in this way should also help pupils to use the mathematical sense of the context in which they are working as feedback to improve an answer.

Develop ICT skills using a mathematical context

Some examples of this might be pupils exchanging solutions to an investigation by e-mail or fax; creating a maths puzzles WWW page; getting pupils to design a computer-based presentation to explain their calculation strategies; using an art or DTP package for pupils to design their own maths activities and games. Having an audience or a purpose for maths work which pupils understand or accept is clearly beneficial. Although this approach is clearly not specific to numeracy, it could provide an appropriate context for developing and applying numerical skills.

Be critical of new software

Teachers clearly need to ask pertinent questions about any new software. What does it offer mathematically? Does it present material in a way that will support pupils' understanding? How could you teach the same skills or ideas without ICT? Is the approach with ICT really better?

Conclusion

As we outlined in the introduction, the issue for this chapter is that no ICT equipment or software yet adequately develops numeracy for primary pupils across the range of 'competence', 'confidence' and 'understanding'. Teachers must therefore choose the type of program that complements their current pedagogy, or more pragmatically they may need to adjust their teaching strategies and approaches to complement or compensate for the strengths and weaknesses of the ICT equipment and programs which they have available.

Notes on the software and web sites mentioned

The information on the software and web sites referred to in this chapter is given for completeness and should not necessarily be taken as an endorsement of the programs or sites mentioned.

 1 Blocks (MEP Blue File Software).
 2 Grid Games by David Kirkby (Eigen Publications/System Software).
 3 Monty available on the Slimwam 2 disk from the Association of Teachers of Mathematics (ATM) and is included in the National Council for Educational Technology (NCET) Number Grids Pack. A PC version called Number Snake is also available on the Shropshire Maths Suite: Number Programs disk: (01743) 233 628.
 4 10 out of 10 Educational Software available for PC, Acorn and Amiga platforms: (0113) 239 4627.
 5 Success Maker (Maths) from Research Machines: (0865) 791234.
 6 Tomorrow's Promise (Maths) by Jostens available for Mac and PC from Xemplar: (01223) 724724 and Longman Logotron: (01223) 425558.
 7 Numerator (Longman Logotron). The Mathematical Association produced a booklet entitled *Numerator in the Mathematics Classroom* in 1993. Available for Acorn and PC platforms.
 8 Number Connections (Wings for Learning) available for the Macintosh platform from TAG Developments: (01474) 357350. (Not to be confused with Sherston Software's Connections for BBC, Acorn and PC referred to in Figure 9.3.)
 9 Animated Numbers (Sherston Software) available for BBC, Acorn, PC and Macintosh: (01666) 840433.
10 CSILE (Computer Supported Intentional Learning Environments): further details are available on their web site at http://csile.oise.on.ca/.
11 The NRICH on-line Maths Club site can be found at: http://nrich.maths.org.uk
12 Math World Interactive http://www.mathworld-interactive.com/. This is a US site 'dedicated to helping educators and parents motivate their students to solve open-ended word problems, communicate mathematically, and share cultural and geographical information'. New problems are posted every nine weeks for different age groups in the primary age range.
13 Counter is available on the Slimwam2 disk and is available from the ATM. A PC version is also available (see Note 3).
14 Pond (Resource): (01509) 672222.
15 Numbers (Smile) on '11 More' and MicroSMILE Pack 4. Available for Acorn and PC: (0181) 347 8624.
16 Logogrid (NCET): contact BECTA: (01203) 416994.
17 Number Maze (Great Wave Software) available for PC and Macintosh platforms.

References

Ainley, J. and Pratt, D. (1995) Planning for portability: integrating mathematics and technology in the primary curriculum. In L. Burton and B. Jaworski (eds), *Technology in Mathematics Teaching*, pp. 435–48. Lund, Sweden: Chartwell-Bratt.

Ainsworth, S., Wood, D. and O'Malley, C. (1998) There is more than one way to solve a problem: evaluating a learning environment that supports the development of children's multiplication skills. *Learning and Instruction*, 8: 141–57.

Balacheff, N. and Kaput, J.J. (1996) Computer-based learning environments in mathematics. In A.J. Bishop, K. Clements, C. Keitel, J. Kilpatrick and C. Laborde (eds), *International Handbook of Mathematics Education*. Dordrecht: Kluwer Academic Publishers.

Black, P. and Wiliam, D. (1998) *Inside the Black Box: Raising Standards through Classroom Assessment*. London: King's College.

Bradshaw, J. (ed.) (1993) *Numerator in the Mathematics Classroom*. Leicester: The Mathematical Association.

DfEE (Department for Education and Employment) (1998) *The Implementation of the National Numeracy Strategy: Final Report of the Numeracy Task Force*. London: DfEE.

DfEE (Department for Education and Employment) (1999) *The National Numeracy Strategy Framework for Teaching Mathematics from Reception to Year 6*. London: DfEE.

Green, D. (1998) IT provision in English schools. *Mathematics in School*, 27 (3): 9–12.

Wood, D. (1998) *The UK ILS Evaluations: Final Report*. Coventry: British Educational Communications and Technology Agency (BECTA)/DfEE.

Yelland, N. (1995) Mindstorms or storm in a teacup? A review of research with Logo. *International Journal of Mathematical Education for Science and Technology*, 26: 853–69.

ASSESSMENT ISSUES

In Chapter 10 Gill Close uses her substantial experience of writing and evaluating National Curriculum test questions at Key Stages 2 and 3 to provide pointers for helping teachers develop their own end of unit, end of term or end of year tests. Gill provides examples of the types of questions that have been found to 'teach' as well as 'test' in that they confront children with their own misconceptions and lead to their resolving the conflict. She illustrates several important points which should be taken into account when writing test items by analysing specific questions used in National Curriculum tests. The advice offered should help teachers to perform the following tasks more efficiently: interpret their own children's performance on National Curriculum tests; evaluate questions from commercial tests with a view to using them for formative evaluation; develop their own items which probe understanding and highlight misconceptions; and prepare their children to take their own National Curriculum tests.

In Chapter 11 Marja van den Heuvel-Panhuizen illustrates the extent to which the adoption of a 'realistic' approach to mathematical education in the Netherlands has led inevitably to the development of a range of more flexible and dynamic context problems for assessment purposes. Examples are given of test items developed specifically for the assessment of children involved in the Realistic Mathematics Education programme, and these are used to provide a context for a discussion of some of the assessment issues currently being tackled by mathematics educators in the Netherlands. Some of the questions are analysed in terms of their strengths and weaknesses, and this leads to a discussion of the extent to which different views of mathematics education lead to different views on assessment.

Choosing a good test question

Gill Close

Many of the assessments we make in mathematics are based on written responses to written questions. Often we have little time to design these questions or to vet carefully the questions in published tests, such as those accompanying teaching schemes. However, we spend much of our lesson time teaching towards assessments we have chosen, or those which we are required to carry out. If we could choose test questions which measured the depth of understanding we wanted them to, and allowed us to make valid inferences about the pupils' understanding based on their responses, the pupils would benefit in many ways.

First, we would be better able to probe understanding of important concepts, and the extent of any misconceptions. Second, we would then have more valuable information on which to plan future differentiated work or to improve our teaching. Third, teaching time would not be deflected onto preparing for poor tests.

Beneficial effects of test questions on teaching and learning

The design and content of test questions is known to have a major effect on teaching, an example being the many pupils in the USA who spend a high proportion of their time practising for multiple choice tests. If questions were well designed, some of the backwash effect on teaching could be beneficial. The first Key Stage 3 test development team set itself a number of aims, in addition to the requirements of government agencies, which were intended to improve the impact of the tests on teaching and learning. These included:

1 *encourage good practice and offer stimuli for further classroom work*
   (good quality materials for direct use, ideas for question structure or for content which could be extended in class);

2 *assess some key concepts and highlight some common misconceptions*
  (selecting key building blocks from the National Curriculum rather than
  just random sampling, e.g. estimating proportions; choosing misconceptions
  from research, inspections, previous test responses, e.g. symbolization, fre-
  quency diagrams relating to time, choice of 'whole' in proportion questions);

3 *offer diagnostic information to teachers*
  (through question style and categories of response in mark scheme);

4 *maximize access for all pupils*
  (so pupils consider the activity as purposeful for them; open response so
  pupils may stamp their own identity on the question and to indicate that
  there is more than one correct answer in maths; choice of response type and
  entry pathway into question to support pupils' different conceptualizations
  of it, e.g. diagram or words);

5 *use language, layout and artwork which makes the requirements clear*
  (vocabulary, syntax, quantity of words, position and line breaks, indicate
  response format by giving example, overall clarity of page with few marker-
  oriented intrusions);

6 *portray mathematics as an interesting, relevant and participative subject*
  (use people and range of names to encourage empathy and engagement,
  show people working together, thinking hard and talking as a natural part
  of maths);

7 *convey the importance of reasoning and of the methods of working used*
  (through question style, e.g. presenting working out or reasoning to be
  evaluated, such as wrong responses to be commented upon);

8 *use informally ideas which are the basis for more advanced mathematics*
  (indicating a further purpose and power, avoiding familiar dead-end or
  unthinking applications, e.g. co-ordinate questions leading to deeper concepts about shapes or the plane rather than pictures or maps).

The design for each question attempted to meet more than one of these aims.
In particular one style of question was developed in which a named person
gave an incorrect answer and pupils were asked to describe why it was
wrong. In fact much development work and trialling was needed to arrive at
this format in preference to others. For example, giving two or more possible
responses and asking which was correct, and why, generally led to less useful
information because the pupils with a misconception tended to identify this
as the correct answer without considering the other possibilities and therefore were never confronted with, or encouraged to address, their own misconceptions. Two examples of this style of question (SCAA 1993) may help
to illustrate its value, and to show how general aims can be operationalized.
The text and some aspects of the layout of items will be referred to as *Wrong
addition* and *Percentage decrease*.

Wrong addition

Kate is adding up the number of pupils in Year 9 and the number of
pupils in Year 10.

Year 9   127 pupils
Year 10   154 pupils

Kate says that there is a total of 2711 pupils in years 9 and 10.

(a) How can you tell that Kate's answer is wrong **before** you work out the correct total?

This is Kate's work: 127
                        + 154
                        ―――――
                         2711
                        ―――――

(b) What do you think Kate did wrong?

Percentage decrease shows the head and shoulders of two young people with hairstyles and clothing common amongst 14-year-olds. A balloon shows what each of them says.

Percentage decrease

(a) Tanya says, 'An increase from 40 to 80 is a 100% increase.'

Scott says, 'So a decrease from 80 to 40 is a 100% decrease.'

Tanya is right. Scott is wrong.

Say why a decrease from 80 to 40 is *not* a 100% decrease.

(b) Fill in the correct percentages.

An increase from 80 to 100 is a _____% increase.

A decrease from 100 to 80 is a _____% decrease.

Do you think these percentages should be the same? _____

Explain your answer.

Wrong addition aims to assess whether pupils can consider the reasonableness of an answer, rather than just work it out. To make this check, it offers both reference to the context by knowing possible sizes of year groups in a school, and reference to the numbers themselves. Pupils' responses reveal the many different ways in which they do this checking. Some use approximating through rounding or looking at the most significant digit, making statements such as 'because 100 and 100 is 200 not 2000', while others focus on the number of digits with remarks like 'because there should only be three numbers for the answer'.

Some state that this is too many pupils for the school. The question also allows high attainers to make sophisticated responses such as 'any 3 figured number added to another 3 figured number cannot be over 2000'. Overall this question offers access to pupils at a range of attainment levels, thereby providing useful diagnostic information about a wide range of successful and inappropriate pupils' methods and ways of conceptualizing addition.

By selecting a very important concept to test, and allocating marks to this rather than to a correct calculation, and through its style, *Wrong addition* goes some way to meeting many of the eight question design aims.

Percentage decrease focuses on a key misconception in proportional reasoning which many children and adults possess. It is based on their lack of awareness of what to consider as the whole in comparison to which changes are made. When these people increase an amount by a half, they assume that decreasing the result by a half, rather than by a third, will return them to the initial amount. When these adults need to claim their expenses they often know the gross expense, including VAT at 17.5 per cent, then mistakenly deduct 17.5 per cent in attempting to calculate the net expense. It is far more important for pupils to overcome this misconception than to be able to calculate given percentages of an amount by following an algorithm which does not address the fact that they are dealing with proportions rather than absolute values.

Pupils' responses to *Percentage decrease* show a range of logical reasoning to explain why Scott is wrong. Some work out the correct percentage decrease from 80 to 40, while others work out the result of a 100 per cent decrease and show this is not 40. Some show they are clear about what to consider as the whole, commenting on what 100 per cent of 80 is or is not. Confusions between additive and multiplicative strategies, and about the meaning of 100 per cent, are revealed, such as '100 enlarges a number. A number below zero will decrease something.' and 'Because 100 per cent is always top so you can't have 100 per cent decrease.' Some pupils who can reason well enough from their common sense to get part (a) correct cannot generalize from this and get part (b) wrong. However, there is clear evidence from altered responses that a few pupils actually noticed an inconsistency between their expectation that the percentages should be different, as in part (a), and their initial response in (b) that they were both 25 per cent. These pupils had learned while doing the question as a result of being confronted by their misconception.

By selecting an important misconception to test and showing youngsters discussing a mathematical disagreement, and through its style, *Percentage decrease* also meets most of the eight question design aims.

Before National Curriculum testing, the style used in *Wrong addition* and *Percentage decrease* was not at all common. The above examples of pupils' responses and learning, and of the valuable diagnostic information which questions structured like this provide, show how hard it is to use these questions in teaching without pupils or teachers benefiting in some way. Research undertaken in 1995 on the impact of the Key Stage 3 tests on teaching and learning (Close *et al.* 1995) found that 22 per cent of Year 9 teachers were already using this style of question in their teaching, even though the majority of teachers claimed not to be paying much attention to the tests or to be preparing pupils for them. These findings indicate that a good test question style can actually provide benefits for learning and teaching in the classroom, as hoped for in the aims of the test development team.

Identifying shortcomings in test questions

It is natural for us to expect that published tests, especially the National Curriculum tests, are of high quality, but research has shown that this is not always the case (Close *et al.* 1997). In a study of the validity of the 1996 Key Stage 2 tests in English, mathematics and science, 53 per cent of the mathematics questions and 60 per cent of their mark schemes were found to have problems which caused concern about the validity of inferences based upon them. These inferences might include whether a pupil understood a particular concept, could carry out a type of calculation or had attained a particular level. In preparing pupils for tests, by working on previous years' tests, it is important to be able to identify weaknesses in the questions because pupils' inability to obtain the marks might be more due to the poor question or mark scheme than to any shortcoming in the pupils' knowledge, skill or understanding.

The main weaknesses in the 1996 Key Stage 2 mathematics test questions provide good examples of problems to look out for in any test questions. They include:

1 the language used providing miscues or vocabulary hurdles;
2 misleading layout, illustrations or context;
3 vagueness, errors, loopholes and omissions in the mark schemes;
4 undemanding questions in which errors or guesses gained credit;
5 failure to credit sophisticated responses or deeper concepts; and
6 unavailability of marks apparently allocated for working.

You can identify weaknesses in a test question through examining various different aspects including:

- the question itself;
- the mark scheme;
- pupils' responses;
- patterns of errors;
- the facility.

Careful study of the question can give you information about weaknesses 1, 2 and 4 above, but you may not notice some of these until you also look at the pupils' responses. For example, a wording which appears straightforward to you may in fact provide a miscue for the pupils. Conversely, wording which you know to be mathematically imprecise may convey a unique meaning to pupils who know less mathematics than you. Looking at patterns of errors can suggest unexpected interpretations pupils have made which you might not notice from only a few pupils' responses, each containing a different error.

The fact that a question is undemanding may be apparent from the question alone, or from the generosity with which marks are awarded in the mark scheme. Analysis of the mark scheme will provide information about weaknesses 3, 4, 5 and 6, but you may not be aware of the correct sophisticated responses which are possible until you see what pupils have written. The mark scheme will show you which concepts and skills within a question are being valued and credited, although evidence of others may well be elicited by the question. In fact they may not be the concepts and skills which you would wish to credit, or which the pupil assumes the question is testing. Vagueness, omissions and loopholes in the mark scheme are sometimes apparent from just thinking clearly about it, but at other times they are revealed when you encounter a pupil's response for which you cannot decide whether or not to give the mark.

While examination of a few pupils' responses can provide valuable information, other features show up only when you look at the facility for each mark, i.e. the percentage of pupils who were awarded it. This can show you marks that were never or rarely awarded, such as those allocated for partially correct answers. From studying the mark scheme you might welcome the fact that partial credit is available for correct methods without correct calculation, but sometimes this credit is structured so tightly that few pupils obtain it because most pupils who can get this far with the working can also complete the question correctly and obtain full marks.

If you are thinking of using a test question for the first time, it might be helpful to try it out on a few pupils and study their responses before using it on a wider scale. It is very hard to write a good question at the first draft, even though we often write questions quickly and assume it is easy. National Curriculum test questions need to go through many drafts, each tried out by pupils. Once you have used a question with a group, you will have lots of pupils' responses to help you to decide whether to use the question again, or how to improve it. You will also have some facilities for each mark which will give you more insight into the quality of the question and mark scheme, and whether it is testing what you intended it to. A useful guide to appropriate facilities, which was used by the first Key Stage 3 test developers, is to aim for 65–70 per cent of pupils working at a particular level to be awarded a mark at that level. For example, if you are intending a mark within a question to have Level 4 demand, 65–70 per cent of pupils who are working at Level 4 in that topic area should obtain the mark.

Examples of shortcomings in test questions

To exemplify some of the categories of shortcomings in test questions described above, I will quote and discuss specific questions which test an aspect of number. The comments are based on the findings of the analysis of questions carried out in the study by the Association of Teachers and Lecturers of the validity of the 1996 Key Stage 2 tests in English, mathematics and science (Close *et al.* 1997).

The most common problem with mathematics questions was their wording. This occurred in 45 per cent of questions. Four questions illustrate this in different ways (SCAA 1996).

Fairground

John and Paula go to a fair.

Galaxy £1.50 per ride	Laser 90p per ride	Big Wheel £1.20 per ride	Spaceship 75p per ride

John has £2.
He goes on **one ride** and has **exactly 80p** left.
Which **ride** does he go on?
He goes on the _____

This question about a fairground aims to assess addition and subtraction. It has a language miscue in the sentences 'John has £2. He goes on **one ride** and has **exactly 80p** left. Which **ride** does he go on?' The use of the present tense, rather than the past tense, encouraged some pupils to think the question was asking for the next ride he would go on. These pupils selected the spaceship ride which cost 75p and was the only ride available for 80p or less. If no ride had been available for 80p or less, or if the past tense had been used, the question would not have left itself open to this alternative valid interpretation. One pupil who answered both big wheel (£1.20) and spaceship was awarded no marks but might well have been aware of the two alternative interpretations of the question, indicating both a ride leaving 80p afterwards and a ride using the remaining 80p. In fact the use of the present tense in this question is incorrect, but many pupils are conditioned to expect that a calculation is required and hence made the intended inference (Close *et al.* 1997: 6.3).

This language miscue may not be apparent when checking the question quickly, but a high proportion of pupils answering 'Spaceship' draws attention to pupils interpreting the question differently from the question writers. For pupils who gave this answer there is no evidence for whether they could carry out the required subtraction. This question has a high facility so its faults are not spotted if you look only at facilities. You need also to see what kind of errors pupils are making and whether there is a trend in them, and to look at sufficient pupils' responses to detect this.

Shape

Complete the table.

Shape	Property of shape		
	4 sides only	one or more right angles	two pairs of parallel sides

In this question, pupils who do not understand the meaning of 'two pairs of parallel sides' are penalized. This wording can confuse pupils who consider 'two' and 'pairs' to be repeated words, one of which is redundant. Wording such as 'two sets of parallel sides' would remove this language barrier. Although 'two pairs' is used in many teaching schemes, in a test response it is not clear whether pupils have actively counted the number of sets of parallel sides, or just considered that the question required them to note the existence of any sets of parallels. In designing a question you need to decide when you are testing vocabulary and when you are testing concepts, ensuring that the vocabulary does not provide a hurdle preventing pupils from showing their understanding and thereby preventing you from finding out whether the pupils understand the concept.

Spinner

In this question Jill has a spinner split into identical sections labelled 1, 2, 3, 4, 5 and 6, while Peter has a spinner split into identical sections labelled 1, 2, 3, 4, 5, 6, 7 and 8. Part of the question wording is:

Peter says,
  'We are both equally likely to spin an even number.'
Give a reason why he is correct.
Peter is correct because _____

Jill's spinner is numbered 1 to 6 while Peter's is numbered 1 to 8, giving an equal number of odd and even numbers on each spinner. The question uses the notion 'equal' twice, once in 'equally likely' outcomes between the two spinners and once in the equal number of odd and even numbers on each spinner, which pupils need to recognize on the way to answering the question. In addition to this unnecessary double use of the concept 'equal', there is also a language confusion because pupils commonly interchange the words 'even' and 'equal', such as when they say they will divide 15 sweets evenly between three friends (meaning equally).

The pupil responses below show the interchanging of equal and even. G17 clearly understands probability but refers incorrectly to even numbers as 'equal numbers'. B19 indicates that 'an even chance' is used to mean 'an equal chance' or a '50–50 chance'.

    G17 'Both of their spinners have 50% (half) of their numbers as equal numbers, so they both have a 50% chance that their spinners will land on an equal number.'
    G22 'His has more equal numbers on but Jill has less divided parts.'
    B19 'They both have half the numbers even which gives them an even chance to get an even number.'

The language and numbers used in this question make it unclear. These two confusions can be avoided by using a situation where the desired probabilities are not a half and where even numbers are not involved. The mark scheme does not deal with the pupils' range of uses of 'equal' and 'even', so some pupils with a clear understanding of equally likely were denied marks. In designing contexts and wording for questions testing 'equal' or 'even' and their mark schemes, pupils' interchangeable use of these words needs to be borne in mind.

Sport

Sue jumped **212 cm**.
Draw Sue's long jump result on the graph.

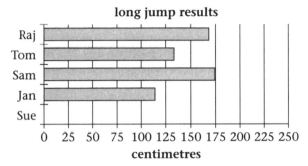

Use the graph to estimate how **much further** Sam jumped than Jan.

In the long jump graph the similarity of the names 'Sue' and 'Sam', and the fact that both were adjacent to 'Jan', caused a miscue. After being asked to draw Sue's result on the graph, below Jan's, some pupils naturally assumed that the last part of the question was still about Sue and was asking them to compare Sue's and Jan's jumps. In total, 13 per cent of pupils distributed across all levels compared Sue and Jan rather than Sam and Jan; they did not receive a mark even though some had compared these correctly and actually met a harder requirement than the one intended. These pupils had provided evidence for the mathematical concept the question was testing, but awarding of the mark also depended on very careful reading of the instructions. If you want to credit this process, as well as estimating on the graph scale, you need to assign separate marks to each skill.

It is helpful to use easily read names in questions. However, there is no need for two names which are so similar to be placed nearby at key points within questions. Pupils often assume that parts of questions relate to the same person, so any deviations need to be signposted clearly.

This question also illustrates that the mark scheme, rather than the question, can render the test undemanding. The scale on the graph was marked and labelled every 25 cm from 0 to 250 cm. This appears to be a difficult scale on which to mark 212 cm, but an understanding that this is approximately half-way between the grid lines for 200 and 225 could be tested, and would be in keeping with the demand of the second part of the question. However, the mark scheme accepts all bars which end between the grid lines for 200 cm and 225 cm. This interval is so wide that the question tests only pupils' recognition that 212 is between 200 and 225, a low-level number

skill, rather than a higher level scale reading or proportion skill. Every pupi
who attempted this question was awarded a mark; only one pupil omitted it
Such a high facility for what appears to be a reasonably demanding question immediately indicates that something is wrong with the mark scheme.
Although questions requiring bars, or drawings, to within a specified degree
of accuracy can be hard to mark, acceptance of such a wide range of responses
completely changes the purpose of the question.

As the question and mark scheme stand, pupils might think the question
requires accuracy and spend a long time on this, when in fact any rough
attempt would be acceptable. In all, 17 per cent of pupils drew a bar ending
about a quarter or less of the way along the interval and one drew a bar about
two-thirds of the way along the interval, having drawn 12 small marks on the
scale. This 20 per cent of pupils seem far from realizing that 212 is just under
half-way across the interval, yet their errors have passed unnoticed and they
have scored the same as pupils who do realize this (Close *et al.* 1997: 6.7).

When choosing questions it is important to decide what you want to test,
for example number order or interpolation on a scale; to make this explicit to
pupils so they do not waste time or become anxious about what is required;
and to match the mark scheme to your aims so you do not credit errors as if
they were partially correct answers.

Another question which illustrates how easy it is to credit errors uninten-
tionally when providing a range of acceptable answers in the mark scheme is
Waste. This included a diagram divided into five unequal sections to indicate
the proportion of each type of waste a family threw away, with the question:
'Estimate what fraction of the waste is **organic**.'

The correct proportion was approximately 25 per cent, with the mark
scheme accepting a range of 20–30 per cent expressed in any appropriate way.
This therefore credited the response one-fifth which is the error expected of
pupils who ignore whether the parts are equal. In all, 13 per cent of pupils
gave this response and were awarded the mark, even though many of them
may have held one of the major misconceptions in fractions. Inclusion of a
very small sixth category of waste would have eliminated the choice of one-
fifth for the wrong reason. When choosing questions, numbers and sizes to
use it is helpful to think about the main misconceptions associated with the
concept you are testing and values you use.

The following example of a good question which can be solved by methods
with different levels of sophistication suggests that it would be useful to add
an extra part to such questions to try to find out the pupils' methods. This
would enable more marks to be given for higher level methods, and would
provide diagnostic information.

Missing digit

Write in the missing digit.

☐ 7 × 9 = 333

The question offers fast access to pupils who can estimate or use inverse operations but it does not enable either of these skills to be assessed or credited, because pupils using trial and improvement gain equal credit, although they are likely to spend more time which may inhibit their access to later questions. Even though 88 per cent of Level 5 pupils answered this question correctly, only 47 per cent of them used division (Close *et al.* 1997: 6.12–6.13).

This question offers access in a range of ways, but in so doing it highlights the inability of such a test item to credit, or even identify, sophisticated performance. A mark for explaining method could alleviate this. If we want to encourage pupils to work towards more sophisticated methods, we need to credit them in tests and make this clear to pupils by prompting for them in the questions.

References

Close, G., Furlong, T. and Simon, S. (1997) *The Validity of the 1996 Key Stage 2 Tests in English, Mathematics and Science.* London: Association of Teachers and Lecturers.

Close, G., Furlong, T. and Swain, J. (1995) *The Impact and Effect of Key Stage 3 Tasks and Tests on the Curriculum, Teaching and Learning and Teachers' Assessments.* London: National Union of Teachers.

SCAA (School Curriculum and Assessment Authority) (1993) *Key Stage 3 1994 Sample Test Materials Mathematics.* London: SCAA.

SCAA (School Curriculum and Assessment Authority) (1996) *Key Stage 2 1996 Mathematics Tests.* London: SCAA.

Context problems and assessment: ideas from the Netherlands

Marja van den Heuvel-Panhuizen

Introduction

For as long as we have had class-administered written tests, objections have been raised against this way of gathering information on the progress of children's learning. The general objection is that traditional class-administered written tests reveal only the results and tell us nothing about the children's strategies. The consequence of this lack of information about these strategies is not only that incorrect conclusions are likely to be drawn about their performance but also that too little information is obtained about the progress of instruction. For example, nothing is learned about the children's informal knowledge or solution methods. Another consequence is that such tests make it difficult to diagnose the children's mathematical difficulties: any error analysis that depends solely on the results can never be sufficient to discover the children's problems and misconceptions. A final drawback of these tests is that they are too narrowly focused: they are usually restricted to subject matter that can easily be tested and so do not allow the children to show what they are able to accomplish. In other words, a lack of certain abilities may very well be balanced by other abilities not revealed by the tests.

Because there has been a tendency to look outside the sphere of formal tests for alternative means of evaluation, such as observations and interviews, much less attention has been paid, particularly at primary school level, to alternatives within the range of class-administered written tests. Among the evaluation methods available to the teacher, written tests should not be wholly dismissed. They do allow the teacher to screen a whole class and should, therefore, be modified rather than rejected completely. In this chapter I shall provide some examples of written test items that illustrate a different perspective, presenting a variety of possibilities to counter such objections as the lack of information about children's strategies. The tests are meant to be administered by the teacher to the whole class. Each student gets a test booklet, and the teacher gives the instructions for each item orally. But before looking at alternatives to traditional class-administered tests I shall provide some background information about the Dutch education system and the Dutch approach to mathematics education from which these new ideas for written assessment emerged.

The Dutch education system

In the Netherlands children can start in kindergarten either when they are 4 years old or when they are 5. The majority start when they are 4, and stay there between one and two years. Children who reach the age of 6 before 1 October are allowed to go into Grade 1 in the August (or September) of that year. Primary education continues up to Grade 6, and each year the students will have one teacher for all subjects.

At the end of primary education, when the children are 12 years old, most of the schools administer a test, the so-called CITO test (CITO is our National Institute for Educational Measurement). This test, which has a multiple-choice format, is not compulsory, and different tests can be used instead. Once every four years there is also a national assessment, called PPON, which is carried out on a sample of students half-way through and at the end of primary. The purpose of this national assessment is to evaluate the school system, especially the output of education.

What is taught in primary school mathematics?

What is taught is, to a great extent, the responsibility of the teachers and the school teams. The most important tool that guides their teaching is the mathematics textbook series that is used. For primary school, for instance, we have at least seven different textbook series, and all are published by commercial publishers.

A significant document concerning the mathematical content that is taught at primary school in the Netherlands is what is called the *Proeve*. . . . This series of documents, the development of which is still in progress, will eventually give a description of the complete mathematics curriculum that should be taught in our primary schools. In 1989, after several years of discussion of the draft versions, the first part of the *Proeve* was published (Treffers *et al.* 1989). Although it is written in a very accessible way with a lot of examples, it is not especially meant as a series for teachers. Instead, it is meant more as a support for textbook authors, teacher trainers and school advisers.

Together with the thinking about the content to be taught, ideas evolved about the teaching and learning of mathematics. These ideas finally developed into an approach to mathematics education which is now known as Realistic Mathematics Education or RME. More than three-quarters of our primary schools now use a mathematics textbook series that was inspired to a greater or lesser degree by RME.

RME and mathematization

As described by Treffers (1978, 1987; see also Chapter 3, this volume), the use of context problems is very significant in RME. However, notwithstanding the importance of contexts, the most crucial criterion for a good problem within RME is not the nature of its context as such but, more importantly, whether the problem offers opportunities for 'mathematization'. This means that the problems must describe a situation which needs some elaboration, for instance, with respect to the data and the operations to be used. The process in which the students can apply mathematical concepts and tools is very crucial within RME. As long ago as 1968 Freudenthal stressed that the process of mathematization should be the focal point of mathematics education and not the conveyance of mathematics as a closed system of knowledge. Later on, Treffers (1978, 1987) formulated the idea of the two types of mathematization explicitly in an educational context and distinguished 'horizontal' and 'vertical' mathematization. In broad terms, these can be described as follows. In horizontal mathematization, the students come up with mathematical tools to help to organize and solve a problem located in a real-life situation. Vertical mathematization is the process of reorganization within the mathematical system itself, such as finding shortcuts and discovering connections between concepts and strategies and then applying these discoveries.

Within RME, mathematizing is not only a goal, but is also considered an important means by which the students can develop mathematical knowledge. In our view, problems suitable for mathematization should offer students a rich context for organization and elaboration, not a context in which everything is already prepared and the only thing a student has to do is to find the correct solution. In problems suitable for mathematization, answers can be given on several levels of understanding.

Test items with a difference

Given the different didactics associated with RME we have tried in the Netherlands to develop tests that provide a maximum of information about children's knowledge and abilities, covering the whole breadth and depth of the mathematical area. The major concern is that *children are allowed to show what they are able to do*. At the same time, the tests must be as easy to administer as the usual written tests that consist solely of numerical problems. In order to achieve this, we looked for possible test problems which could be applied in the classroom with a minimum of explanation. We tried to avoid tests with extensive oral or written instructions that would result in overemphasizing listening or reading comprehension rather than an understanding of mathematics. For this reason, we have looked for tasks that require no additional information beyond the minimum of instruction needed to get the intent across. Little text is used; rather, pictures that are self-explanatory and related to meaningful situations convey the problem to be solved.

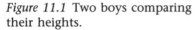

81 children

Figure 11.1 Two boys comparing their heights.

Figure 11.2 Packets of chocolate milk.

These real-life contexts offer the opportunity to test the children's under-standing while avoiding obstructions caused by formal notation. In this way, concepts that have not yet been formally taught can be probed to provide important information for instruction. The understanding gained about chil-dren's informal knowledge and solutions can be used for building the teach-ing on the children's prior knowledge.

Moreover, these items show how contexts can contribute to the under-standing of test problems by suggesting clever strategies that make the items easier to solve by using informal strategies that are linked to the contexts. The picture in Figure 11.1[1] of two children comparing their heights refers to the number sentence 145 – 138 which is rather difficult for children when they have not yet been taught number sentences including carrying and working with numbers over 100. Nevertheless, a lot of children who cannot solve the bare problem can solve this context problem. The reason for this is that the context elicits a complementary addition strategy for the subtraction task. In other words, instruction that has not yet been given can be anticipated. It is this opportunity for testing that precedes education that makes context problems so appropriate for providing indications for further instruction.

The item in Figure 11.2 is another example of how a picture referring to a context situation can elicit an action that has the potential to lead to a solution. Here the question is: How many cartons of chocolate milk are needed for 81 children? In this example, the necessary arithmetical operation is not obvious. This, however, gives room for the children to use their own strategies to solve the problem. Some will solve it by repeated subtraction, staying close to the context. Others will make use of their knowledge of division tables. Another striking feature of this problem is that even a correct calculation of $81 \div 6$ does not directly yield the appropriate answer. For interpreting the answer, again the context is important.

The next two examples are specifically designed not only for eliciting the process of mathematizing but also for making it visible by means of a written

Figure 11.3 The *Polar bear* problem.

test. Figure 11.3 illustrates a test item about a polar bear. Here the problem information, read aloud by the teacher, is: 'A polar bear weighs 500 kilograms. How many children together weigh as much as one polar bear?' The students have to write their answer in the empty box. If they like, they may use the scrap paper for making notes, calculations, or drawings. The problem was developed for students in the beginning of Year 4.

The item illustrated in Figure 11.4 was aimed at Grade 5 (Y6). The problem was presented to the students after a short initial introduction to percentages. In this problem, the students are prompted to work out in which of the two shops the sale price of the tennis shoes is the lower. In the shop on the left there is a discount of 40 per cent whereas on the right the discount is 25 per cent. We shall return to the *Polar bear* and the *Best buy* problems later.

The emphasis within RME is on problem solving that is strongly connected to number sense and that has an explicit function in the development of mathematical concepts. This kind of problem solving could be called 'realistic problem solving', but I am not sure whether this is the right word for it. Problem solving and mathematization have much in common: both involve much more than the simple recall of facts, or the application of routine procedures, and both ask for non-routine problems. But there are also dissimilarities between the two. For mathematizing, metacognitive techniques, like thinking of similar problems, making the numbers in the problem simpler, free association, and working backwards do not play such a key role as in learning problem solving. Instead of these, to learn to mathematize it is important that the students develop tools for organizing or modelling a situation. Another difference with problems suitable for mathematization might be that the typical problems for problem solving often have only one correct answer. A further point to be clear of is that, in any case, 'realistic problem solving' should not be interpreted as 'real-world' problem solving. As Freudenthal said (1981), 'In teaching mathematizing "the real world" is represented by a meaningful context involving a mathematical problem.

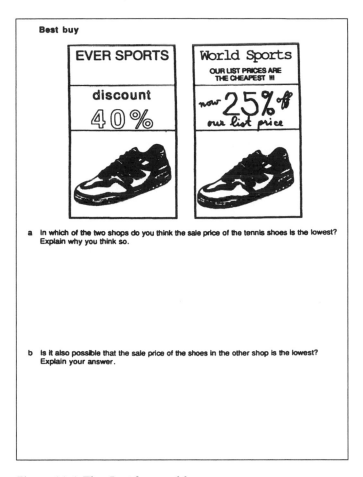

Figure 11.4 The *Best buy* problem.

"Meaningful" of course means: meaningful to the learners.' Therefore, I think 'solving realistic problems' would be a better name; where 'realistic' should be understood in the three-fold meaning of: imaginable, meaningful and real.

Strength of context problems

Contexts can enrich assessment (see van den Heuvel-Panhuizen 1996), and there are several ways in which they can do this.

- *Contexts enhance accessibility*
  In the first place, contexts can contribute to the accessibility of assessment problems. By starting from easily imaginable situations which are presented visually, the students can quite quickly grasp the purpose of a given problem. The advantage of this direct, visual presentation is that the students

need not wrestle with an enormous amount of text before they can deal with the problem. Furthermore, a pleasant, inviting context can also increase the accessibility through its motivational element.

- *Contexts contribute to the latitude and transparency of the problems*
Compared with most bare problems, where just the numbers and the operation are given, context problems offer the students more opportunity to demonstrate their abilities. In bare problems – such as long division problems – they can only show whether they can do long divisions or not. In a context problem – for instance, where one must work out how many buses are needed to transport a large contingent of soccer fans – the students can also find the answer by applying an informal method of division, namely, repeated addition until they arrive at the target number. Because the problem can be solved on different levels, its elasticity is increased. Not only can the good students solve the problem, but the weaker students can as well – although this may be on a lower level. This means that contexts can reduce the 'all-or-nothing' character of assessment. At the same time, however, by giving the students more latitude in the way they approach the problem, the contexts can also increase the transparency of the assessment. They can reveal more about the students' thinking.

Another point, related to this latitude and transparency issue, is that the use of contexts makes 'advance testing' possible. In bare problems, the operation to be performed is generally fixed in the problem in question, so one can only verify whether students are able to perform certain procedures that they have learned earlier. For this reason, bare problems are not suitable for advance testing. For example, one cannot present a long division problem to a student who has never done one and expect to find footholds for further instruction.

- *Contexts can provide strategies*
The most important quality of contexts in assessment (assuming they are chosen well) is that they can provide strategies. By imagining themselves in the situation to which the problem refers, the students can solve the problem in a way that was inspired, as it were, by the situation. Sometimes this will mean that the students use an accompanying drawing in a very direct way as a kind of model while, at other times, it is the action enclosed within a given context that elicits the strategy. How close the students stick to the context with their solution depends upon the degree of insight and the repertoire of knowledge and skills they possess. This role of 'strategy provider' is not only important with respect to expanding the breadth of assessment problems and the potential this creates for advance testing, but it touches the core goal of RME as well, which is the ability to solve a problem using mathematical means and insights.

Some difficulties caused by contexts

However, using contexts familiar to the students does not always provide support. Contexts can also create some difficulties in assessment:

- *Getting away from the mathematics by 'escaping' into reality*
  Gravemeijer (1994), for instance, described an experience involving a problem in which 18 bottles of Coca-Cola had to be shared fairly by 24 students at a school party. These students refused to interpret the problem as it was intended because, they said, some students did not like Coca-Cola and, moreover, not everyone drank the same amount.
- *Ignoring the context*
  The opposite can occur as well, namely that the students ignore the context entirely. Greer (1993), for instance, discovered that context problems were often answered using stereotypical procedures that assumed a 'clean' modelling of the situation in question. The students simply took the problem out of its context and solved it as a bare arithmetic problem. Verschaffel *et al.* (1994), who repeated Greer's research along broad lines, also had to acknowledge a strong tendency by the students to exclude real-world knowledge and realistic considerations when solving word problems in the classroom. This behaviour, however, is not surprising if the students' previous experience has suggested that the context *must* be ignored.

Different views on mathematics education, different views on assessment

Because, in RME, mathematization is an important goal of education then the assessment must make the mathematizing activities of the students visible. The difficulty, however, is that many of the problems which we think are suitable for RME assessment do not meet the psychometric requirements for good assessment problems. For instance, from the psychometric point of view, assessment problems should be unambiguous and should have answers that are either correct or clearly not correct. In addition, many people – especially those outside the mathematics education community – think that these psychometric requirements are in tune with the real nature of mathematical problems. As a consequence, numerous colleagues from other school subjects are even jealous of us mathematics teachers. According to them, mathematics is seen as a subject that is easily assessed. Let us return to the *Polar bear* problem (Figure 11.3) and consider whether this is true or not.

The **Polar bear** *problem*

This is not only a problem that children are very familiar with and can imagine – they often encounter these kinds of problems in television programmes and magazines – but it is also a real problem. The solution procedure is not known beforehand and not all the data is given. In other words, it is a problem that asks for mathematization.

To understand the purpose of this problem we must put ourselves in the shoes of Year 4 children in November of the school year. The children have already become rather proficient at multiplication and division tables up to 10, and have some experience as well in doing multiplication and division with two-digit numbers. Written algorithms, like long division, have yet to be introduced however. This is an ideal moment for assessment which, in RME, includes both looking backward (to see what the students have already mastered) and looking forward in search of footholds for further instruction. The *Polar bear* problem is especially suited to the latter. Characteristic of this problem is the room the students are given to make their own constructions. As it stands, the problem gives no indication of what kind of procedure must be performed, and it implicitly requires the students to think up the weight of an average child first. The room provided for children's own constructions or, in other words, this 'zone of free construction' means that, on the one hand, the students are provided with the opportunity to show what they know and, on the other hand, the teachers thus acquire information on how their students tackle problems; information on their knowledge of measurements; information on which 'division' strategies they apply, and on which models and notation schemes they use to support their thought processes in a hitherto unfamiliar division problem. Let us now look at the work of a selection of Year 4 students on this problem (Figure 11.5).

What do these examples tell us? In the first place, the scrap paper reveals that the students used different average weights, varying from 25 to 35 kilograms. Some used round numbers and some did not. There was also a considerable variety in the solution strategies. As was to be expected, none of the students performed a division operation. Instead, they all chose a form of repeated addition: keep adding a given weight until you get near 500 kilograms. This was done in a great variety of ways: Student A kept adding up 35 mentally, and kept track by writing down 35 each time. The '35' in the upper left-hand corner is probably intended to indicate the choice of 35 kilograms. Student B also kept adding up, but wrote down the new result each time. Student C applied a more structured form of adding up by combining this with doubling; the final doubling to reach the solution was done mentally: 8 children is 240 kilograms, so you'll need 16 children. Student D also applied a doubling strategy. Moreover, a clever way was found to keep track of how many times the given weight had been counted. The last part of the solution was found by mental arithmetic but, because of a mistake made when doubling 162, the final result of 26 children was a bit too high. Student E changed to mental arithmetic half-way through: 4 children are 100 kilograms, so you'll need 20 children. And student F even used a notation in the form of a ratio table to solve the problem, without this ever having been taught.

The quality of this *Polar bear* problem lies in the fact that it makes the mathematization by the students visible and gives clues for how to continue in teaching them long division, in other words, how to guide them in the reinvention of it. Compared to the traditional way of testing, this 'advance testing' can be seen as a real breakthrough. It is completely different from the 'readiness testing' that was done in former times. In this latter testing, which fits closely to the mechanistic approach to mathematics education, the focus was on prerequisite skills, whereas advance testing is aimed at revealing the informal skills that can form the first steps to the next skill or concept to be learned. This kind of assessment, which anticipates what is on

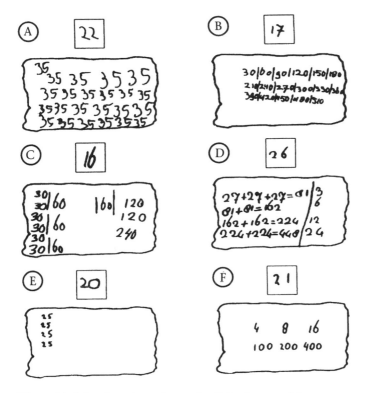

Figure 11.5 Students' work on the *Polar bear* problem.

the horizon, does not fit the paradigm of psychometric-based testing, but is perfectly appropriate within the didactical assessment paradigm.

The Best buy *problem*

After having said all these positive things about how, for instance, a greater zone of free construction can make assessment more informative and more in tune with a constructivist approach to the learning of mathematics, I must admit that this openness in assessment can also bring with it some uncertainty. By using open-ended problems teachers do not always obtain the specific information that is required. The obvious reaction to this limitation can be a return to a more closed problem format, leaving the reform for what it is. However, there is also an alternative: the 'safety-net' question. This was applied in the *Best buy* item mentioned earlier (Figure 11.4).

The first question of this problem is a rather open one. It generated a great variety of answers, but did not always show whether the students had any insight into the relative character of percentage. To overcome this uncertainty something was done that teachers usually do after they have asked a question and are unsure how to interpret the answer, namely, append an additional, more specific, question. The same is also often done in oral interviews. The function of this safety-net question is to identify those students who have some understanding of the relative nature of percentages but who need some extra hints in order to be able to apply this understanding. The next examples of students' work illustrate how the safety-net question works (Figure 11.6).

In one of the classes in which this problem was piloted almost half of the students answered the first question in an absolute way. However, in the second question, about 80 per cent of the students who had at first compared the two percentages absolutely, showed that they did have a clear understanding of the relative nature of percentage. The work of student A is a typical example of this. The work of student B shows that the safety-net question worked the other way around as well. This student's answer to the first question suggested that he or she did understand the relative character of percentage. This is indicated by the addition of the words 'because there [= they are] the same shoes'. The answer to the second question, however, made his or her understanding very questionable. Finally, the work of student C demonstrates that the safety-net question can help towards a better understanding of the students' reasoning. The answer to the second question makes it clear that this student probably meant something different from what it appears to suggest in the first answer.

Compared to moving back to the traditional way of assessment in order to be more certain about a particular understanding, the advantage of following an open question with a safety-net question is that the students then really do have the opportunity to answer the first question in their own way. We thought of the safety-net question when searching for some means of making written assessment more informative.

Final remarks

In the assessment research that has been carried out during the last decade in connection with the further development of RME (see van den Heuvel-Panhuizen 1996), it became apparent that for the enrichment of assessment – and now I am particularly speaking of written assessment – two keys points are very crucial:

- the application of interview techniques in written assessment; and
- the breaking of some taboos in assessing mathematical knowledge.

Both give access to a more informative written assessment.

Let me say a few concluding words about the first point: the application of interview techniques in written assessment. In the safety-net question in the *Best buy* problem, the integration of written assessment and oral interviewing, which have been considered up to now to be two separate worlds, has been achieved. This has proved to be extremely fruitful for the improvement of written assessment. In fact, the strategy of asking the student a follow-up question to check his or her understanding is similar to what is very common in oral interviews. Another thing that can be done is to present the student

A a In which of the two shops do you think the sale price of the tennis shoes is the lowest? Explain why you think so.

Ever Sports is the best deal because, it has the most discounts. 40% is more than 25%.

   b Is it also possible that the sale price of the shoes in the other shop is the lowest? Explain your answer

Yes, because the shoes might have been cheaper before the discount.

B a In which of the two shops do you think the sale price of the tennis shoes is the lowest? Explain why you think so.

Ever Sports because there the same shoes and theres a 40% and 25% off and the 40% is higher so it better!

   b Is it also possible that the sale price of the shoes in the other shop is the lowest? Explain your answer

No because it a lower % discount than. 40%.

C a In which of the two shops do you think the sale price of the tennis shoes is the lowest? Explain why you think so.

I think the shoe that 25% off because there is less percentage being took off and if you take less % off the shoe would cost less

   b Is it also possible that the sale price of the shoes in the other shop is the lowest? Explain your answer

yes, because the regular price could be lower and then if you took 40% off you would be getting a good deal

Figure 11.6 Students' work on the *Best buy* problem.

with a different question if the initial one is too difficult or too easy. This is also possible in written assessment.

One result of applying interview techniques in written assessment is that it makes written assessment more dynamic. It is no longer the one-way communication that it always was. An additional consequence of the application of interview techniques is that the problems become more adaptive or elastic. This means that possibilities are emerging to adapt the problems to the student's level, so that problems move away from 'all-or-nothing' testing.

The elastic character of such assessment problems is, however, in conflict with the prevailing psychometric-based ideas on assessment.

However, for didactical assessment, it is essential to broaden our view of what are good assessment problems. Psychometric-based testing can never be a complete model for didactical assessment. Developing didactical assessment problems implies ignoring a number of traditional requirements for assessment problems and dispelling a number of misconceptions about mathematical problems which have long determined assessment, namely that assessment problems:

- should be unambiguous;
- should provide students with all the data needed;
- should have only one correct answer, and so on.

In the assessment world there is still a taboo on thinking differently about these issues, but in order to improve the assessment of mathematical knowledge these taboos must be broken. Within RME a start has been made, and the results so far provide encouragement to continue down this track.

Note

1 The instructions for the problems in Figures 11.1, 11.2 and 11.3 were given orally in class by the teacher. For Figure 11.1 the question was: 'what is the difference in height?'

References

Freudenthal, H. (1981) Major problems of mathematics education. *Educational Studies in Mathematics*, 12: 133–50.

Gravemeijer, K.P.E. (1994) *Developing Realistic Mathematics Education*. Utrecht: CD-ß Press/Freudenthal Institute.

Greer, B. (1993) The mathematical modelling perspective on wor(l)d problems. *Journal of Mathematical Behavior*, 12: 239–50.

Treffers, A. (1978) *Wiskobas doelgericht* [Wiskobas Goal-Directed]. Utrecht: IOWO (Instituut voot de outwikkeling van het wiskuude oudewüs [Institute for the Development of Mathematics Teaching]).

Treffers, A. (1987) *Three Dimensions. A Model of Goal and Theory Description in Mathematics Instruction – The Wiskobas Project*. Dordrecht: Reidel Publishing Company.

Treffers, A., De Moor, E. and Feijs, E. (1989) *Proeve van een nationaal programma voor het reken-wiskundeonderwijs op de basisschool. Deel I. Overzicht einddoelen* [Design of a National Curriculum for Mathematics Education at Primary School. Part I. Overview of Goals]. Tilburg: Zwijsen.

van den Heuvel-Panhuizen, M. (1996) *Assessment and Realistic Mathematics Education*. Utrecht: CD-ß Press/Freudenthal Institute, Utrecht University.

Verschaffel, L., De Corte, E. and Lasure, S. (1994) Realistic considerations in mathematical modelling of school arithmetic word problems. *Learning and Instruction*, 4 (4): 273–94.

Section 4

PEDAGOGICAL ISSUES

The final section deals more specifically than earlier sections with *pedagogy* – 'the art or science of teaching'. It comprises five chapters dealing with different aspects of calculation – mental, part-written, written, and calculator – relating to the four basic operations.

In Chapter 12 Ian Thompson provides a brief historical account of the development of the teaching of mental calculation in school. After considering the reasons given in the literature for the teaching of mental methods he explores the range of interpretations of the phrase 'mental arithmetic'. A synopsis of the research evidence concerning children's mental strategies for addition and subtraction with numbers to 20 is followed by a more detailed consideration of strategies for dealing with the same operations with two-digit numbers. Two models of mental calculation are discussed, and one of these is used as a vehicle for making suggestions as to how teachers might develop their pupils' mental strategies.

Meindert Beishuizen (Chapter 13) begins with a brief history of the development of the 'empty number line' (ENL) in mathematics education in the Netherlands, and provides a rationale for its current role in the development of children's mental calculation strategies. Meindert outlines the knowledge, skills and understanding that needs to be developed by young children learning to use the empty number line, and suggests practical activities to help teachers develop these specific skills and concepts in their pupils. Examples are given of the work of Year 3 children involved in an experimental programme at Leiden University to illustrate the point that the empty number line is a great help in making pupils' solutions clearer for the teacher. Not only does the use of the ENL facilitate whole-class discussion but also individual diagnosis of misunderstandings and errors.

The National Curriculum for mathematics states that children should 'record in a variety of ways, including ways that relate to their mental work'. In Chapter 14 Ian Thompson considers some of the problems involved in developing written calculation methods which relate to mental methods. He discusses the main differences between the procedures employed for mental calculation and those demanded by the standard algorithms for the four basic operations. A classification system for written calculations is developed in order to facilitate discussion of the issues involved. Low-stress algorithms for each of the mathematical operations are described.

In her chapter on multiplication and division (Chapter 15) Julia Anghileri suggests that traditional teaching of the 'four rules of arithmetic' does not always provide children with an understanding of the connections that are vital for developing good number sense. She argues that linking multiplication and division to fundamental processes like counting, and identifying the structure behind different problem-solving strategies, will help underpin children's understanding of number relations and extend beyond whole numbers to fractions, decimals and algebra. She discusses the relative importance of two different models of division: the 'sharing' and the 'grouping' models. Examples of children's strategies for multiplication and division are provided and the ensuing discussion reveals different levels of sophistication in these strategies. The chapter concludes with a consideration of written procedures for both operations.

In the final chapter of the book Ken Ruthven sets the use of the calculator in a professional and political context. He discusses the arguments for and against the use of calculators in primary schools, providing a balanced consideration of relevant research findings. He uses examples of pupils' work to illustrate some of the pedagogical issues involved in using calculators to develop realistic problem-solving skills, to support number exploration and to develop mental calculation.

Getting your head around mental calculation

Ian Thompson

Introduction

By the end of the nineteenth century the psychological theory of 'mental discipline' had substantially influenced the content, scope and sequence of the developing mathematics curriculum in the USA and to a lesser extent in Britain. Advocates of the movement considered mental arithmetic to be an integral part of mathematics teaching, seeing it as an important form of exercise to develop the faculties of the mind. In the 1920s there was a backlash against the movement and the concept of 'mental discipline' was rejected in favour of the more sophisticated theory of 'transfer'. This led to a decline in the teaching of mental arithmetic. In the 1940s, however, when the social usefulness of mathematics was beginning to be recognized, there was a revival in the emphasis given to teaching the topic in schools. Mental arithmetic came to have its own separate heading on school reports, and even mathematics textbooks written in the 1960s had exercises which perpetuated the 'mental, mechanical, problems' structure of earlier books.

The decline of mental arithmetic since the 1950s is often blamed on a variety of 'progressive' innovations: the move in the 1970s to individualized learning which, it is claimed, reduced the opportunity for teachers to communicate with the class as a whole group; the parallel move to mixed ability teaching, which made it difficult to pose questions that did not demoralize some of the children; and the teaching of modern mathematics which, with its broader syllabus and focus on structure and understanding, placed much less emphasis on arithmetic in general and instant recall in particular.

A section devoted to mental arithmetic in the Cockcroft Report (DES 1982) asserted that the topic, which was once a regular part of the mathematics curriculum, had come to occupy a far less prominent position by the late 1970s. The report argued for the reinstatement of mental arithmetic in the curriculum, explaining that the committee:

... believe(s) that the decline of mental and oral work within mathematics classrooms represents a failure to recognise the central place which working 'done in the head' occupies throughout mathematics.

With the arrival of the National Curriculum in the 1980s mental arithmetic, in theory at least, was back on the agenda: the ability to add or subtract mentally any pair of two-digit numbers was fixed at Level 4 in the very first version of the National Curriculum. However, in practice, because of the subject knowledge demands of the curriculum, mental arithmetic did not receive the emphasis that it deserved.

England's poor performance on the number sections of international tests and surveys was a major contributing factor to the swing back to mental arithmetic in the 1990s. Although we did perform well in 'Shape and Space' and in problem solving this success was totally ignored by the media and by the government. The Bierhoff Report, a publication from the right-wing National Institute of Economic and Social Research, was published in 1996 (Bierhoff 1996). This was ostensibly a comparison of primary school textbooks in Britain, Germany and Switzerland, and it emphasized, among other things, the importance that European countries attached to mental calculation, and to the addition and subtraction of two-digit numbers in particular.

The booklet also succeeded in detracting from the real issue by arguing that an emphasis on mental arithmetic was incompatible with calculator use. This unsubstantiated claim, made without reference to research or inspection evidence, caught the mood of the moment and continued to be repeated in later government publications. The Bierhoff Report (1996) appeared to be offering a panacea for our ills: ban calculators in primary schools and all would be well. Unfortunately, several politicians were sufficiently convinced by the argument to threaten such a ban, and the DfEE's press machine was criticized by several members of the Numeracy Task Force in 1998 for misleading schools and distorting the view of calculators given in the final report. To my mind, the *real* issue was not 'mental calculation versus calculators' but 'mental calculation versus written algorithms'.

In 1996 the National Numeracy Project was launched (see Straker, Chapter 4, this volume). The project's approach to the teaching of numeracy was originally based on three key principles, later to become four: mathematics lessons every day; direct teaching and interactive oral work with the whole class and with groups; and an emphasis on mental calculation. The arrival of the Numeracy Project and its development into the National Numeracy Strategy succeeded in making 'mental arithmetic' the most important mathematics item on many school agendas. The final report of the Numeracy Task Force, *The Implementation of the National Numeracy Strategy* (DfEE 1998) stated that: '... the Task Force's view (is) that mental calculation methods lie at the heart of numeracy' (p. 51).

Why teach mental arithmetic?

The literature suggests four main reasons for the teaching of mental methods:

1 *Most calculations are done in the head rather than on paper*
In 1957 Wandt and Brown investigated adults' use of calculations in their everyday activities, and found that 75 per cent of these involved mental arithmetic. This led them to argue for a greater emphasis to be placed on mental work in school at that time.

2 *Mental work develops a sound number sense*
Mental calculation encourages children to use and develop computational shortcuts, and in doing so, they gain a deeper insight into the workings of the number system (McIntosh 1990).

3 *Mental work develops problem-solving skills*
Driscoll (1981) argued that regular sessions of mental computation improve problem-solving performance. Mental calculation places great emphasis on the need to select an appropriate computational strategy for the actual numbers in the problem and the following of a sequence of steps to execute the calculation. Similar skills are also important for successful problem solving.

4 *Mental work promotes success in later written work*
The Cockcroft Report (DES 1982) argues that '. . . it follows that the practice of mental methods of computation will also assist in the understanding and development of written methods' (see Thompson, Chapter 14, this volume, for further discussion of this issue).

In a general review of research on mental calculation Zepp (1976) concluded that the data were consistent and fairly conclusive that direct teaching of this topic 'produced good results in general arithmetic growth'.

The language of mental methods

During the late 1990s the media and government ministers talked in terms of 'mental arithmetic' because of its air of respectability and tradition. However, the negative emotions that this phrase conjured up in many people's minds (see Buxton 1981) – reminding them of stressful times when they were unable to recall a number bond or tables fact quickly enough to avoid the wrath of their maths teacher – persuaded some educators that a different, more positive-sounding phrase was needed. Consequently, 'mental calculation', with its suggestion of 'calculation' or 'working something out in your head', came to be seen as a more accurate description of 1990s mental arithmetic. Given that you cannot really calculate unless you have something to calculate with, the phrase 'mental calculation' was seen to encapsulate the two important aspects of mental work, namely, recall and strategic methods.

When we compare the language used in England with that used in the Netherlands we find that, because they have no word equivalent to 'mental', they use the phrases 'working in the head' and 'working with the head' to distinguish what they see as the two different aspects of mental calculation.

The former covers knowing by heart, or being able to work out very quickly, specific number bonds or tables facts. The latter is concerned more with the use of some of these known facts, along with an understanding of the properties of our number system, to work out unknown facts such as the sums of pairs of two-digit numbers. In England we use the phrases 'knowing facts' and 'figuring out' to describe these two different aspects of mental calculation.

Both countries had come to a similar view on the importance of knowing some facts and using these to work out others, but what made it all the more interesting was that they had reached this consensus from opposite ends of the spectrum: England from the 'facts' end, the Netherlands from the 'strategies' end. In this country, even in the 1990s, 'mental arithmetic' was interpreted by many in a limited way as being solely concerned with the instant recall of number bonds and tables facts. In 1991 – the year of the first Key Stage 1 National Curriculum tests (formerly SATs) – teachers were told to 'assess each child's ability to add and subtract by using recall of number facts, not by counting or computation': an instruction which flew in the face of research conducted over the previous twenty years. It was only in the 1995 Dearing version of the National Curriculum that the concept of 'deriving facts' was formally acknowledged as being an important component of mental calculation. On the other hand, Beishuizen (1997) explains that 1980s textbooks in the Netherlands 'emphasised very much a variety of models and mental strategies at the expense of daily practice in mental recall of number bonds'.

Following their 1987 National Evaluation Test of Primary Mathematics, the decision was made to shift the focus of teaching more towards the learning of number facts.

What do we know about mental strategies?

Research since the late 1970s has provided a substantial amount of information on the mental calculation strategies used by young children, particularly for the addition and subtraction of one- and two-digit numbers, and a brief description of some of these findings follows. Much less information is available about multiplication and division, but several researchers are currently working in this area (see Anghileri, Chapter 15, this volume).

Addition and subtraction with numbers to 20

Carpenter and Moser (1984) identified the following levels of addition strategies used by young children when solving simple word problems:

- *count all* – where a child solving a simple addition problem such as 2 + 3 first counts out two blocks followed by another three blocks, and then finds the total by counting the number of blocks altogether;
- *count on from the first number* – where a child, finding 2 + 3, begins the count by repeating the first number and then continues counting from

that number. For example, a child might say: 'Two ... three, four, five. There are five';

- *count on from the larger number* – where a child proceeds as in the previous example, but begins the count from three, reasoning that starting from the larger number will mean that less counting is involved;
- *use known addition fact* – where children give immediate responses to those number bonds which they know by heart – usually the simpler number bonds such as the smaller doubles like 2 + 2 and 3 + 3;
- *use derived fact* – where children use a number bond that they know by heart to calculate one that they do not know. In the initial stages there is a tendency to use the doubles, so that 6 + 5 might be found by saying: 'Five and five is ten and one more makes eleven', or 'Six and six is twelve, but it's one less so it must be eleven'.

Thompson (1995) has described levels for subtraction, but the developmental sequence is less clearly defined. The subtraction 9 – 3 is used below to exemplify the strategies:

- *count out* – child counts out nine fingers, lowers three, and counts the remainder;
- *count back from* – child says 'Nine' and then counts back three numbers from nine: 'Eight, seven, six ... It's six';
- *count back to* – child says 'Nine' and then counts back to three, 'Eight, seven, six, five, four, three', keeping a tally (probably on fingers) of how many number names have been said;
- *count up* – child says 'Three' and counts forward six more number names, keeping a finger tally: 'Four, five, six, seven, eight, nine' (this is not a 'natural' strategy for children in England because of subtraction normally being interpreted as 'take away');
- *use known subtraction fact* and use derived fact are as for addition.

These strategies are discussed in more detail in Thompson (1997).

Addition and subtraction with numbers from 20 to 100

There appear to be four main two-digit mental addition and subtraction strategies used by children. In England the most common addition strategy is the *split* method, so-called because the numbers to be added or subtracted are split into multiples of ten and ones. This strategy is sometimes called the *partitioning* method, and in the Netherlands is known as the *1010* (ten–ten) procedure (Figure 12.1).

Scott   27 + 28
Two 20s is 40 ... seven and eight ... if there's seven ... take three off eight which would be 10 ... and three took off eight would be five ... so the answer would be 55

Figure 12.1 Scott uses the split method for two-digit addition.

Scott has split the 27 into 20 and 7; has split the 28 into 20 and 8; has added the two 20s together; has added the 7 and the 8 together by *bridging through ten*; and has added the two sub-totals together (40 and 15) to get the correct answer 55. Less common among children in this country – although it is the preferred method taught to children in the Netherlands – is the *jump* method (see Beishuizen, Chapter 13, this volume). The strategy is given the name *jump* because it can be easily represented – practically or mentally – on a number line, where you start at one number and move to the answer by jumping along the line adding or subtracting conveniently sized chunks of the second number as Chris does below (Figure 12.2). Alternative descriptors for this strategy in the literature are *sequencing* or *cumulative* methods (*N10* in the Netherlands).

Chris   *54 – 27*
27 . . . I took 20 away from 54 . . . to make 34 . . . and I took four from 34 which made 30 . . . and I took another three away to make 27

Figure 12.2 Chris uses the jump method for two-digit subtraction.

Chris has split the 27 into 20 and 7; has subtracted the 20 from 54 to get 34; has spit the 7 into 4 and 3; has subtracted the 4 and then the 3 from 34 to get the correct answer 27. Because of the apparent superiority of this method for subtractions of this type (the split method leads to a potential problem with 4 – 7) some mathematics educators recommend that the jump method should be taught in preference to the split method. However, some 'splitters' get round the problem by using a combination of the two strategies – known as the *split-jump* method, the *mixed* method or, in the Netherlands, the *10S* method (Figure 12.3).

Mark   *27 + 28*
55 . . . Because, you know, I did 20 and 20 is 40 . . . and 48 and another two from the seven is 50 . . . and I've got five left, so 55

Figure 12.3 Mark adds two numbers using the split-jump method.

In this case Mark has partitioned both numbers: 20 plus 7 and 20 plus 8; has added the two 20s; has added the 8 (the larger of the two units) to the 40; has bridged to ten and has then added the remaining 5. A fourth common strategy for dealing with 'near multiples of ten' is the *over-jump* or *compensation* method used by Nigel (Figure 12.4).

Nigel   *19 + 8*
27 . . . Twenty and eight would be 28 . . . and take away one gives you 27

Figure 12.4 Nigel adds two numbers using the over-jump method.

Nigel has treated 'adding 19' as 'adding 20 and then subtracting one' – a useful strategy for the addition and subtraction of 'near multiples of 10' –

but again, not as common with English children as with those from the Netherlands.

This research evidence provides a useful knowledge base to inform teachers' practice (Thompson 1999). Awareness of these strategies will help them better understand children's explanations and provide appropriate support to develop, where appropriate, more efficient strategies.

Models of mental calculation

The model illustrated in Figure 12.5 is discussed in *The Teaching and Assessment of Number at Key Stages 1–3* (SCAA 1977), and has appeared in various other publications. Whilst being succinct and accurate as a model for mental calculation for numbers to 20, it is not detailed or comprehensive enough to account for calculations with two-digit numbers. The model is accurate as far as it goes: we know that most children can use what they know to derive new facts and, by remembering some of these derived facts, can build up their store of known facts. However, one problem is that there is a temptation to read more than this into the model. The diagram is sometimes interpreted as suggesting that learning more facts will automatically increase one's repertoire of mental strategies. For example, an Ofsted review of research (Askew and Wiliam 1995) states: 'recalled facts (help) expand the range of strategies for deriving facts'.

It is debatable whether this actually is the case, even for single-digit numbers. It is not necessarily the accumulation of more known facts (important though this may be) that contributes to the expansion of an individual's range of strategies, but rather a more detailed understanding of the workings of our number system linked to an increased level of confidence to 'have a go'. The diagram illustrated in Figure 12.6 is more comprehensive, and would appear to model more accurately the process of mental calculation with numbers of any size.

The model shown in Figure 12.6 comprises four components which, it is argued, together contribute towards the development of an individual's range of mental calculation strategies. These components comprise: facts, skills, understandings and attitudes, and it is conjectured that those who are most

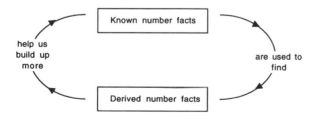

Figure 12.5 A model of mental calculation.

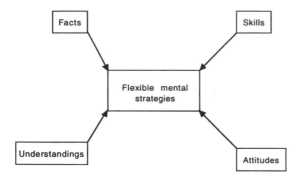

Figure 12.6 An extended model of mental calculation.

successful in mental calculation are likely to possess all four attributes. Weaknesses in any one area are likely to have an adverse effect on the development of a wide range of efficient mental calculation strategies. However, research is needed to test this hypothesis.

Facts

Included under this heading are: knowledge of specific number bonds, including doubles and complements in ten; awareness of addition and subtraction facts to twenty; and knowledge of multiplication tables and division facts. It is sometimes difficult to tell which facts are known and which are calculated extremely quickly. For example, I think I know that 7 and 5 make 12, but I'm not too sure that I *know* what 17 − 9 is. I definitely know that 7 × 8 = 56, but I am sure that I do *not* know what 48 ÷ 6 is, as I have to use my multiplication tables to help me work it out.

Understandings

This heading refers to the many and varied properties of the number system that we might expect someone possessing good 'number sense' to be aware of – if not explicitly, then at least implicitly. These 'understandings' range from those exhibited by very young children when they come to appreciate that they can count on from the larger of the numbers involved in an addition instead of counting on from the first number on each occasion, to those shown by Year 6 children when they realize that when you divide a number by a half it doubles in size.

Included under this heading are the properties of commutativity (3 × 4 = 4 × 3), associativity ((3 + 4) + 5 = 3 + (4 + 5)) and distributivity (3 × 24 = 3 × 20 + 3 × 4). Good mental calculators also need to understand the following:

- adding or subtracting zero has no effect (additive identity);
- multiplying or dividing by one makes no difference (multiplicative identity);
- subtractions can be solved by using a known addition fact (additive inverse);
- divisions can be solved by using a known multiplication fact (multiplicative inverse);
- adding together multiples of ten is similar to adding corresponding single-digit numbers;
- because 3 + 6 makes 9 then 473 + 6 is 479;
- because 3 × 4 ends in a 2 then so does 13 × 14;
- a number ending in zero can be divided exactly by 10;
- to multiply by six you can multiply by three and then double;
- to divide by four you can halve and then halve again.

More sophisticated 'understandings' would include the following:

- if you double one of the numbers in a multiplication and halve the other then the answer stays the same;
- to multiply 23 by 9, you can multiply by 10 and then subtract 23;
- to multiply by 12 you can multiply by four and then by three, or by three and then double twice.

Skills

To be effective mental calculators children need to have acquired certain labour-saving skills or techniques, such as counting on as a development of counting all or subtracting ten from a number without counting back. There follows a list of some of the mental calculation skills that children might be expected to have developed by specific ages:

Reception Add 1 to, or subtract 1 from a small number;
Year 1 Add 10 to a one-digit number;
Year 2 Add or subtract 9 (or 19) by working with 10 (or 20) and then compensating;
Year 2 Calculate any single-digit 'near-doubles';
Year 3 Multiply whole numbers by 10;
Year 4 Multiply by five by multiplying by ten and then halving (or vice versa);
Year 4 Multiply by 20 by doubling and then multiplying by 10 (or vice versa);
Year 5 Multiply by 50 by multiplying by 100 and then halving;
Year 6 Multiply by 25 by multiplying by 100 and then divide by four (halve and then halve).

To complete this section the mental calculation skills used by Scott and Chris in their solution strategies discussed above will be analysed.

Scott   *27 + 28*
Two 20s is 40 . . . seven and eight . . . if there's seven . . . take three off eight which
would be 10 . . . and three took off eight would be five . . . so the answer would
be 55

Partition two-digit numbers:	27 = 20 + 7
Add multiples of ten	20 + 20 = 40
Know and use complements in ten	7 + 3 = 10
Partition one-digit numbers	8 − 3 = 5
(Know and use subtraction facts)	
Add 10 to a number	10 + 5 = 15
Add M10 to a number	40 + 15 = 55

Figure 12.7 Skills used by Scott in calculating 27 + 28.

Chris   *54 − 27*
27 . . . I took 20 away from 54 . . . to make 34 . . . and I took four from 34 which
made 30 . . . and I took another three away to make 27

Partition two-digit numbers:	27 = 20 + 7
Subtract M10 from any two-digit number	54 − 20 = 34
Partition one-digit numbers	7 = 4 + 3
Bridge down through M10	34 − 4 = 30
Calculate/know complements in 30	30 − 3 = 27

Figure 12.8 Skills used by Chris in calculating 54 − 27.

Attitudes

An important, but neglected, ingredient in mental strategy use is self-
confidence. Children can have all manner of facts and skills at their fingertips,
but if they do not have the confidence to 'have a go' or take risks they are
unlikely to use these facts and skills to generate an appropriate strategy. It is
to be hoped that an emphasis on the teaching of mental calculation will effect
a change in the attitude of children and adults towards mathematics. An
ethos needs to be developed where people no longer have the attitude of
'I can't remember the method so I cannot solve the problem' – discussed in
the Cockcroft Report (DES 1982) – but instead adopt a more positive attitude
of 'I can't remember how my teacher did it, but if I . . .'

In order to help build children's confidence teachers need to develop a
supportive climate in their classrooms. Some of the measures that teachers
can use during their lessons are clearly illustrated in the 1998 Numeracy
Project/Hamilton Trust video *Numeracy in Action*.[1] In one sequence an excellent Year 5 teacher (see Straker, Chapter 4, this volume), teaching a mixed
ability class how to double a three-digit number, uses, amongst other techniques, the following confidence-building strategies:

- she starts the session with activities they can all manage: generating the
  four times table from the two times table;
- she uses supportive phrases like 'You all know your four times table'
  whenever possible;

- she never says 'no' or 'wrong';
- she adopts an approach which is about developing a positive, confident attitude where different methods are acceptable and even expected;
- she keeps a mental record of children's answers for later discussion;
- she returns to a child who gave a wrong answer earlier and asks a question she can get right.

These are just some of the strategies that teachers can use in order to improve the teaching of mental calculation.

Implications for teaching

To summarize, it has been argued that a minimum requirement for children to be successful mental calculators is the development of the following:

- a secure knowledge of number facts;
- a good understanding of the number system – how it works, which operations are permissible and which are not – so that known number facts can be combined using appropriate operations to work out other facts;
- the ability to perform accurately the skills underpinned by these understandings;
- the confidence to use what they know in their own way to find solutions.

The teacher's job is to ensure that these aspects form an important part of their teaching. They need a good knowledge of the common mental strategies that children use so that they can understand their own children's methods; can support them in refining these strategies; and can help them develop more sophisticated methods if they consider this necessary. Teachers also need to hone their own teaching strategies for developing children's attitudes to calculation, particularly their pupils' confidence to use methods with which they feel happy. Teachers need to create a suitable classroom ethos where children will be prepared to take risks. Whilst working to develop efficient and effective strategies for mental calculation for all children teachers need to ensure that they do not emphasize the efficiency aspect to such an extent that children reject a method they understand in favour of a more efficient one that they do not. Research suggests that children make fewer errors when using their own methods – either mental or written.

One important aim of the National Numeracy Strategy, launched in 1999, was to ensure that children were confident with and competent at mental addition and subtraction of any two-digit numbers before they left primary school. At the time this seemed like a rather lofty aim. However, over 100 years before this, Bidder (1856) had declared at an inaugural lecture of the Society for Civil Engineers:

> I have for many years entertained a strong conviction that mental arithmetic can be taught, as easily as, if not with greater facility than, ordinary arithmetic, and that it may be rendered conducive to more useful purposes than that of teaching by rule . . .

Note

1 *Numeracy in Action*. See page 47.

References

Askew, M. and Wiliam, D. (1995) *Recent Research in Mathematics Education 5–16. (Ofsted Reviews of Research)*. London: HMSO.

Beishuizen, M. (1997) Two types of mental arithmetic and the empty numberline. Paper presented at the BSRLM conference, University of Oxford Department of Educational Studies, June.

Bidder (1856) *Minutes of Proceedings of Civil Engineers*, Vol. XV, 1856.

Bierhoff, H. (1996) *Laying the Foundations of Numeracy: A Comparison of Primary School Textbooks in Britain, Germany and Switzerland*. Discussion Paper No. 90. London: National Institute of Economic and Social Research.

Buxton, L. (1981) *Do You Panic about Maths?* London: Heinemann.

Carpenter, T.P. and Moser, J.M. (1984) The acquisition of addition and subtraction concepts in grades one through three. *Journal for Research into Mathematics Education*, 15 (3): 179–202.

DES (Department of Education and Science) (1982) *Mathematics Counts* (Cockcroft Report). London: HMSO.

DfEE (Department for Education and Employment) (1998) *The Implementation of the National Numeracy Strategy: Final Report of the Numeracy Task Force*. London: DfEE.

DfEE (Department for Education and Employment) (1999) *The National Numeracy Strategy Framework for Teaching Mathematics from Reception to Year 6*. London: DfEE.

Driscoll, M.J. (1981) *Research within Reach: Elementary School Mathematics*. Reston, VA: NCTM (National Council of Teachers of Mathematics).

McIntosh, A. (1990) Becoming numerate: developing number sense. In S. Willis (ed.), *Being Numerate: What Counts?*, pp. 24–43. Hawthorn, Victoria: ACER (Australian Council for Educational Research).

SCAA (School Curriculum and Assessment Authority) (1997) *The Teaching and Assessment of Number at Key Stages 1–3: Discussion Paper No. 10*. London: SCAA.

Thompson, I. (1995) The role of counting in the idiosyncratic mental calculation algorithms of young children. *European Early Childhood Education Research Journal* 3 (1): 5–16.

Thompson, I. (1997) The role of counting in derived fact strategies. In I. Thompson (ed.), *Teaching and Learning Early Number*, pp. 52–62. Buckingham: Open University Press.

Thompson, I. and Smith, F. (1999) *Mental Calculation Strategies for the Addition and Subtraction of 2-digit Numbers (Report funded by the Nuffield Foundation)*. Newcastle upon Tyne: University of Newcastle upon Tyne.

Wandt, E. and Brown, G.W. (1957) Non-occupational uses of mathematics. *Arithmetic Teacher*, 4: 151–4.

Zepp, R. (1976) Algorithms and mental computation. In N. Suydam and A.R. Osborne (eds), *Algorithmic Learning*. Columbus, OH: The ERIC Clearinghouse for Science, Mathematics and Environmental Education.

The empty number line as a new model

Meindert Beishuizen

The empty number line was introduced in Holland not just as a new idea, but as a result of evaluation and discussion on how to improve existing practice. Reasons for this came from the experiences with new 'realistic' textbooks during the 1980s and from the outcomes of the first National Arithmetic Test in 1987. At the Freudenthal Institute a proposal for a revised early number curriculum was formulated by Treffers and De Moor (1990). Mental arithmetic had already been in focus for a long time in Dutch lower grades, given the realistic view on mathematics education in our country (see Treffers and Beishuizen, Chapter 3, this volume) that teaching should begin with children's informal strategies. Now, more emphasis was put on the basic computation skills up to 100, and for that purpose the empty number line (ENL) was introduced as a new model.

In international research there was also the recognition that after a long period of studying the number domain under 20, mental strategies with larger numbers should be given more attention. In this area our knowledge of how children carry out number operations 'lags far behind' as Fuson (1992) put it. In Holland such research was carried out at Leiden University (Beishuizen 1993), which led to a new project with an experimental ENL programme implemented in Dutch 2nd grades (Year 3) in collaboration with the Freudenthal Institute (Klein *et al.* 1998). A description of the empty number line in this chapter is based on this project, which took place in several schools during 1992–6. But first we will summarize some background arguments, because there are interesting similarities with current British discussions on how to improve early number teaching. For instance, some British authors have also argued for children's informal strategies instead of the early introduction of standard vertical algorithms (for a broader discussion see Beishuizen and Anghileri, 1998).

Dissatisfaction with existing models was one of the arguments for the ENL. In the 1960s and 1970s manipulatives like Dienes Multibase Arithmetic Blocks (MAB) or Unifix blocks were widely in use in Dutch schools, but teachers complained about children hanging on too long to these materials and passively reading off the answer from the blocks when doing sums (Beishuizen 1993). Apart from this low level of mental activation there was the other drawback of a low modelling function. Concrete blocks are helpful for the representation of abstract number structure, but they are weak in the representation of number operations when these become more complicated. Such critique was voiced by other authors in the 1980s, for instance by Hart (1989) when she analysed a solution of the number problem 56 – 28. After the removal of three from five ten-blocks (50 – 30), two unit-blocks are returned (+2) and then the blocks left on the table are counted for the answer (2 + 20 + 6 = 28). Hart concluded that this manipulation of blocks has very little connection to the intended (written) algorithm, and 'that the gap between the two types of experience is too large' (p. 142).

In Leiden, such research was done in relation to the mental strategies involved. The computation procedure described by Hart, where in both numbers the tens are 'split off' and are added or subtracted separately (50 – 20 = 30), was therefore given by us the acronym *1010*. This *partitioning* or *split* method (following Thompson in Chapter 12) proceeds mostly by adding or subtracting the units (6 – 8) as the next step. In this case that causes a conflict which correctly could be solved by borrowing a ten (16 – 8 = 8, change 30 → 20, answer 20 + 8 = 28). Many children, however, solve this conflict in the procedure by the wrong 'smaller from larger' bug (6 – 8 = → 8 – 6 = 2, answer 30 + 2 = 32). These difficulties of the 1010 partitioning method, in particular with subtraction and regrouping problems, are well-known (Plunkett 1979). Nevertheless this 1010 strategy is widely used, because at first sight splitting up numbers in tens and units seems an easy procedure to children. It follows the decimal (formal) structure of our hundreds, tens and units (HTU) number system and is also elicited and reinforced by the use of arithmetic blocks (Beishuizen 1993). The difficulty of the 1010 strategy is not so much in the decomposition procedure but more in the correct recomposition of numbers (Beishuizen *et al.* 1997). A less vulnerable and more efficient computation procedure (fewer steps) is the mental strategy which proceeds in a sequential way (56 – 28 = via 56 – 20 = 36, 36 – 8 = 28). We have used the acronym *N10* for this strategy because the first number is not split up but kept intact while the tens are added or subtracted through counting by tens. The N10 strategy or *jump* method is less common as a spontaneous method of children, because it is not elicited by the HTU number structure and needs some initial support by making the sequential number patterns (56, 46, 36, etc.) more noticeable.

There is now a growing body of (international) research underlining the important role of these two main strategies (and mixed methods in between) for mental arithmetic with larger numbers up to 100 and beyond. Fuson has described them as the 'separate tens' (1010) and the 'sequence tens' (N10) strategies at a recent experts' meeting (Beishuizen *et al.* 1997). In Holland both 1010 and N10 are widely used as mental strategies, while in the US (and in the UK) 1010 seems more common because of dominance of the HTU (place value) number structure as well as arithmetic blocks in teaching. In Holland it has now been found (Beishuizen *et al.* 1997) that many better pupils prefer the more efficient strategy N10, while most weaker pupils choose 1010 as the 'easier' procedure at first sight, which, however, may take them into difficulties (see above). Another conclusion has been that most pupils are rather consistent but rigid in preferring either only 1010 or only N10 as their computation procedure, with just a minority using both strategies in a flexible way: 1010 for addition and N10 for subtraction. Outcomes of the National Arithmetic Test in 1987 confirmed this lack of flexibility, and this became another argument for the introduction of the ENL: to raise pupils' level of flexibility in mental arithmetic (Treffers and De Moor 1990).

Earlier in the 1980s the Dutch dissatisfaction with blocks had led to the introduction of the hundred square as a richer model visualizing both number relations and number operations for mental arithmetic up to 100. The abacus was introduced for illustrating better the HTU number structure and the corresponding vertical algorithms. Both models, being more abstract, had the potential function of eliciting a higher level of mental activation, but because of this same characteristic also turned out to be more complicated for weaker children. The hundred square, when used in its mentally most activating format with empty boxes (instead of numbers), may confuse children so that they get lost when drawing arrows or jumps on it. Moreover, the increasing influence of the RME approach in mathematics teaching in our country ran counter to the pre-structured character of the hundred square, a model which leaves little room for informal and flexible strategies of children.

Consequently, Treffers and De Moor (1990) came up with the idea of the old number line in a new format: the empty number line up to 100 as a more natural and transparent model than the hundred square. The growing research into mental strategies also played a role as summarized above. First and foremost, however, the well-known argument for emphasizing mental arithmetic in the lower grades should be mentioned (Treffers 1991; Thompson 1997a): dealing with whole numbers supports pupils' understanding and insight in number and number operations much more than the early introduction of vertical algorithms dealing with isolated digits. Therefore, columnwise (written) arithmetic, which was already being introduced later in the Dutch curriculum, was now postponed even further until Year 4 in the new proposal.

Another argument, already mentioned as central in the Dutch RME approach as well as in the views of some British authors, is that early mathematics teaching should start by building on children's informal (counting) strategies instead of imposing formal procedures. A further didactic RME principle is to level up informal strategies to higher (formal and efficient) procedures as well as to their flexible use. For that purpose the ENL is very well suited because on its sequential model counting strategies can be accepted and abbreviated towards counting in jumps of twos, fives and tens, i.e. a gradual transition to the N10 strategy of counting by tens. Treffers and De Moor (1990) have sketched the development of N10 for a subtraction problem like $65 - 38$ through the following stages: (i) $65 - 10 - 10 - 10 - 5 - 3$, (ii) $65 - 30 - 8$, (iii) $65 - 40 + 2$. After procedural abbreviation on the first levels we see at the highest level a short-cut adaptation of N10 used as a compensation strategy (acronym *N10C*). Notice that the lowest level of N10 is long-winded and inefficient as often happens in the beginning of new strategies. Is this a reason not to trust these informal strategies and to teach 'straightforward and efficient standard methods' as an alternative, as sometimes seems to be the official British viewpoint (SCAA 1996)? In the RME view it is not, and the early number curriculum should provide opportunities (learning sequences and tasks) as well as learning time for children to develop their own strategies through 'progressive mathematization' (see Treffers and Beishuizen, Chapter 3, this volume) to more efficient and flexible levels. In Dutch classrooms working with the experimental ENL programme, this happened by having children draw their jumps on the ENL, by practising their recording of mental strategies on the ENL, and by whole-class discussion of different problem solutions drawn on the blackboard.

In summary we have given four arguments for the ENL, which are described more extensively in Klein *et al.* (1998):

1 a higher level of mental activation in providing learning support;
2 a more natural and transparent model for number operations;
3 a model open to informal strategies and also providing support for children to develop more formal and efficient strategies;
4 a model enhancing the flexibility of mental strategies, in particular variations of N10.

In addition to the last argument we should add that one of the conclusions of the research into mental strategies was also (Beishuizen *et al.* 1997) that to enhance flexibility in mental arithmetic Dutch pupils should learn to use both strategies N10 and 1010. For reasons given above, the didactic sequence in the experimental ENL programme is first to invite N10-like strategies. Later in the same programme (three months before the end of the 2nd grade or Year 3) 1010 is introduced, using another (not sequential) grouping model like blocks or money as learning support. An argument for this order of introduction is also that children will learn the more complicated 1010 procedure more quickly, and become more proficient, when they have already acquired a conceptual and procedural knowledge base of two-digit number operations up to 100 through N10. Further experiences in Holland in 2nd and 3rd grades with revised textbooks like *Wis and Reken* (Buys *et al.* 1996), integrating both N10 on the ENL and 1010 with blocks, do confirm how children indeed attain such higher levels of proficiency and flexibility.

British discussions and official viewpoints about mental arithmetic are interesting but not always clear. We will return to this at the end of this chapter. But before giving a description of the ENL programme, we have to clear up one misunderstanding – namely that children doing mental arithmetic should not be allowed to use a pencil for making written notes (see Bramald 1998). This misunderstanding also surfaced at the international experts' meeting in Leiden (Beishuizen *et al.* 1997), when Fuson from her American perspective said that 'students in Holland do not learn mental strategies first, because they start with a lot of written activities on the empty number line' (p. 296). But written work on the ENL has only a secondary function: supporting or recording the strategies chosen as mental decisions in the first place. One

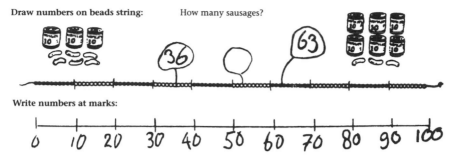

Figure 13.1 Number concept and number positioning.

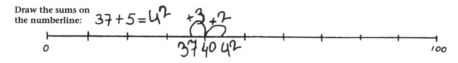

Figure 13.2 Crossing-ten on a structured empty number line.

Figure 13.3 Crossing-ten on a completely empty number line.

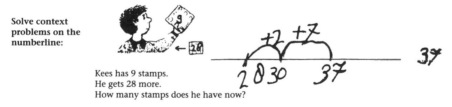

Kees has 9 stamps.
He gets 28 more.
How many stamps does he have now?

Figure 13.4 Flexible solution of a context problem.

might object that this is also true for vertical algorithms. So 'mental' versus 'written' does not seem to be a good contrast (but a commonplace one), because the real distinctions are between the different types of strategies and procedures as described above.

Figures 13.1–13.8 give an impression of the development of mental strategies in our experimental ENL programme for the 2nd grade (Year 3). A fuller description is available in Klein (1998). The sequential model is introduced at a concrete level through a 10-structured bead string up to 100 (Figure

**Make jumps
from.... to....**

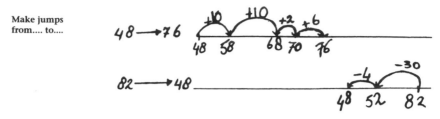

Figure 13.5 Sequential N10-jumps in small and large steps.

Try different solutions:

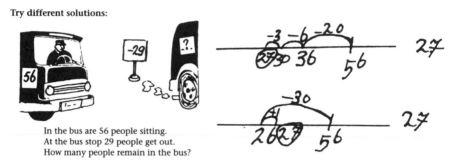

In the bus are 56 people sitting.
At the bus stop 29 people get out.
How many people remain in the bus?

Figure 13.6 Two different solutions: standard N10 (above) and N10C (below) using compensation.

13.1). Two-digit numbers are introduced by building on the (quantity) number concept using both an ordinal and cardinal representation. Through positioning, this knowledge is immediately practised on a corresponding number line. During the first three months a structured empty number line is used (Figures 13.1 and 13.2), before the complete empty line is introduced on which children position and mark the numbers themselves (Figure 13.3). Number operations are first practised with addition and subtraction of single-digit numbers in combination with two-digit numbers up to 100 (Figures 13.2, 13.3 and 13.4). This deliberately builds on arithmetic under 20 in the 1st grade (Year 2), because counting on, splitting up in complements of ten, and using number facts instead of counting still need further practice for most children in order to reach a level of mental recall. Here we have to add that whole-class oral exercises and games (with speed limits) support this process of further automatization. The results of this first part of the ENL programme (from September until January) were very promising: speed tests showed a substantial increase in total number of correct answers, whereas interviews with children showed an almost complete vanishing of counting strategies by January (Klein *et al.* 1998).

Notice that the mental strategies for crossing-tens are quite different from the way this is done with vertical algorithms in Britain. In problems like 37 + 5 and 48 + 6 (Figures 13.2 and 13.3) the algorithm would proceed with splitting off the units and adding them up separately, which means continuing

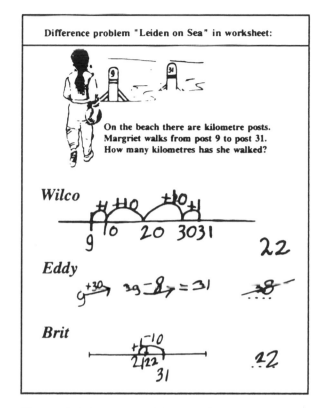

Difference problem "Leiden on Sea" in worksheet:

On the beach there are kilometre posts.
Margriet walks from post 9 to post 31.
How many kilometres has she walked?

Figure 13.7 Context problem evoking various solution strategies.

but limited practice of number bonds like 7 + 5 and 8 + 6 under 20. The
sequential mental strategy involves crossing-tens quite differently by splitting up the (second) units in complements to (new) decadal tens (37 + 5 =
via 37 + 3 = 40, 40 + 2 = 42; 48 + 6 = via 48 + 2 = 50, 50 + 4 = 54). By this
latter strategy children practise not only procedural knowledge but also the
extension of number relations and number sense up to 100.

Realistic context problems play an important role in the RME approach (see
Treffers and Beishuizen, Chapter 3, this volume), inviting a greater variety of
'using your head' problem-solving strategies than standard number problems
which suggest mainly the application of routine computational procedures.
Context problems have been part of Dutch realistic mathematics teaching for
a long time, and so they are also used in our experimental programme. In
this respect the (open) ENL model proved to be a good help for the representation of different problem structures. Context problems, combined with the
ENL model, were used a lot to evoke more variety and flexibility in children's
solution strategies and computation procedures (Figures 13.4, 13.6 and 13.7).

In particular, the 'Leiden on Sea' problem in Figure 13.7 gives an example
of how children come up with various strategies for solving a new type of

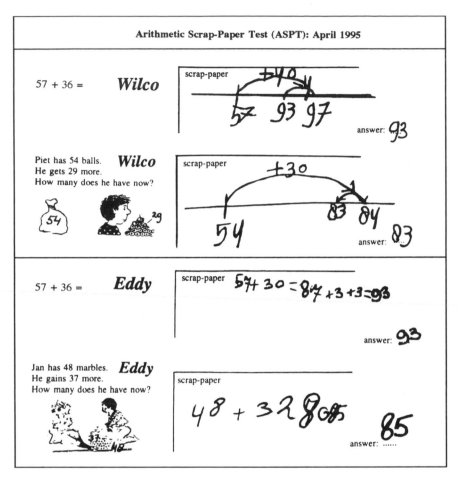

Figure 13.8 Good results at different levels: ENL – support (Wilco) and mental steps (Eddy).

'difference' problem. The weaker pupil Wilco sticks very closely to the structure of the problem by working in small steps and creating several footholds on the ENL. He does this by using the new strategy of 'adding-on to tens', for which we use the acronym *A10*. The better pupil Brit, on the other hand, transforms the problem structure into a subtraction and uses the compensation strategy N10C for a very efficient and elegant solution. The pupil Eddy lies somewhere in-between, solving the problem in his own way and preferring mental steps without the ENL, but his use of the N10C strategy is still inefficient and incorrect. Later, Eddy gets things right by using N10 and his own version of A10 on the April test (Figure 13.8), which illustrates his development to a higher level of understanding and flexibility (beyond the ENL). The weaker pupil Wilco still uses the support of the ENL a lot in the

April test (Figure 13.8) and has developed a rather rigid preference for the N10C strategy for all kinds of problems. These examples also illustrate how the recordings on the ENL contain much information about the sources of errors and about the strategy development of children. The teachers in our experiment agreed that providing diagnostic feedback is another very helpful feature of the ENL.

After practice with single-digit addition and subtraction as described above, the acquisition of number operations with two-digit numbers proceeded much more quickly than we expected. The introduction of N10 takes place as a game of jumping by tens on the ENL (November). Because the pupils are now familiar with all number positions up to 100, making jumps like 15, 25, 35, etc. (forward) and 82, 72, 62, etc. (backward) goes rather easily. This game of jumping is continued by presenting new problem types asking pupils to go from . . . to . . . (Figure 13.5). Adding constraints like the instruction to do this in three jumps or in two jumps enhances the further abbreviation and automatization of larger steps (+30, –20). These conditions, however, leave much room for individual variation in levels of abbreviation, as can be seen in Figure 13.5. Notice that no sums with two digits are presented in the beginning, but then between December and April all two-digit problem types are mastered rather rapidly. The teachers were surprised that the acquisition of the difficult sums like addition and subtraction with regrouping went much more smoothly than usual (Figure 13.6). For the pupils these problems were hardly new because they asked for a combination of N10-jumps and single-digit operations already practised a lot. In the April test (Figure 13.8) the results on two-digit context and number problems reached a high level of procedural competency of about 80 per cent correct. This also included the more difficult subtraction with regrouping problems. These good results were confirmed on the test in June as well as on a National Arithmetic Test for the end of Grade 2 (Year 3). The last three months between April and June had mainly been used for enhancing the flexibility of strategy use by presenting many non-standard problems, and by whole-class discussions of different solutions (cf. Figure 13.7). Also the other strategy 1010 (see above) was introduced. An interesting metacognitive aspect was the introduction of labels for the strategies in a childlike style (for instance 'Jump Further' for N10C), which the children used with pleasure in their worksheets and classroom discussions.

More details about the ENL programme, about the flexibility of strategy use, and about the (good) performance of weaker pupils can be found in Klein (1998) and in Klein et al. (1998). The best proof of its success was the request of all experimental schools to continue with the ENL programme, now provided by a publisher and in use in hundreds of other Dutch schools. The breakthrough of the ENL can also be seen in the new so-called second generation of realistic textbooks in Holland, published in the 1990s. For instance in the revised textbook Wis and Reken (Buys et al. 1996) the ENL model is extended throughout the 3rd grade (Year 4) for number problems up to 1000, followed by the delayed introduction of vertical algorithms until 4th grade (Year 5).

Looking back we can say that the greatest effort was invested during the first half of the 2nd grade programme, when the ENL model was introduced and when single-digit addition and subtraction were practised. In that period procedural errors due to counting and not splitting up units correctly were happening a lot but disappeared gradually. So, single-digit practice prepared the ground for two-digit operations, because they both have a similar sequential character as mental strategies. In our opinion this curriculum outline as well as the curriculum condition of a continuous programme with only small interruptions for other subjects contributed much to the positive transfer of learning.

Returning to British discussions we see a growing awareness of the role of mental arithmetic. Many authors offer suggestions for everyday mental activities in the expectation that children will improve by practising them. This enthusiasm is heart-warming, but in another publication (Beishuizen and Anghileri, 1998) we have argued that combining new and old ideas is not going far enough. We agree with Straker (1996) that given the great variety of mental strategies it is important to decide on 'exactly which methods should be taught and in what order'. And the introduction of the ENL in Holland is an example of not only a new model but also a curriculum change for an improved approach to the development of mental strategies. Priority for the sequential argument (counting, crossing-ten, N10-jumping) and postponement of the partitioning (1010) strategy and the standard algorithm played an important role (cf. above).

Because of these strong sequential characteristics, we are afraid that the ENL model does not fit in with current British teaching practice on early number. For instance, in a small experiment with the ENL in a British mixed-age Year 3/Year 4 class (see Rousham 1997), pupils easily adopted sequential strategies like N10 and A10 and improved on problem solutions. But two months later many pupils had reverted to the standard algorithms, which illustrates that it is of little help to keep up two different systems. The latter situation is comparable to what happened in Holland in the 1970s and 1980s, when mental arithmetic was already emphasized but not adequately supported, resulting in children using a mixture of N10 and 1010 strategies with many of them being unclear and half-correct with difficult subtraction problems (Beishuizen 1993). Attempts to clear up this situation with two-digit number operations up to 100 became the focus (cf. above), not only in the Dutch RME viewpoint (Treffers and De Moor 1990) but also in the growing international research (Fuson 1992; Beishuizen *et al.* 1997).

This applies also to the British discussions on how to 'bridge the gap' between blocks-supported strategies and standard vertical algorithms (cf. Hart 1989) or between mental and written algorithms (Thompson 1997b). In his problem analysis Thompson argues for an emphasis on a modified form of the mental 1010 strategy – working with quantities from left to right – because of its close resemblance to the vertical written algorithm (p. 108). We agree with many of his arguments, and in fact the Dutch revised curriculum (Treffers and De Moor 1990) proposes a similar transition from 1010 to vertical algorithms including some modifications. The big difference, however, is that in the Dutch curriculum N10-like mental strategies are emphasized first for the reasons given above. Thompson neglects the sequential argument too much in our opinion, because, by focusing only on addition and not on subtraction strategies (p. 97), he presents too narrow a problem analysis. Our conclusion is therefore the same as mentioned above in Beishuizen and Anghileri (1998). More emphasis on 1010 mental strategies as well as whole-class discussion will help a bit but not enough, in particular not for the difficult subtraction problems. Also a real connection to the natural development of mental strategies is missing in Thompson's (1997b) proposal, because he still uses a retrospective viewpoint from the standard algorithm instead of a prospective viewpoint from children's informal (counting) strategies.

There is also an inconsistency in Thompson's analysis in that he advocates the latter 'alternative approach . . . that counting should constitute the basis of the early years number curriculum' in the general conclusions of his book (Thompson 1997a: 157), but he does not develop this counting/sequential argument more specifically in his chapter on mental and written algorithms (Thompson 1997b). Nevertheless, such examples of innovative thinking are essential in their contribution to a real discussion and rethinking. In Holland we struggled and still struggle in the same way towards more consistent reasoning and more balanced teaching in the early number curriculum (see the latest revision in the so-called TAL project 1998, under the authority of the Ministry of Education; TAL-team 1998). We hope that this chapter on the empty number line has illustrated not only the new ENL model but also the background to the wider discussion and research on mental arithmetic that is taking place in our country.

References

Beishuizen, M. (1993) Mental strategies and materials or models for addition and subtraction up to 100 in Dutch second grades. *Journal for Research in Mathematics Education*, 24: 294–323.

Beishuizen, M. and Anghileri, J. (1998) Which mental strategies in the early number curriculum? A comparison of British ideas and Dutch views. *British Educational Research Journal*, 24: 519–38.

Beishuizen, M., Gravemeijer, K.P.E. and Van Lieshout, E.C.D.M. (eds) (1997) *The Role of Contexts and Models in the Development of Mathematical Strategies and Procedures*. Utrecht: Freudenthal Institute.

Beishuizen, M., Van Putten, C.M. and Van Mulken, F. (1997) Mental arithmetic and strategy use with indirect number problems up to one hundred. *Learning and Instruction*, 7: 87–106.

Bramald, R. (1998) Why does mental have to mean no fingers, no paper? *Equals*, 4: 5–7.

Buys, K., Boswinkel, N., Meeuwisse, T., Moerlands, F. and Tijhuis, J. (1996) *Wis and Reken – Groep 3, 4 en 5* ['Wis and Reken' Maths Textbook for Year 2, 3 and 4]. Baarn: Bekadidact Publishing Company.

Fuson, K.C. (1992) Research on whole number addition and subtraction. In D.A. Grouws (ed.), *Handbook of Research on Mathematics Teaching and Learning*, pp. 243–75. New York: Macmillan.

Hart, K. (1989) There is little connection. In P. Ernest (ed.), *Mathematics Teaching: The State of the Art*, pp. 138–42. London: Falmer Press.

Klein, A.S. (1998) *Flexibilization of mental arithmetic strategies on a different knowledge base: the empty number line in a Realistic versus Gradual program design.* Utrecht: Freudenthal Institute.

Klein, A.S., Beishuizen, M. and Treffers, A. (1998) The empty number line in Dutch second grades: realistic versus gradual program design. *Journal for Research in Mathematics Education*, 29: 443–64.

Plunkett, S. (1979) Decomposition and all that rot. *Mathematics in School*, 8 (3): 2–5.

Rousham, L. (1997) Jumping on an empty number line. *Primary Maths and Science*, October 1997: 6–8.

SCAA (School Curriculum and Assessment Authority) (1996) *Report on the 1995 Key Stage 2 Tests and Tasks in English, Mathematics and Science.* London: HMSO.

Straker, A. (1996) The National Numeracy Project. *Equals*, 2: 14–15.

TAL-team (1998) *Tussendoelen Annex Leerlijnen (TAL) – Hele getallen – Onderbouw – Basisschool* [Intermediate Objectives in Learning Strands – Whole Numbers – Lower Grades – Primary School]. Utrecht: Freudenthal Institute.

Thompson, I. (ed.) (1997a) *Teaching and Learning Early Number.* Buckingham: Open University Press.

Thompson, I. (1997b) Mental and written algorithms: can the gap be bridged? In I. Thompson (ed.), *Teaching and Learning Early Number*, pp. 97–109. Buckingham: Open University Press.

Treffers, A. (1991) Didactical background of a mathematics program for primary education. In L. Streefland (ed.), *Realistic Mathematics Education in Primary School*, pp. 21–56. Utrecht: Freudenthal Institute.

Treffers, A. and De Moor, E. (1990) *Proeve van een nationaal programma voor het reken-wiskunde-onderwijs op de basisschool. Deel 2: Basisvaardigheden en cijferen* [Specimen of a National Program for Primary Mathematics Teaching. Part 2: Basic Mental Skills and Written Algorithms]. Tilburg: Zwijsen.

Written methods of calculation

Ian Thompson

Introduction

Take a close look at some of 9-year-old John's answers to a page of multiplications from his school maths book. See if you can work out what he is doing wrong before reading on (Figure 14.1).

Notice that John is actually carrying out all of the correct procedures involved in the execution of the standard multiplication algorithm: it is just unfortunate that he has reversed the order of two fairly crucial steps. In each of the examples John successfully multiplies the units digits and 'carries' the appropriate tens digit, correctly placing it under the other tens. However, in the second example, instead of saying 'Two times three is six, plus one more makes seven', he says 'Two plus one is three and three times three is nine' which unfortunately gives him a totally erroneous solution. His only problem appears to be misremembering the steps in the standard algorithm, or, more accurately, getting the correct steps in the wrong order.

John's work provides us with an excellent illustrative example of what many researchers into children's errors have found, namely, that the mistakes that children make in written calculations are generally not random, but are more often than not the result of consistently following an incorrect or faulty procedure (known in the literature as a 'bug'). John did not question any of his answers. So far as he was concerned he was correctly following the method that his teacher had taught him and so was quite confident that his answers

$$
\begin{array}{cccc}
2\,5 & 2\,5 & 2\,5 & 1\ 7 \\
\times 2 & \times 3 & \times 4 & \times 3 \\
\hline
6\,0 & 9\,5 & 16\,0 & 9\,1 \\
\end{array}
$$

Figure 14.1 John's multiplications.

would be correct. If John were using his own method rather than his teacher's he would probably not be making such an error.

Criticisms have been made for many years of mathematics teaching that focuses on the acquisition of memorized standard procedures at the expense of the development of understanding and children's own methods. Ofsted reports are often critical of the overemphasis on written algorithms and the underuse of mental methods: 'Where teaching was poor there was . . . undue pressure on pupils to record mathematics formally before their understanding had been adequately developed' (Ofsted 1994); 'In the classes where standards were low it was frequently the over-emphasis on written recording and computation . . . which contributed to the low levels of achievement' (Ofsted 1993).

Mental or written?

There is little doubt that one of the main reasons for our underperformance in the number tests of international surveys is the very early introduction of formal written calculation methods in this country. The late 1990s saw the emergence of an interesting consensus of opinion where both ends of the political spectrum were unexpectedly agreed on the need for greater emphasis to be placed on the teaching of mental calculation, particularly in primary schools (see Thompson, Chapter 12, this volume). One of the arguments given for the need for this greater emphasis was the close relationship that was claimed to exist between mental and written methods. The Non-Statutory Guidance for the National Curriculum informs us that: 'Such methods (mental) are the basis upon which all standard and non-standard written methods are built' (National Curriculum Council 1989: E2).

However, a consideration of the research literature (see Thompson 1997) would appear to suggest otherwise. There are many studies which show that children's mental methods operate very differently from standard written algorithms in several respects: written methods work from right to left, whereas mental methods generally move in the opposite direction; in mental work the numbers are manipulated as quantities rather than as single digits (43 + 26 is 40 + 30 . . . or 43 + 20 . . . and not 4 tens and 2 tens or 4 + 2 in the tens column); and when children use written methods to support their calculation they prefer to set the numbers down horizontally rather than vertically (Thompson 1994). Consequently, it seems unrealistic to expect that there will be a smooth progression from idiosyncratic mental methods to the standard written algorithms for the four basic operations.

Because in England we have traditionally forced a distinction between mental and written calculation methods – exemplified in the separate 'mental' and 'mechanical' sections of early arithmetic textbooks – it has proved difficult for us to escape this particular mindset. For example, when National Curriculum tests were adapted to include mental tests for the first time in 1998 the Qualifications and Curriculum Authority (ex-SCAA) carried out a pilot test in the previous year. In a section providing instructions to markers (SCAA 1997) we find the following statement:

Any marks on the paper other than the answers, unless specified else-
where as acceptable, are to be regarded as 'working', and will result in
the loss of the mark. This includes any 'memory-jogging' words, figures
or pictures.

Fortunately, because of critical feedback from researchers and teachers this
somewhat myopic interpretation of what might constitute 'mental' work was
modified in the 1998 tests. Children were allowed to make jottings which
would help them, and marks were not deducted for any working out shown
on the answer sheets.

This narrow view of calculation methods does not exist in the Netherlands, where they include 'scrap' paper in mental tests in order to gain access
to children's idiosyncratic algorithms (see van den Heuvel-Panhuizen, Chapter 11, this volume). They also teach the use of the 'empty number line' as a
vehicle to support mental calculation strategies (see Beishuizen, Chapter 13,
this volume).

Written algorithms: formal, informal, standard or non-standard?

In 1998 the idea of 'partial written methods' was introduced into the National
Numeracy Project Framework at Key Stage 1. This, coupled with modifications
to the National Curriculum Mental Tests made that same year, legitimized the
use of *jottings* as an aide-mémoire in mental calculation. A sensible extension
of this idea would have been to develop these jottings into informal written
methods, and then move to more formal strategies as children got older,
culminating in the adoption of standard algorithms by those who understood them and/or wished to make use of them. Unfortunately, however, the
Framework classified written methods for addition, subtraction, multiplication
and division at Key Stage 2 into 'informal' and 'standard' written methods,
suggesting that all, rather than perhaps some, older primary school children
should learn to use the standard algorithms. An alternative classification
system for written calculation algorithms is illustrated in the Carroll diagram
in Figure 14.2.

Given that 'informal standard algorithms' are a contradiction in terms, the
following discussion will cover the three remaining cells in the diagram.

Informal non-standard written algorithms

It was suggested above that children's mental calculations are unlikely to
develop naturally into formal, standard algorithms. Figure 14.3 illustrates a
range of 'natural' written methods produced by young children for each of
the four basic operations.

One feature of these examples is the extent to which the written methods
model the children's mental calculation strategies. The written marks on paper
constitute little more than a written expression of the children's thinking.

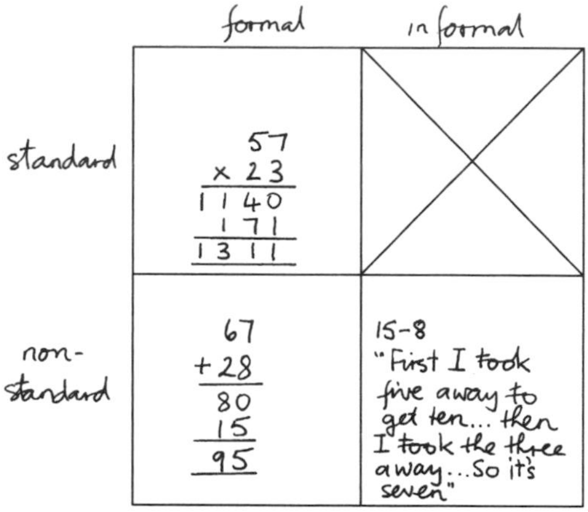
formal
informal
standard
non-standard
57
× 23
1140
171
1311
67
+28
80
15
95
15-8
"First I took five away to get ten... then I took the three away...So it's seven"

Figure 14.2 Written algorithms.

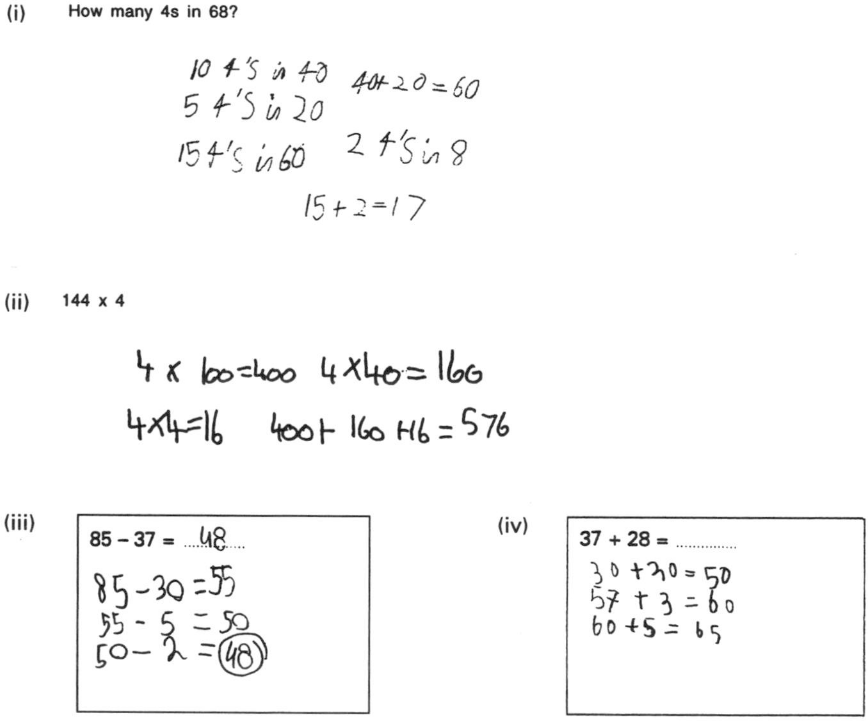
(i) How many 4s in 68?
10 4'S in 40
40+20=60
5 4'S in 20
15 4'S in 60
2 4'S in 8
15+2=17
(ii) 144 x 4
4 x 100=400 4x40=160
4x4=16 400+160+16=576
(iii) 85 – 37 = 48
85-30=55
55-5=50
50-2=48
(iv) 37 + 28 =
30+20=50
57+3=60
60+5=65

Figure 14.3 Informal non-standard written algorithms for the four basic operations.

As Richard Skemp said on the 1985 Horizon video *Twice Five Plus the Wings of a Bird*, 'It's as if their thinking is out there on the table.' Having the children's thinking exposed in this way is very useful. It makes it easier to spot errors or faulty reasoning as the methods are usually quite transparent. Because of the idiosyncratic nature of these informal algorithms it is not recommended that they be taught formally. However, the children should be encouraged to demonstrate them on the board and discuss them with their classmates, as this might lead to one child adopting his or her classmate's more efficient strategy.

Formal standard written algorithms

In a seminal article Plunkett (1979) provided a detailed analysis of the nature of standard written algorithms and the ways in which they differ from mental algorithms. Specific aspects of these standardized written procedures which cause particular difficulties include the fact that they are *symbolic* and *contracted*, and by their very nature involve pure manipulation of symbols without reference to the particular meanings which the place value system attaches to these individual symbols. For example, in order to find the answer to the following sum:

    387

+ 475 using the standard algorithm, you are obliged to say 'seven and five is twelve; put down the two and carry the one' (the fact that this 'one' is actually one ten is ignored); 'eight and seven is fifteen and one more makes sixteen; put down the six and carry the one' (of course, this time the 'one' refers to one hundred, and the 'six' is actually sixty or six tens). The algorithm demands that you do not even *try* to think about what the digits actually represent. If you do, you are highly likely to become confused. Instead you are expected to suspend disbelief and follow the recommended steps in the procedure, not like John above, but in the correct order. Williams (1962–3) argued that such methods encouraged 'cognitive passivity' on behalf of the person using them: the decision as to how to set out the calculation, where to start, what value to assign to the digits, etc. are all taken out of the individual's hands.

There are two main written methods for subtraction that are currently taught in British schools: 'equal additions' and 'decomposition'. They are illustrated below, and are accompanied by a verbal explanation of the thinking process involved:

Equal additions

73^12 'You cannot take 6 from 2 so borrow a ten and
                 pay back (on the doorstep!) . . .

$- 47_16$ . . . 6 from 12 leaves 6 . . .

  256   . . . 7 and 1 is 8 . . . You cannot take 8 from 3, so
                 borrow a ten . . .

          . . . 8 from 13 is 5 . . . 4 and 1 is 5 . . . 5 from 7 leaves 2.'

Decomposition

$$7^2\cancel{3}^12$$
$$-\ 4\ 7\ 6$$
$$\overline{\ \ 2\ 5\ 6\ }$$

'You cannot take 6 from 2 so exchange a ten for ten ones . . .

. . . 6 from 12 leaves 6 . . .

. . . You cannot take 7 from two so exchange . . .

. . . 7 from 12 is 5 . . . 4 from 6 leaves 2.'

There has been a continuing debate for decades in this country about the 'best' subtraction algorithm to teach young children. This debate, however, has focused narrowly on the relative merits of the decomposition and equal additions algorithms. There is some evidence that the latter method is quicker and that the former is generally more accurate, but it is argued that 'equal additions' is more difficult to understand, and that the language associated with the operation does not really help: 'borrowing a ten' from some un-specified place and 'paying it back' to some other place can only contribute to mystification rather than clarification. The subtle concept of adding a ten to the minuend (the number to be reduced) in the units column and to the subtrahend (the number being taken away) in the tens column is felt to be too sophisticated for the majority of children to understand. However, decomposition is considered, in theory at least, to be easier to explain, par-ticularly if Dienes base ten equipment is used.

There are a great many children and young adults around today who have been taught subtraction using this equipment, but the available evidence seems to suggest that many of those who actually use this algorithm still apply the method unthinkingly and make a wide range of errors. It would appear that the blocks constitute an excellent model for clarifying the algorithm to some-one who already uses it with confidence and has some understanding of the meaning of the operations involved. However, there are few, if any, examples in the literature of children actually inventing or 'discovering' the decom-position algorithm for themselves, even when they have spent time playing interesting preparatory 'exchange' games with Dienes equipment.

Hart (1989) has shown that children experience great difficulty in making the anticipated connections between their manipulation of the apparatus and their pencil and paper calculations. She found that, once children had been introduced to the formal written algorithm, it was not very long before they had completely forgotten the pre-formalization linking lessons which had involved the use of the apparatus.

Many pupil-hours are spent in mathematics lessons on the practice of these calculation procedures, and yet there is a plethora of research evidence to suggest that neither young children, teenagers nor adults actually make use of these methods when performing calculations in the real world rather than in a classroom. Unfortunately, many teachers equate an understand-ing of addition, subtraction, multiplication and division with the ability to perform the standard methods for each of these operations. We need to remind ourselves that these particular algorithms were developed long ago so that everyday arithmetic could be carried out with the minimum of fuss and the maximum of speed. There is no doubt about the efficiency and elegance of these procedures. However, the very strengths of the methods – their conciseness, their dependence on symbol manipulation and their generalizability – also constitute their major weaknesses, and these very aspects are often the main cause of the difficulties that many children have with written subtraction.

One further problem with standard algorithms is the great demand that they make on working memory. This means that many children are inevitably going to experience difficulty in remembering the steps in the procedures and, like John, may well remember the necessary steps but mix up the order.

Formal non-standard algorithms

Hart (1989), commenting on her observations of classes being taught subtraction, wrote: '. . . some children graduated from informal but successful methods to failure (e.g. taking away the smaller digit irrespective of position) when teaching took place'.

In this section some alternative 'user-friendly' algorithms will be considered. They are classified as formal because they have a recognizable layout, but they are different from the standard algorithms for the four operations. All of these non-standard methods are based on ideas which underpin many of the informal mental strategies that children use.

Addition

In a sample of 117 9- and 10-year-olds who had not been taught standard methods of calculation Thompson (1994) found that 87 per cent of children preferred to perform written addition calculations by working from left to right, beginning with the most significant digit, rather than working from right to left as is expected when using the standard algorithms for addition and subtraction. The author went on to discuss the possible formalization of a common written procedure used by many children which retains this 'left to right' movement where the addition of 358 and 237 would be written as:

$$300 + 200 = 500; \quad 50 + 30 = 80; \quad 8 + 7 = 15; \quad 500 + 80 + 15 = 595.$$

Another advantage of this algorithm is that the children deal initially with that part of the number which they articulate first. For example, when adding three hundred and fifty-eight to two hundred and thirty-seven in the above example, it is the three hundred that is added to the two hundred before the fifty is added to the thirty. The algorithm in action does not involve the language normally associated with written addition, where the strong emphasis on the manipulation of symbols leads to phrases such as '5 and 3 make 8' even though the digits actually mean 50, 30 and 80. Similarly, phrases like 'put down the five and carry the one' or 'put the one on the doorstep' are not really conducive to the development of relational understanding in children.

Research in England suggests that this *partitioning* method is a more natural and understandable procedure than the usual algorithm taught for this
operation, although Dutch educators have a different view (see Beishuizen,
Chapter 13, this volume). It is a more accurate representation of the way
people, adults and children alike, carry out calculations in their heads with
multi-digit numbers. It therefore provides transparency. Because the children
are working with actual quantities, the meaning and purpose of each stage of
the operation can be easily discerned. Schools or particular teachers wishing
to teach a procedure that looks more like the standard algorithm could adapt
this partitioning method and set the numbers down vertically as illustrated
in Figure 14.4:

$$
\begin{array}{r}
358 \\
+\ 237 \\
\hline
500 \\
80 \\
15 \\
\hline
595 \\
\hline
\end{array}
$$

Figure 14.4 Partitioning addition algorithm.

Figure 14.5 shows an alternative *sequencing* method, which is closely related
to empty number line strategies discussed by Beishuizen (Chapter 13).

$$358 + 237$$
$$358 + 200 \rightarrow 558 + 30 \rightarrow 588 + 7 \rightarrow 595$$

Figure 14.5 Sequencing addition algorithm.

This method can also be set out more formally in a vertical layout.

Subtraction

The algorithm for subtraction which is probably the easiest to understand is
the 'low-stress' method of *complementary addition*. Children need experience
of interpreting 73–24 not only as '73 take away 24' or 'The difference between
24 and 73' but also as 'How many do I add to 24 to get 73?' They should
practise mentally counting up from one number to another – initially in
ones then in tens, but also in 'chunks' which take them to the next multiple
of ten. With this experience, a variety of different written procedures can be
developed – one of which is illustrated below:

$$
\begin{array}{ccc}
6 & 40 & 3
\end{array}
$$
$$24 \rightarrow 30 \rightarrow 70 \rightarrow 73 \qquad 6 + 40 + 3 = 49$$

Figure 14.6 Horizontal complementary addition.

An alternative strategy is to say the numbers . . . *24* . . . *30* . . . *70* . . . *73*, and to write down only the steps between the numbers as they are said, namely, 6 40 3. Adding these three numbers together gives you the total. Teachers keen to develop vertical algorithms might wish to introduce the notation illustrated in Figure 14.7:

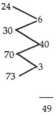

24
6
30
40
70
3
73

49

Figure 14.7 Vertical complementary addition.

or, more formally:

```
   73
 - 24
 ____
    6    to 30
   40    to 70
    3    to 73
 ____
   49
```

Figure 14.8 Formal layout for complementary addition.

Another common strategy for two-digit subtraction, illustrated in Figure 14.3 (iii), can be formalized in the following way for more difficult three-digit calculations. This is a *sequencing* subtraction strategy which, like its additive counterpart shown in Figure 14.5, can be easily modelled on an empty number line.

353 – 177
353 – 100 → 253 – 50 → 203 – 20 → 183 – 3 → 180 – 4 = 176

Figure 14.9 Sequencing subtraction algorithm: horizontal.

Or slightly more formally as:

```
   353
 - 177    Subtract 100
 _____
   253    Subtract 50
   203    Subtract 20
   183    Subtract 3
   180    Subtract 4
   176
 _____
```

Figure 14.10 Sequencing subtraction algorithm: vertical.

Teaching either of these written methods avoids the need to involve children in the acknowledged difficulty of the concepts underlying words like: decomposition, exchanging, borrowing and paying back. However, because children have usually had more experience of the 'take away' aspect of subtraction, both at home before starting school and during their early school years, it is important that they get practice at working with contextualized difference problems, as these often stimulate a solution by complementary addition (see Treffers and Beishuizen, Chapter 3, this volume).

Multiplication

By a single digit

Given 23×7 to calculate most people using the standard multiplication algorithm would probably begin in the following way: 'seven threes are 21 . . . put down the one and carry the two . . .' This demands that children unthinkingly follow a procedure where the meaning and purpose of the actions are not really obvious nor particularly easy to understand. A more meaningful procedure is:

23×7

$\qquad 20 \times 7 = 140 \qquad\qquad 3 \times 7 = 21 \qquad\qquad 140 + 21 = 161$

or simply

$140 + 21 = 161$, where the thinking process runs as follows: 'Seven 23s is seven twenties plus seven threes . . . Seven twenties make 140 (write this down), and seven threes make 21 . . . Adding 140 and 21 gives 161 . . .'

As with addition, this method begins with the digit on the left and makes use of the word order of the numbers being operated on. In this case 23 is treated as twenty-three, or, more specifically, as a twenty and a three. The place value meaning of the numbers is maintained as with addition, and children are once again operating with quantities rather than with pure symbols. This helps them to stay in control of their thinking at each stage of the calculation. This procedure is sometimes called the *partial products* or *partitioning* method of multiplication, and can easily be set out in vertical form.

$$
\begin{array}{r}
23 \\
\times\ 7 \\
\hline
140 \\
21 \\
\hline
161
\end{array}
$$

Figure 14.11 Partial products in vertical layout.

Practical work using Cuisenaire rods or squared-paper strips can be used to help children gain a good understanding of this method of multiplication (see Thompson 1989).

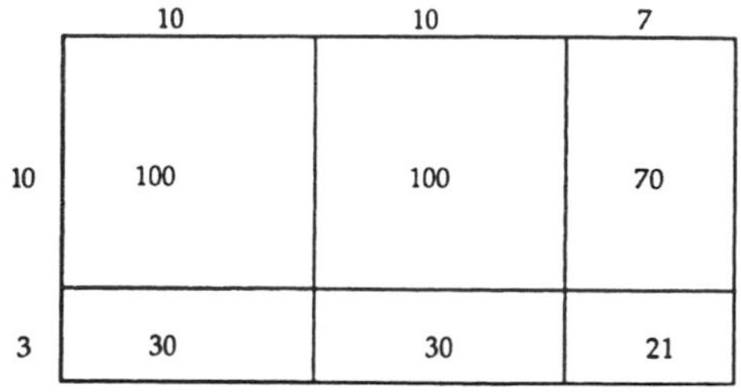

Figure 14.12 The 'area' model for long multiplication.

Multiplying two-digit numbers
It is possible to extend the method described above to multiply, say, 27 by 13. However, experience suggests that the following related procedure (Figure 14.12), modelled on squared paper, is easier for most children to understand.

The partial products can be added together in any order, and the working can be set out horizontally or vertically.

27 × 13   100 + 100 + 70 + 30 + 30 + 21 = 351

or

```
    27
  × 13
  ----
   100
   100
    70
    30
    30
    21
  ----
   351
  ----
```

As the children gain more confidence with, and understanding of, the underlying concepts they can progress to abbreviating the process slightly, drawing their diagrams in the following manner:

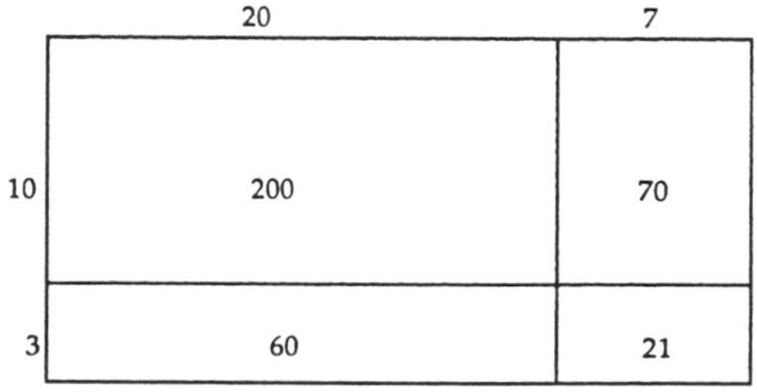

Figure 14.13 Abbreviated 'area' model for long multiplication.

Algorithms associated with this diagram might progress from:

27 × 13   200 + 70 + 60 + 21 = 351

or

$$\begin{array}{r} 27 \\ \times\ 13 \\ \hline 200 \\ 70 \\ 60 \\ 21 \\ \hline 351 \\ \hline \end{array}$$

to   27 × 13   270 + 60 + 21 = 351
or

$$\begin{array}{r} 27 \\ \times\ 13 \\ \hline 270 \\ 60 \\ 21 \\ \hline 351 \\ \hline \end{array}$$

or even to

27 × 13   270 + 81 = 351

or

$$\begin{array}{r} 27 \\ \times\ 13 \\ \hline 270 \\ 81 \\ \hline 351 \\ \hline \end{array}$$

For those children who understand the concepts involved it is a short step to progress from scale diagrams to a simple two-by-two grid illustrated in Figure 14.14.

Division

'Sharing' is an activity that young children have experienced even before they come to school, and it is natural that their early interpretation of the division sign is in terms of this particular activity. Secondary school pupils often perpetuate this narrow interpretation, and this can be seen in the language that they use to read a mathematical statement such as 24 ÷ 8. Some might say, '24 shared between 8' or '24 divided by 8' (see Anghileri, Chapter 15, this

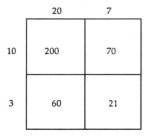

Figure 14.14 Grid model for long multiplication.

volume); others, probably the majority, would say '24 share(d) by 8'. Very few would interpret the symbol as 'How many eights are there in 24?', and yet this 'grouping' model of division is more important than the 'sharing' model for teaching long division. However, children need to be made aware of both of these aspects if they are to develop a thorough understanding of the division operation.

'User-friendly' algorithms for division – long or short – are based on interpreting the division operation as a 'grouping' activity. This necessitates children reading or interpreting a mathematical statement such as 48 ÷ 3 or $3\overline{)48}$ as 'How many threes are there in 48?' and involves removing 'chunks' of the divisor. The algorithm in action then looks and 'sounds' like this:

$$
\begin{array}{r}
16 \\
3\overline{)48}
\end{array}
$$

30	(10)	There are 10 groups of 3 in 30. Write 10. (Take the 30 from the 48.)
18		Now find how many 3s there are in the remaining 18.
18	(6)	There are six 3s in 18. Write 6.
0		Add the 10 and the 6. So altogether there are 16 threes in 48.

Figure 14.15 Written division by 'chunking'.

Alternative written algorithms can be developed by children using the same thinking process. The following was produced by one particular child:

48 ÷ 3
10 × 3 = 30
6 × 3 = 18   Answer is 16

You might like to try working through the following example where the 'rough work' involves the complementary addition strategy for the subtractions, the partitioning strategy for the necessary additions and the partial products method for the multiplication of 34 by 5. Because the example really needs a detailed 'running commentary' you may find it difficult to follow, particularly as three different non-standard algorithms are involved!

```
        27
   34)918                     Rough work
      340    (10)        60        60       34
      ───                                   
      578              500       100      × 5
                                          ───
      340    (10)     + 18     + 78      150
      ───              ───      ───
      238              578      100       20
                                          ───
      170    (5)                130      170
      ───                        
       68    (2)                   8
                                  ───
                                  238
```

Figure 14.16 Long division involving 'user-friendly' algorithms.

The method involves the removal of chunks of the divisor from the dividend. When no more lots of ten can be removed it makes sense to try working with chunks of five, two or just one, if needs be, until no more chunks can be removed. The sum of the numbers in brackets tells you how many groups of the divisor there are in the dividend.

The various sub-skills that need to be developed in order to perform divisions involving two- and three-digit numbers include:

- multiplying any number by ten;
- halving fairly large multiples of ten (in order to find five lots of the divisor);
- doubling two-digit numbers (to find two lots of the divisor);
- subtraction (complementary addition will suffice), and
- addition (by partial sums or any other method).

Conclusion

The 'low-stress' or 'user-friendly' algorithms discussed in this chapter are based on the methods generally used by children who have *not* been taught standard methods. The steps involved in carrying out these algorithms, rather than the so-called standard algorithms, relate much more closely to recognized mental strategies. Consequently, children are more likely to be able to understand these more 'natural' methods than the traditional standard algorithms which involve the automatic and unthinking manipulation of abstract symbols. The English approach, whilst acknowledging the importance of avoiding the premature teaching of standard written methods, is to insist that: 'For each operation at least one standard written method of calculation should be taught in primary schools' (DfEE 1998).

The Dutch approach is to think more in terms of different *levels* of strategy (see Figure 3.1 in Treffers and Beishuizen, Chapter 3, this volume), ranging from 'informal context-bound' methods to 'high-level abbreviated' strategies, and to acknowledge that some pupils will not reach the highest level of formal written standard algorithm, but will still have a method which helps them succeed in solving problems.

References

DfEE (Department for Education and Employment) (1998) *The Implementation of the National Numeracy Strategy: Final Report of the Numeracy Task Force*. London: DfEE.

Hart, K.M. (1989) Place value: subtraction. In D. Johnson (ed.), *Children's Mathematical Frameworks 8–13*. London: NFER – Nelson.

National Curriculum Council (1989) *Mathematics Non-Statutory Guidance*. York: NCC.

Ofsted (1993) *The Teaching and Learning of Number in Primary Schools*. London: HMSO.

Ofsted (1994) *The Annual Report of Her Majesty's Chief Inspector*. London: HMSO.

Plunkett, S. (1979) Decomposition and all that rot. *Mathematics in School*, 8 (3): 2–5.

SCAA (School Curriculum and Assessment Authority) (1997) *Mathematics Mental Arithmetic Pilot Test: Teachers' Handbook*. London: SCAA.

Thompson, I. (1989) W(h)ither long multiplication. *Struggle: Mathematics for Low Attainers*, 25: 19–21.

Thompson, I. (1994) Young children's idiosyncratic written algorithms for addition. *Educational Studies in Mathematics*, 26 (4): 323–45.

Thompson I. (1997) *Teaching and Learning Early Number*. Buckingham: Open University Press.

Williams, J.D. (1962–3) Arithmetic and the difficulties of calculative thinking. *Educational Research*, 5 (3): 216–28.

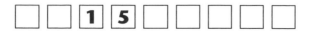

Issues in teaching multiplication and division

Julia Anghileri

With modern technology so readily available that every important calculation is done with a computer or a calculator, is there a role in modern
society for human calculators?

Do we need to teach long multiplication and long division to every child in
school today?

These questions identify some fundamental issues that have stimulated discussion about the purposes of arithmetic teaching in school. Current recommendations promote 'the importance of numeracy as an essential life skill'
suggesting that 'a good grasp of numeracy is needed to manage personal
financial affairs' and that 'people find life much easier if they can answer basic
numerical questions' (DfEE 1998a). Complex calculations, however, can go
much further to involve logical problem-solving strategies that develop more
general thinking skills which are transferable to many problem situations.

Controversy has arisen because some written calculations, particularly 'long
multiplication' and 'long division', have caused difficulties for generations of
children who have tried to master complex rules to solve apparently irrelevant
questions. Figure 15.1 shows some pupils' attempts to use a standard algorithm
but there is evident confusion in applying the rules.

The types of errors shown in these examples are very common and illustrate
the way rules may be forgotten if they are not well understood. While calculators and computers take the burden of calculation from the world of business
and commerce, new developments in the arithmetic curriculum present opportunities for school children to *abandon rules* and focus on the way procedures
can be developed with *understanding* so that they may gain the satisfaction of
true mastery over numbers. The curriculum today requires pupils to develop
'number sense' by integrating skills with knowledge and understanding, and
by 'using and applying' mathematics in problem solving, communicating and
reasoning. Pupils are expected to 'make sense of number problems, including
non-routine problems, and recognise the operations needed to solve them'

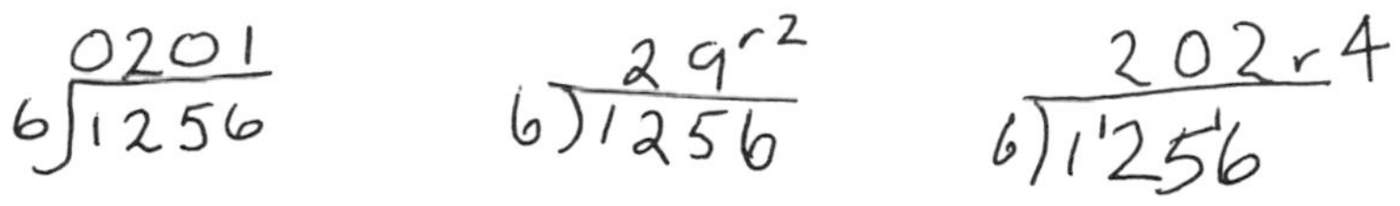

$$\begin{array}{r} 0\,2\,0\,1 \\ 6\overline{)1\,2\,5\,6} \end{array} \qquad \begin{array}{r} 2\,9\,r\,2 \\ 6\overline{)1\,2\,5\,6} \end{array} \qquad \begin{array}{r} 2\,0\,2\,r\,4 \\ 6\overline{)1\,2\,5\,6} \end{array}$$

(i)   (ii)   (iii)

Figure 15.1 Some common errors in division.

(DfEE 1998b). This means that endless practice with pages of sums will not satisfy the needs of today's curriculum. One only needs to consider the types of problem set in the Key Stage 2 National Curriculum Tests, to see that flexibility and understanding are crucial requirements in arithmetic. For example:

Write in the missing digit

$$\boxed{}\,7 \quad \times \quad 9 \quad = \quad 333$$

to see that flexibility and understanding are crucial requirements in arithmetic. The curriculum today identifies the need for pupils to have sound strategies for mental arithmetic, supported when necessary by efficient recording procedures.

Starting early

Young children are fascinated by numbers, and playground chanting of '2, 4, 6, 8 . . .' or '5, 10, 15, 20 . . .' can be encouraged by the teacher who knows the importance of such patterns for later work in multiplication and division. It will be some time before the structure in these number patterns relates to tables facts and to division problems, but their familiarity has enduring importance as numbers that form a 'family'. The patterns that occur less frequently, like the pattern of sevens, will take longer to learn when number facts have to be memorized. Awareness of these structures in repeated addition, together with introduction of the language of 'lots of' and 'times' and 'multiplied by' can accompany the earliest activities where sets of objects, images or numbers are grouped as patterns.

Procedures for grouping and sharing will help identify the concepts of multiplication and division but these will remain impotent unless the related number patterns are an early focus. In later schooling pupils who can use number facts and relationships will have a considerable advantage over those who continue to 'share' and 'group' with objects or with visual imagery. The transition from arranging 12 objects in four groups of three to the mathematical relationships between 12, 4 and 3 depends on verbalization that is best generated by teacher interactions. It is these number triples, not the procedures for generating them, that will be the key to success in more formal calculating later.

Stages in learning

Ideas of multiplication and division occur long before children meet them in textbooks, and introducing the symbols should provide a shorthand for recording relationships that are well known. The earliest multiplication facts that children learn are the 'doubles' that occur in addition. 'Two and two', 'three add three', 'two lots of four' and 'two fives' are all different ways of expressing a doubling relationship. This flexibility in language is important and extensions to 'how many fives make ten?' and 'three is half of six' will help children make the connections between multiplication, division and later work with fractions. Formalization using 'multiplied by' and 'divided by' as well as words like 'factors', 'multiples' and 'remainders' should be introduced by the teacher into discussion about activities and images well before pupils need to use the symbols. The *Framework for Teaching Mathematics* (DfEE 1999) identifies language that needs to be learned in Years 2 and 3 before written recording is introduced, as well as the formal language that will accompany written recording.

Selecting appropriate interpretations for symbols will be fundamental in problems like $6000 \div 6$ and $4 \div \frac{1}{2}$ in order to identify an appropriate way to solve them. Finding 'how many sixes in 6000' can be a complicated practical activity and deciding how to 'share four between half' can be impossible if half a person is the perceived image. When pupils limit their understanding to a sharing model it can hamper progress and the illustration below (Figure 15.2) shows a Year 5 pupil's attempt at a complex calculation using a sharing strategy where alternative methods would be more effective.

The notion of division as 'sharing' is difficult to reconcile with a grouping procedure, but 'grouping' and the use of multiplication facts will provide the key to success in most division calculations as this way of 'breaking down' numbers can be related to the 'building up' of multiplication. In the example above the relationship between 6 and 12 can be extended to enable $1200 \div 6$ and $56 \div 6$ to be calculated. Working on multiplication and division facts together and de-emphasizing sharing procedures will help to develop pupils' number sense and awareness of links between the operations.

Importance of mental strategies

In stressing the importance of 'strategic mental methods of computation' (SCAA 1997), distinction is made between mental recall and mental calculation (see Thompson, Chapter 12, this volume). Mental strategies may require pencil and paper for 'jottings' to support pupils' short-term memory as 'mental' is interpreted as calculating 'with the head' and not solely 'in the head'. For multiplication and division it is important that pupils remember number facts but they must also be able to derive further facts and see connections that will help them to simplify calculations.

Starting with 'five 4s are 20', a doubling procedure will determine that 'five 8s are 40' and this is the same as 'eight 5s'. The relationships that link 5 and 4 and 20 provide a 'multiplicative triple' in which 20 is the **product** and 5 and 4 are the **factors**. By rephrasing the statement as a question, 'How many 4s make 20?', the language for division may be introduced at the same time that multiplication is learned. This important notion of multiplication

1256 apples

1256 apples are divided among 6 shopkeepers.
How many apples will every shopkeeper get?
How many apples will be left?

Working: Answer:................

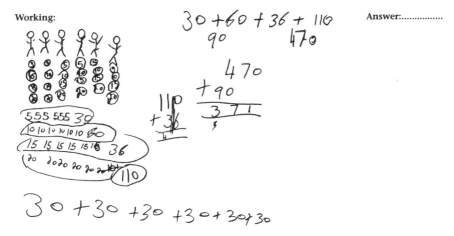

Figure 15.2 Year 5 pupil's cumbersome 'sharing' strategy.

as putting together equal groups and division as reversing the procedure and splitting the total back into groups is crucial to understanding the inverse nature of the operations. Although most schemes and textbooks introduce the operations separately, early connections through mental calculations will show that the same number triples can be used for both types of calculation.

Additional strategies will need to be introduced where division involves remainders. Problems like 34 ÷ 7 may be solved mentally by referring to 'close' number facts and practice should include work on 'clusters' of problems with close numbers, e.g.

35 ÷ 7   36 ÷ 7   and   34 ÷ 7

and with related numbers, e.g. 350 ÷ 7 and 35 ÷ 14. The idea of a remainder needs some exploration as it is not an everyday notion and some pupils confuse the remainder with the 'distance' from the nearest multiple. It is a common error to identify 34 ÷ 7 as 5 remainder 1 rather than 4 remainder 6 which is a bit more complex to calculate. Traditional textbooks do not always provide the opportunities for making connections that match to their pupils' developing knowledge. Teacher-generated activities and investigations are better able to provide the reflection and discussion that best fits their pupils' needs.

$$84 \div 14 \qquad \text{Ans } 29 \, r4$$

$$10 \overline{\smash)84} \quad \overset{8r4}{} \qquad \qquad 14 \overline{\smash)84} \quad \overset{81}{}$$

$$4 \overline{\smash)84} \quad \overset{21}{}$$

       (i)   (ii)

Figure 15.3 Errors involving separate digits.

Developing strategies for calculating

Underlying many of the connections for multiplication and division are the commutative, associative and distributive laws which can be used to simplify mental calculations.

- commutative law – e.g. $7 \times 2 = 2 \times 7$ – reduces the tables facts to be learned although the differences in the images of '7 lots of 2' and '2 lots of 7' may hamper some pupils in making this connection;
- associative law – e.g. $(17 \times 2) \times 5 = 17 \times (2 \times 5)$ – will simplify some calculations particularly where pupils are able to split numbers, e.g. $6 \times 15 = 3 \times 2 \times 15$;
- distributive law – e.g. $32 \times 24 = (30 + 2) \times 24 = (30 \times 24) + (2 \times 24)$ or $32 \times 24 = 32 \times (20 + 4) = (32 \times 20) + (32 \times 4)$ – provides steps for working with larger numbers.

These rules are fundamental to both mental and written procedures and although they may not be known to pupils by their names, their consequences need to be thoroughly explored.

Many pupils will make erroneous connections and, for example, assume that since multiplication is commutative then so too is division and $6 \div 12$ is just an alternative way to record $12 \div 6$. It is possible even to read the first sum as '6 divided into 12' and relate this to the alternative way of writing $6 \overline{\smash)12}$ if early recording of division has been introduced. Explicit discussion is necessary if this confusion is to be avoided. Another temptation is the tens and units partitioning used in the distributive rule. Although multiplication by 24 can be achieved by first multiplying by 20 and then by 4 and adding the results, it is not possible to divide by 24 in an equivalent way. In a recent study of Year 5 pupils' strategies for division, many individuals trying to use a standard algorithm to solve $84 \div 14$ made the error of trying to divide 84 first by 10 and then by 4 (Figure 15.3 (i)). Associated with this sum was the common error to divide digit by digit (Figure 15.3 (ii)).

Working with larger numbers

Progress from knowing the 'tables' facts for smaller numbers to using them in calculations with two- and three-digit numbers needs to be made in gradual stages if errors like those above are to be avoided. Knowing that 3×4 is 12 gives access to 30×4 and 300×4, or to 3×40 and later to 30×40 and 0.3×0.4 but establishing these deduced number facts should reinforce the meaning of multiplication. Linking $3 + 3 + 3 + 3$ with $30 + 30 + 30 + 30$ may provide a necessary intermediate step to understanding the multiplicative relationship. The evidence suggests that pupils who are able to make such links between recall and deduced number facts make good progress because each approach supports the other (SCAA 1997). Encouraging discussion of different mental strategies will help pupils to develop flexible approaches and to become aware of those that are efficient.

The following methods shows a variety of mental strategies for solving the problem 32×24:

- 30×20 plus 30×4 plus 2×20 plus 2×4 giving $600 + 120 + 40 + 8$
- $32 \times 20 = 640$, now add 64 and another lot of 64 to get 768
- $3 \times 24 = 6 \times 12 = 72$ so $30 \times 24 = 720$, add another $2 \times 24 = 48$ to get 768
- $32 \times 24 = 64 \times 12$ which is $(64 \times 10) + (64 \times 2)$ that is $640 + 120 + 8 = 768$

Halving and doubling can be very effective ways of calculating with larger numbers as the doubles facts appear to be better known by most children. Arithmetic teaching to encourage such connections is a far cry from the rote procedures valued in school in the past. The role of the teacher today is to help pupils move progressively from seeing multiplication as repeated addition to making use of number facts and to increased efficiency through appropriate use of rules and connections. (It is worth noting that the 'close' problem 32×25 could provoke quite different strategies when 'number sense' enables pupils to connect 32×25 to $8 \times 4 \times 25$. Indeed, $32 \times 24 = (32 \times 25) - 32$ would be a most effective strategy for solving the first problem.)

Each of these methods may require 'jottings' to help keep track of the partial sums that are found mentally but none of them depend on a taught written procedure. Pencil and paper jottings do not need to record all stages but pupils will need opportunities to explain their strategies and compare them with others. When complex calculations are tackled the need to structure their written recording will become increasingly important and comparison of different methods will help establish an efficient standard method for each individual.

Written procedures for multiplication

With growing emphasis on mental strategies the National Numeracy Strategy Framework advocates a delay in introducing written calculations until the 'end of Year 3' (NNP 1998). This reflects the tradition in continental teaching to focus much more on mental arithmetic in the lower grades with deliberate postponement of written algorithms. The continental approach (see Treffers and Beishuizen, Chapter 3, this volume) also uses problems set in context as a starting point so that the calculations are seen as useful rather than arbitrary exercises. A good example is the following:

On a farm 432 eggs are packed into boxes of 12. How many boxes will be needed?

The context for a problem will usually suggest a strategy for solving the problem although the numbers involved should also trigger connections with known number facts. The problem above may be tackled by considering 120 eggs at a time or more efficiently by considering 360 eggs.

By talking together about context problems, pupils should have gained considerable experience with multiplying two-digit numbers before they start to record their methods in a formal way. Some early attempts at using pencil and paper will reflect their understanding rather than an efficient and succinct record. It is important that recording is introduced to support and to extend the mental strategies they have developed and not to superimpose a standard format that will confuse some children. Pupils will need help to structure their recording and develop efficiency without loss of understanding. Whole-class discussion of various recording methods suggested by the pupils themselves will provide opportunities for the teacher to monitor individuals' understanding. The process of describing to others their chosen method will prove difficult for some but the need to reflect and communicate their understanding will help pupils of all abilities.

For more complex problems like 372×24 (suggested in the Framework for Teaching Mathematics for Year 5), doubling and halving or use of the distributive law may be needed. This will need to be reflected in the way the calculation is recorded. Early recording may require a great many steps and efficient short-hand recording methods may take some time to develop. It is important that the priority remains for children to develop flexible problem-solving strategies rather than becoming rule followers. The National Numeracy Strategy Framework suggests alternative arrangements for recording multiplication calculations:

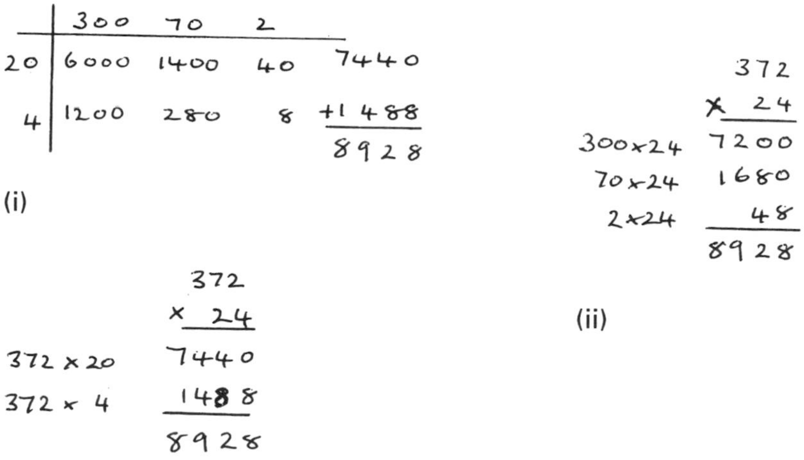

Figure 15.4 Different written methods for recording long multiplication.

Each method relates to a different way of breaking down the problem into manageable steps and presents an efficient way of recording some of the strategies that have been developed mentally. With such organization it should be possible to tackle problems with larger numbers but it will be essential to retain number sense and recognize where shortcuts may be helpful (e.g. 199 × 4). It will also be necessary to consider how sensible the answer to the calculation looks in relation to the original problem. Where a procedure becomes mechanical it is easy to produce answers that are nonsense.

The difficulty for teachers arises when there is no standardization and every pupil needs individual attention which is neither feasible nor generally effective. This may be overcome by group and whole-class discussions where recordings may be compared and efficiencies developed.

Written procedures for division

As mental strategies become more sophisticated, pencil and paper will need to be used for supporting short-term memory and for organizing solution procedures. Figure 15.5 shows the way Year 5 pupils have recorded their working for a problem involving the calculation 98 ÷ 7. The pictorial tallying is evidence that the problem is understood but such counting procedures reflect a poor grasp of number relations. Progressive shortening of the procedures involves initially working with numbers instead of tally marks and then finding short-cuts for adding them. At the higher levels, the number 98 is recognized as 'chunks' of 70 and 28 and multiplication facts are used.

The process of 'chunking' or breaking down of larger numbers may vary among children as this example shows. Efficient strategies used by pupils who have selected different number facts as a starting point for their calculations involve the use of 10 × 7 = 70 and 7 × 7 = 49, half of 98. Temptation for teachers to rush into the formal algorithm as an efficient recording method must be balanced with the need to retain the holistic values of numbers and to reflect mental strategies. When recorded as 'short division' in the format $7\overline{)98}$ it is easy to think of 7 divided into 9 rather than 90 and errors like those in the illustration frequently occur. There is sometimes confusion over the remainder when 9 is divided by 7 and introducing a 'small 2' in front of the 8 is not always easily recognized as the 28 that would remain when 70 was subtracted from 98. Another problem arises when there are zeros involved in the solution as in the problem 1256 ÷ 6 (Figure 15.6 (i)). A zero is not required when '6 does not go into 1' but is crucial where '6 will not go into 5' and it is very common to find the answer 29 r2 instead of 209 r2. Where there has been a strong emphasis on place value notation (hundreds, tens and units) it may lead pupils to strategies that are more complex than necessary (Figure 15.6 (ii)). By considering 1256 as 1000, 200, 50 and 6, each step in the division process has been difficult, providing opportunities for errors. It is 'number sense' that helps pupils recognize that 'chunking' 1256 as 1200 and 56 will provide a much easier calculation, perhaps even calculated mentally. It is true that the extension to some large numbers becomes

98 flowers are bundled in
bunches of 7. How many
bunches can be made?

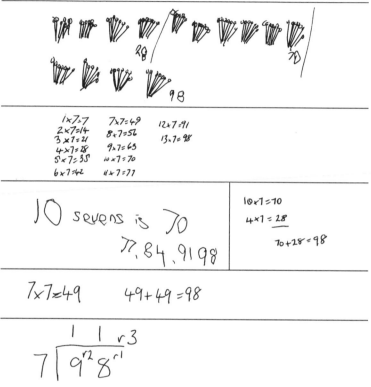

Figure 15.5 Progression in solution strategies for division.

very easy, for example 6936 ÷ 3, but for problems with a divisor larger than
10 (or perhaps 12) the algorithm becomes 'long division' and involves many
steps in 'breaking down' the dividend. It starts with a 'guess' or approximation that many pupils find difficult and then proceeds through steps of
subtracting and 'bringing down' digits

$$
\begin{array}{r}
02 \\
17\overline{)432} \\
34 \\
\hline
92
\end{array}
$$

At each step the positioning of digits becomes vital as a way of keeping track
of the stage reached in the calculation. This traditional approach reflects the

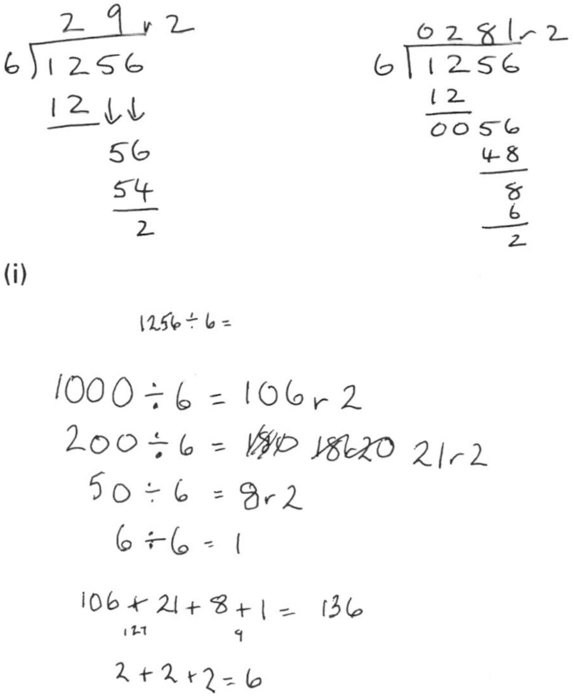

$$\begin{array}{r} 29\ r\,2 \\ 6\,\overline{)1256} \\ 12\downarrow\downarrow \\ \hline 56 \\ 54 \\ \hline 2 \end{array} \qquad \begin{array}{r} 0\,2\,8\,1\ r\,2 \\ 6\,\overline{)1256} \\ 12 \\ \hline 0056 \\ 48 \\ \hline 8 \\ 6 \\ \hline 2 \end{array}$$

(i)

$$1256 \div 6 =$$

$$1000 \div 6 = 106\,r\,2$$
$$200 \div 6 = \cancel{180}\ \cancel{18620}\ 21\,r\,2$$
$$50 \div 6 = 8\,r\,2$$
$$6 \div 6 = 1$$

$$106 + 21 + 8 + 1 = 136$$
$$1279$$

$$2 + 2 + 2 = 6$$

(ii)

Figure 15.6 Problems caused by zeros and place value.

place value system emphasized in schools in this country but it may lead to errors where pupils start to work with digits and lose sight of the meanings of the numbers.

In some schools the procedure has been adapted to keep the true values of the numbers involved and to include some 'tally' of the multiples involved:

$$\begin{array}{r l} 17\,\overline{)432} \\ 340 & \times\,20 \\ \hline 92 \\ 68 & \times\,4 \\ \hline 24 \\ 17 & \times\,1 \\ \hline 7 & 25\ \text{rem.7} \end{array}$$

This alternative approach has been developed as a written algorithm in other countries like the Netherlands that takes the idea of repeated subtraction and works towards steadily increasing efficiency (see Treffers and Beishuizen, Chapter 3, this volume).

This approach leaves the flexibility for individuals to choose their own 'chunks' and progressively develop efficiency without losing understanding. It is equally appropriate for large and small divisors where the traditional format used in English schools has required a change from short to long division. Although the format resembles the algorithm shown above, it differs in that the numbers are built up towards the final total in chunks that are chosen by the individual.

Understanding versus efficiency

In both multiplication and division it is possible to teach standard algorithms that are highly efficient for those pupils who can follow the various stages of estimating, calculating partial sums and products, and piecing together all the parts that make a complete solution. There is now evidence that the procedural approach encouraged by the traditional algorithm leads pupils to ignore the meaning of the numbers as they try to remember complex procedures they have learned without really understanding. Frequent errors relate to the treatment of numbers as separate digits and confusion over when to include the zero and when to leave it out. This chapter has included a small sample of the errors that are commonly found in children's work and the reader might like to try to decipher the efforts in the various examples.

A final anecdote may strike a chord for those who sympathize with children trying to master a complex procedure with little understanding. Having struggled for a while with the calculation $15\overline{)432}$ David put up his hand and asked, 'Could I add the 2 to 43 because I know that 15 goes into 45 three times?'

References

DfEE (Department for Education and Employment) (1998a) *Numeracy Matters: Preliminary Report of the Numeracy Task Force*. London: DfEE.

DfEE (Department for Education and Employment) (1998b) *The Implementation of the National Numeracy Strategy: Final Report of the Numeracy Task Force*. London: DfEE.

DfEE (Department for Education and Employment) (1999) *The National Numeracy Strategy Framework for Teaching Mathematics from Reception to Year 6*. London: DfEE.

SCAA (School Curriculum and Assessment Authority) (1997) *The Teaching and Assessment of Number at Key Stages 1–3*: Discussion Paper No. 10. London: SCAA.

The pedagogy of calculator use

Kenneth Ruthven

This chapter outlines the professional and political context of calculator use in British primary schools, and summarizes relevant research into the influence of calculator use on pupil attitude and attainment. It then examines a range of pedagogical issues concerned with the development of pupil skill and judgement in making use of a calculator, and with the use of calculators to support realistic problem solving and the exploration of pattern and structure in number.

The professional and political context of calculator use in the primary phase

The Calculator Aware Number Project (CAN) (Shuard *et al.* 1991) has provided an important reference for professional thinking about the teaching of number at primary level. Launched in 1986, this project took an exploratory approach to the teaching of number, emphasizing practical and investigative activities; renounced the standard written methods of column arithmetic; encouraged children to develop their own informal methods of mental calculation; and provided them with unrestricted access to calculators, as a means both of exploring number and tackling computations beyond the reach of their mental methods. In 1989, as the project concluded its development work in three clusters of primary schools in England and one in Wales, a National Curriculum came into effect for all maintained schools in the two countries.

The non-statutory guidance intended to support schools in implementing the original National Curriculum was strongly influenced by the CAN experience. It suggests that pupils 'should be encouraged and helped to develop *their own* methods for doing calculations'. Mental methods are 'a first resort when calculation is needed' and 'the basis upon which all standard and non-standard written methods are built'; written methods (taken to 'encompass a wide range of formal and informal techniques and methods') are 'a versatile and convenient resource for doing calculations'; and calculator methods 'provide a fast and efficient means of calculation, liberating pupils and teachers from excessive concentration on pencil and paper methods'. The guidance recommends that 'For most practical purposes, pupils will use mental methods or a calculator to tackle problems involving calculations . . . Work should be based in a firm understanding of number operations, applied to problems in a variety of contexts' (NCC 1989: E1–E6).

Nevertheless, the testimony of those working with and within primary schools indicates that this guidance has had limited impact on professional practice (SCAA 1997). Moreover, the very presence of the calculator in the primary school has become increasingly contentious. A Conservative Secretary of State set a more critical tone by introducing 'calculator-free' testing and announcing a 'review on the use of calculators'; and her Labour successor was quick to sustain this censorious note in characterizing numeracy as being about 'young people . . . doing calculations in their heads rather than by pushing the buttons of a calculator'. The effect of such thinking, which assumes an antagonistic relationship between calculator use and mental calculation, has been to reinforce the 'calculator-beware' approach to number found in many schools, rather than the calculator-aware approach informing the original National Curriculum.

Research into the influence of calculator use on pupil attitude and attainment

Research has drawn broadly positive conclusions about the impact of calculator use on pupils' attitudes and attainments in mathematics. But it is important to ask in what respects the situations which have been researched match those of today's classrooms.

An extensive body of research was carried out during the late 1970s, largely in North America, and has been analysed as a whole (Hembree and Dessart 1986, 1992). The studies reviewed were predominantly ones 'where calculator and non-calculator groups had received equivalent instruction except for calculators' rather than 'special calculator instruction'; in which 'the calculator's primary function was computational' rather than being 'used primarily as a pedagogical device to help develop concepts or problem-solving strategies'; and in which 'the lengths of calculator treatment ranged from less than one class period to a full school year; the median length [being] 30 school days'. Whatever their merits, then, these studies cannot answer the plea that research should 'assess how *typical* uses of calculators in schools have affected students' long-term mathematical thinking and behaviour' (London Mathematical Society 1995: 14). To assess the impact of calculator-aware approaches sustained over longer periods, we must look to later studies.

The CAN project reported the favourable findings from a participating local authority in which the first cohort of project pupils were compared with their peers in other schools. Pupils who had followed the CAN approach for between four and seven terms took a county-wide written mathematics test at age 9. On 28 of the 36 items, the CAN pupils had a higher success rate than their peers; on the remaining eight items, the position was reversed. The differences were not tested for statistical significance, but on 11 of the items the success rate of the CAN group was at least 10 per cent greater, with no difference in favour of the comparison group being as large (Shuard *et al.* 1991: 59–60). The following year, the second cohort was involved in a similar study. On this occasion, it seems that the CAN pupils outperformed their peers on only 21 of the 36 items, and with smaller margins of success (Foxman 1996: 47).

An Australian project (Groves 1993, 1994) took up and developed the idea of a calculator-aware number curriculum from Reception class onwards. Achievement data were collected through written tests and interview assessments with pupils aged 8 to 9 who had been involved in the project for several years. Their performance was compared with that of their seniors who had entered the same schools two years earlier, and had already been assessed with the same instruments at the same stages of their school career. The project pupils were found to perform better on a range of computation and estimation tasks and on some 'real-world' problems; they exhibited better knowledge of number, particularly place value, decimals and negative numbers; they made more appropriate choices of calculating device; and they were better able to interpret their answers when using calculators, especially where knowledge of decimal notation or large numbers was required.

Nevertheless, the conditions under which these encouraging findings emerged were unusually favourable. The CAN project team recorded the advice they received that:

> it would be difficult to make valid numerical comparisons between project children and control groups of children in other schools. Misleading impressions might be gained from measurements of the comparative performance of children who worked in CAN against other children, as the two groups would have other differences in addition to the fact that they were following different curricula. The project teachers would be supported by team members and advisory teachers; they would also meet regularly and work together in ways in which teachers in control schools might not.
>
> (Shuard *et al.* 1991: 55)

A more recent British study analysed the progress through primary education of a cohort of children from neighbouring schools, including some schools previously involved in the CAN project and retaining its methods (Ruthven *et al.* 1997). Analysis of performance at age 7 found that pupils in the post-CAN schools were more likely to be found at the extremes of the attainment distribution. One plausible explanation is that the emphasis on investigative and problem-solving tasks within CAN produced a greater differentiation of experience between pupils, creating higher expectations of, and greater challenges for, successful pupils, but providing less systematic teacher intervention to structure and support the learning of pupils who were making poor progress. However, this pattern did not persist through to the results at age 11. Nonetheless, one important contrast was found at this age. A higher proportion of pupils in the post-CAN schools expressed positive attitudes towards calculating mentally. This finding was strengthened by an analysis of the mental, written and calculator strategies of numerical computation used by a subsample of pupils in tackling number problems. Pupils in the post-CAN schools were more liable to compute mentally, and to adopt powerful mental strategies (Ruthven 1998).

This brief review of research highlights variation in what is meant by 'calculator use' and the conditions under which 'it' has been studied. The evaluations have tended to be positive, but we should beware of uncritical generalization. More important are insights from research into exactly how calculator use may be shaped so as to be beneficial for pupils' learning, and what this might mean in the everyday practice of a primary school.

Opportunities and dilemmas in using calculators to support problem solving

An important contribution that the calculator can make to primary mathematics is in supporting realistic problem solving. We will now observe some pupils at work, in order to identify and explore issues of everyday use of calculators in the classroom. The examples are drawn from individual task-based interviews with over fifty Year 6 pupils (Ruthven and Chaplin 1997), and have been chosen to typify the kinds of incidents which might be expected if such pupils were to tackle this task in a classroom setting. Hence, in the following discussion the episodes will be treated not only as yielding insights into pupils' actions and the reasoning behind them, but as presenting dilemmas and opportunities for teaching.

The pupils were tackling 'the coach problem':

313 people are going on a coach trip. Each coach can carry up to 42 passengers. How many coaches will be needed? How many spare places will be left on the coaches?

During the interviews, pencil, paper and calculator were readily available to the pupils, and they had been told that they could work however they liked; using their head, pen and paper, or calculator, or a mixture of these.

Teacher regulation and intervention

These very conditions raise the first issue: to what extent should pupils be left free to make decisions for themselves about when and how to use a calculator in tackling such a problem? Certainly pupils must have opportunities to make such choices if they are to achieve curricular specifications that they should take increasing responsibility for organizing tasks, and should learn to select appropriate mathematics and materials. Recognizing, too, that pupils' actions reflect the habits that they have developed as much as the choices that they deliberately make, there is a strong argument that the working assumption of the classroom should be that pupils are free to make use of calculators, but also that use – or non-use – of the machine will be open to comment and discussion (as examples later in this section will illustrate). A corollary of such a position is that on those occasions when a teacher does offer pupils specific instructions to use – or not to use – a calculator, the reason should be made clear.

To turn now to pupils' responses to the problem, Kylie was typical of several pupils in attempting to carry out a direct division using a written method. She set out $313 \div 42$ in a 'long division' format and deliberated for some time, making a few tentative moves. Should a teacher intervene at this point, and if so, how? That involves a judgement about learning purposes and priorities. Given the prime purpose of the activity as one of developing pupils' capacities for problem solving, then the issue is whether Kylie can find a way of retrieving the situation through an alternative approach. Given a subsidiary purpose of the activity as one of honing pupils' computational skills, it might be tempting to assist Kylie to make a start with her long division. However, to intervene in this way at this stage would deflect her from the prime purpose of the activity. A better alternative would be to take this up later. Indeed, since this difficulty was shared by many pupils, there is a clear need for further teaching of the technique.

In fact Kylie, like many pupils in the same situation, switched – without prompting – to make use of a calculator to carry out the division. First, however, she asked if she could use the calculator. How should a teacher respond? Simply giving – or refusing – permission is unlikely to help Kylie to take increasing responsibility for such choices. One option would be to deflect the question back, and to help Kylie to make and articulate her decision. However, this may not be the moment for that. At the least, however, the reasoning behind any granting – or withholding – of permission needs to be made clear: 'That long division is quite a tough one. If you're going to get ahead with solving the problem, then it would make sense to use a calculator.'

Mike was another pupil who floundered with the long division. He, however, made to abandon the problem without trying another approach. An appropriate teaching intervention would encourage him to persist with the problem; if necessary, helping him to review the situation and identify alternatives. One of these would be to use a calculator to carry out the division. But for some pupils, reluctance to make use of the machine can be very strong. It might become necessary to authorize use of a calculator; spelling out the reasons why it is justified, as before.

Direct division and the calculator

Many of those pupils who did use the calculator to execute the division encountered an unexpected difficulty. Karen is a revealing example.

    Karen keys [313][÷][42][=]7.452380952
Karen: Whoopsee!
Interviewer: What have you got?
Karen: I've got loads of numbers.
Interviewer: Are they any good to you?
Karen: No.
Interviewer: Why?
Karen: I don't know.
Interviewer: Can you understand what they say?
    Karen shakes her head
Interviewer: Okay.
    [pause]
    Karen rekeys [313][÷][42][=]7.452380952
    [pause]
    Karen keys [42][÷][313][=]0.134185303

Karen's immediate interpretation of the string of digits on the calculator screen is that she has miskeyed; and when rekeying only produces the same result, her next thought is that she must have reversed the numbers within the calculation. Behind such responses lies an expectation – or perhaps an aspiration – that the result of a division should be a whole number. Certainly, the 'commonsense' of this problem points in this direction, as in Tom's initial reaction: 'You can't split a coach up.'

But other factors are in play. In these pupils' experience of mental and written calculation, division is a process yielding an integer quotient and remainder. By contrast, the calculator provides the (not necessarily integral) ratio between dividend and divisor. The results of the two processes are the same only for 'exact' division. Karen simply did not recognize the string of digits as resulting from an 'inexact' division. Not surprisingly, then, she abandoned this approach and switched to one based on repeated addition. Yet – on the evidence of a written test taken a few weeks earlier – Karen was capable of working successfully with the one- and two-digit decimals which predominate in the primary mathematics curriculum. This signals a need for explicit teaching to bring out the relationships between division, fraction and decimal concepts.

Indeed, carefully designed calculator-based tasks can provide a focal point for such teaching, helping pupils to draw out the mathematical principles embedded in the way in which the machine handles division and decimals; for example, by seeking different division calculations which will produce a particular 'point number'; or by exploring the way in which a calculator rounds the patterned decimals resulting from division calculations (van den Brink 1993).

Such teaching would also benefit pupils like Damon. Although he did recognize the result as that of an 'inexact' division, he confused decimal part with remainder.

    Damon keys [313][÷][42][=]7.452380952
Interviewer: What have you got? Any good?
Damon: About seven coaches.

Interviewer: About seven coaches.
  [pause]
Damon: I think it's four.
Interviewer: Four.
Damon: Yeah.
Interviewer: Spare places?
Damon: Yeah.
Interviewer: How did you work that bit out?
Damon: Because it's seven point four.

More immediately, Damon should be prompted to check his solution back against the original data; steered, if necessary, in a suitable direction: 'How many places altogether in seven coaches?'; 'And four spare places means how many passengers?'; 'So, does that match up with the number of people wanting to travel?'

Kylie – whom we met earlier – also recognized the string of digits as the result of an 'inexact' calculator division.

Kylie: Well you'd probably get seven coaches but you'd have some left.
Interviewer: How are you going to sort it out?
Kylie carries out a written multiplication: $7 \times 42 = 294$.
Then a written subtraction: $313 - 294 = 19$.

In effect, through carrying out the further computations, Kylie was able to translate the ratio result of the initial calculator division into a quotient and remainder form.

This is a powerful idea which could be developed into a systematic method of integer division by calculator. It might be helpful to draw pupils' attention to the possibilities of expressing 313 both as $7 \times 42 + 19$ and $8 \times 42 - 23$, stressing the relationships between these forms: 7 and 8 as the successive whole numbers which 'sandwich' the result of the calculator division; 19 as the amount by which 7×42 'undershoots' 313, 23 as the amount by which 8×42 'overshoots' 313; and the final check that 19 and 23 sum to 42, the difference between 7×42 and 8×42.

These episodes highlight the special character of calculator division and the demands that it makes on pupils' mathematical understanding. Carrying out an apparently simple computation with a calculator has proved to be anything but the mindless, automatic process that it is commonly reputed to be.

Indirect strategies and the calculator

Another approach to the problem was through trial multiplication.

  Joanne keys [42][×][12][=]504
Interviewer: Why did you do that?
Joanne: Forty two times any number, but it was a bit too high.
  Joanne keys [42][×][10][=]420

Joanne: Forty two times ten, that's too high so . . .
Joanne Keys [42][×][8][=]336
[pause]
Joanne: They'd need eight coaches, and they'd have . . .
[pause]
Joanne: Twenty three places left over.

Joanne's trial-and-improvement approach is certainly an effective way of solving the problem, and her confident and articulate solution deserves praise. However, it is a relatively indirect method, and so it would be desirable to go on to ask Joanne whether another approach would lead more directly to the number of coaches. Some people might also want to take issue with Joanne's use of the calculator to multiply 42 by 10. However, by using the calculator to carry out computations in a predictably routinized way, Joanne has freed her attention to monitor her strategy and interpret results. As it happens, Joanne was very capable of doing such a calculation mentally; a few minutes earlier she had successfully multiplied 24 by 10 in her head, answering within one second.

Liam approached the problem through repeated addition, and his difficulties were typical of such attempts.

Liam: So you need to add up how many forty twos go into . . . I'll do
        that. I'm sure you could do it a quicker way but, well . . .
Liam keys [42][+] [42][+] [42][+] [42][+] [42][+] [42][+] monitoring inter-
        mediate totals.
Liam keys [252][+]
Liam: Oh no!

Because a calculator leaves no trace of intermediate results, any extended calculation of this type is vulnerable to miskeying or losing track of where the calculation has reached. Even if pupils register that this has happened, the absence of previous results makes it impossible to check or backtrack. Pupils who tried to calculate wholly in their heads had similar difficulties.

Some pupils tried a repeated subtraction approach, focusing on the number of people still unplaced on a coach. Dougal is typical, running into similar difficulties to those noted with repeated addition.

Dougal: Three hundred and thirteen take away forty two.
Dougal keys [313][−][42][=]271
Dougal: Two hundred and seventy one. Now I've got two hundred and
          seventy one people. Now I've taken forty two people away. That's
          one coach. I took forty two away from three hundred and thirteen
          and I gained two hundred and seventy one. I'll try again now.
Keys [271][−][42][=]229
Dougal: That's three coaches.

The computations involved here are still more demanding to carry out mentally or in writing than those of repeated addition, so it is not surprising that this approach was always associated with use of a calculator.

By their nature, written methods leave a record of intermediate steps and their results. But often, when calculation is carried out mentally or by machine, it is possible – and preferable in terms of efficiency – to do so without making any written record. However, repetitive calculations such as these require careful monitoring, and make greater demands on pupils' short-term memory. Under these circumstances, pupils like Liam and Dougal need encouragement, either to modify the computational process – so as to reduce the memory demands – or to make a written record of each stage of their computation.

Use of the calculator constant function does, of course, offer a way of simplifying and expediting repeated computations. Only Kath tried this approach, and she was confused (possibly through associating repeated addition with multiplication):

Kath: 42 times
  Kath keys [42][×][=]1764
  Rekeys [42][×][=]1764
Kath: I thought if you could do forty two times and then equals, it should keep going, forty two, eighty four like that and say how many forty twos to get up to that.

Kath then moved on to an approach involving repeated keying of [+][42]. These observations suggest that the class as a whole would benefit from explicit teaching about use of the constant function.

Finally, some pupils simplified the repeated addition by calculating mentally in round 40s, although none then took account of the additional 2s. There was no evidence of pupils estimating a result more directly from the approximate proportions 40:320, or 40:300 – or from the corresponding division – either as the basis of a direct strategy, or as a rough check on some other approach. Clearly, these pupils would benefit from work on estimation and approximation. And although checks through estimation are often associated with calculator computations, they are equally applicable to pupils' – usually rather less dependable – mental and written computations.

As in all activities concerned with 'using and applying mathematics', pupils' work on this problem has served to highlight specific mathematical topics which would benefit from more focused teaching. Indeed, discussion of the problem itself, and strategies adopted by pupils, may provide a good springboard for such work. For example, suitably recorded, Joanne's trial multiplication, Liam's repeated addition, and Dougal's repeated subtraction each provide the basis for a written technique of long division (see Treffers and Beishuizen, Chapter 3, this volume).

These examples also show that effective use of a calculator calls not only for mastery of operating procedures – such as use of the constant function, but a grasp of underlying mathematical ideas – such as the distinction between decimal part and remainder, and the development of distinctive calculator methods – such as that of integer division. These episodes also illustrate how access to a calculator can enable pupils to tackle a problem using direct strategies which call for computations beyond their current capabilities in mental and written calculation; and can also support indirect strategies based on trialling or building up towards a solution.

Using calculators to support number exploration and develop mental calculation

The other important contribution that calculators can make to primary mathematics is in supporting exploration of pattern and structure in number, often with a view to developing pupils' capabilities in mental calculation. Such explorations have been subjected to some criticism:

> For example, 8–9 year-old pupils are to 'explore number patterns' (sometimes as simple as . . . 91, 81, 71, 61, . . .) . . . When using calculators, pupils contribute to the process of finding the result hardly more than if it were dictated to them by the teacher. The underlying process is totally concealed from them, and the calculator does not help pupils to understand why the result is true.
>
> (Bierhoff 1996: 38–9)

What is crucial in such activities is the way in which the calculator is used to structure the task, so shaping the strategies which pupils can use. If asked to work mentally, pupils could extend the pattern 91, 81, 71, 61 either by visualizing and following a symbol pattern: 91, 81, 71, 61; or by verbalizing and following a name pattern: *ninety* one, *eighty* one, *seventy* one, *sixty* one. Tasked to set the constant function on their calculator to produce the pattern, pupils are obliged to conceptualize it in terms of a repeated number operation. Framed in this way, the task can help the teacher to diagnose the extent to which pupils have grasped the mathematical principle underpinning these name and symbol patterns. If necessary, the task then provides a context in which the principle can be explained. Finally, further tasks of similar type can be used to reinforce the idea, or diagnose if further teaching is needed. This exemplifies a *diagnose–explain–reinforce* sequence of calculator use.

Another appropriate way of using the calculator is through an *observe–predict–surpass* sequence. Suppose we wish to move pupils on from the inefficient and unreliable process of using counting on as a method of adding 10 to a number. Instruct pupils first to observe what happens when they use the calculator to add 10 to different numbers (employing the machine to avoid them simply rehearsing and reinforcing the count-on procedure); then to predict the results of machine calculations (so shifting the function of the calculator towards that of checking their mental calculations); and finally to surpass the calculator, through developing sufficient speed and accuracy in the curtailed mental strategy to be able to beat someone using the machine.

Used in such ways, the calculator can be the key to structuring an activity to produce effective learning. For some pupils, too, use of the machine can increase motivation, particularly if an activity can be recast into a game format. A popular example is commonly known as 'Wipe Out' (although I prefer to think of it as 'Place Invaders'), intended to strengthen pupils' grasp of our numeration system. The teacher opens by writing up a multidigit number – say 789123 – which pupils enter on their calculator. The teacher then challenges the pupils to carry out a single subtraction which will 'wipe out' a particular digit – say the 9 – replacing it with 0 while leaving the others intact (in this case, by entering – 9000 to produce 780123). The game continues until finally the leading digit is wiped out, leaving only 0. Clearly the type of number to be entered can be varied, making it possible to focus on increasingly large whole numbers or on decimal fractions. If desired, the game can be scored, with a point awarded for each successful move. Once pupils have grasped the rules, they can play one another. However, it has been noted that pupils can tackle this version of the game successfully by treating the number that they are subtracting simply as a block of digits – in the example cited, starting with the 9 and replacing each digit to the right with a 0 (Hopkins 1992). This suggests a modification of the scoring to award an extra point for satisfactorily naming the number subtracted in a successful move.

Conclusion

This chapter has illustrated how calculators can be used to support realistic problem solving and the exploration of pattern and structure in number. What has been highlighted is the crucial part that teachers play in structuring such activities and capitalizing on the opportunities they provide to analyse pupil thinking and promote pupil learning. It is this pedagogy which is the key to shaping and exploiting calculator use so as to be educationally beneficial.

Acknowledgements

This article draws on work supported by the Economic and Social and Research Council (award number R000221465) and the School Curriculum and Assessment Authority.

References

Bierhoff, H. (1996) *Laying the Foundations of Numeracy: A Comparison of Primary School Textbooks in Britain, Germany and Switzerland*. Discussion Paper No. 90. London: National Institute of Social and Economic Research.

Foxman, D. (1996) *A Comparative Review of Research on Calculator Availability and Use Ages 5–14*, unpublished report to School Curriculum and Assessment Authority.

Groves, S. (1993) The effect of calculator use on third graders' solutions of real world division and multiplication problems. In I. Hirabashi, N. Nohda, K. Shigematsu and F.-L. Lin (eds), *Proceedings of the Seventeenth International Conference for the Psychology of Mathematics Education*, 2: 9–16.

Groves, S. (1994) The effect of calculator use on third and fourth graders' computation and choice of calculating device. In J. da Ponte and J.F. Matos (eds), *Proceedings of the Eighteenth International Conference for the Psychology of Mathematics Education*, 3: 33–40.

Hembree, R. and Dessart, D. (1986) Effects of hand-held calculators in precollege mathematics: a meta-analysis. *Journal for Research in Mathematics Education*, 17 (2): 83–99.

Hembree, R. and Dessart, D. (1992) Research on calculators in mathematics education. In J. Fey and C. Hirsch (eds), *Calculators in Mathematics Education*, pp. 23–32. Reston, VA: National Council of Teachers of Mathematics.

Hopkins, M. (1992) Wipe Out – refined. In J. Fey and C. Hirsch (eds), *Calculators in Mathematics Education*, pp. 239–40. Reston, VA: National Council of Teachers of Mathematics.

London Mathematical Society, Royal Statistical Society, Institute of Mathematics and its Applications (1995) *Tackling the Mathematics Problem*. London: London Mathematical Society.

NCC (National Curriculum Council) (1989) *Mathematics Non-Statutory Guidance*. York: NCC.

Ruthven, K. (1998) The use of mental, written and calculator strategies of numerical computation by upper-primary pupils within a 'calculator-aware' number curriculum. *British Educational Research Journal*, 24 (1): 21–42.

Ruthven, K. and Chaplin, D. (1997) The calculator as a cognitive tool: upper-primary pupils tackling a realistic number problem. *International Journal of Computers for Mathematical Learning*, 2 (2): 93–124.

Ruthven, K., Rousham, L. and Chaplin, D. (1997) The long-term influence of a 'calculator-aware' number curriculum on pupils' mathematical attainments and attitudes in the primary phase. *Research Papers in Education*, 12 (3): 249–82.

SCAA (School Curriculum and Assessment Authority) (1997) *The use of calculators at Key Stages 1–3*. London: SCAA.

Shuard, H., Walsh, A., Goodwin, J. and Worcester, V. (1991) *Calculators, Children and Mathematics*. London: Simon and Schuster.

van den Brink, J. (1993) Different aspects in designing mathematics education: three examples from the Freudenthal Institute. *Educational Studies in Mathematics*, 24 (1): 35–64.

Index

TEACHING AND LEARNING EARLY NUMBER

Ian Thompson (ed.)

... the book includes plenty of clear suggestions for practical action in the classroom ... Don't be fooled by the comfortable familiarity of the title. This is a radical and influential book, that ought to be read and acted upon, and that will continue to be quoted and discussed for some time to come.

Time Educational Supplement

... a well-produced and effectively edited examination of a wide range of issues concerned with children's acquisition of the fundamental concepts of number.

Mathematics in School

- Is it time to question the traditional approach to the teaching of early number?
- What does research tell us about how young children acquire number concepts?
- What can teachers do to facilitate the development of number understanding?

This book presents an accessible guide to current research into the teaching and learning of early number concepts. The beliefs and number understanding of nursery and reception children are examined, and the book provides a detailed account of the role of counting in the acquisition of number understanding and in the development of derived fact strategies for addition, subtraction and multiplication. Practical activities are described to help teachers develop various aspects of number understanding.

Contents
Prologue: the early years number curriculum today – Section 1: the numercial understanding and beliefs of pre-school children – Children's beliefs about counting – Children's early learning of number in school and out – Section 2: the place of counting in number development – The importance of counting – Uses of counting in multiplication and division – The role of counting in derived fact strategies – Compressing the counting process: developing a flexible interpretation of symbols – Section 3: written number work – 'When should they start doing sums?' A critical consideration of the 'emergent mathematics' approach – Writing and number – Mental and written algorithms: can the gap be bridged? – Section 4: perspectives on teaching number – Approaching number through language – Developing young children's counting skills – The role of calculators – Teaching for strategies – Epilogues: the early years number curriculum tomorrow – Index.

Contributors
Julia Anghileri, Carol Aubrey, Janet Duffin, Sue Gifford, Eddie Gray, Effie Maclellan, Penny Munn, Ian Sugarman, Ian Thompson, Alan Wigley.

174pp   0 335 19851 1 (Paperback)   0 335 19852 X (Hardback)